STUDY GUIDE

PRENTICE HALL

Seventh Edition

STUDY GUIDE

PRENTICE HALL

BIOLOGY
THE STUDY OF LIFE

Seventh Edition

PRENTICE HALL
Upper Saddle River, New Jersey
Needham, Massachusetts

Credits

Outside Credits	Writing Services	Stephen Wolfinger, Gary Kransnow Ann L. Collins, Deborah S. Haber
	Editorial Services	Dotty Burstein, Dorothy Marshall
	Design Services	Mark McKertich, Carolyn Champigny
	Illustrations	Boston Graphics, Inc.

ISBN 0-13-435081-2

8 9 10 11   10 09 08

PRENTICE HALL

Contents

Introduction

Did you know that learning to study more effectively can make a real difference in your performance at school? Students who have mastered study skills are generally more confident and tend to enjoy their learning experience. This book, a study guide for *Biology: The Study of Life,* is designed to help you acquire the skills that will allow you to study biology more effectively.

The first step is to understand what a study skill is. A study skill is the ability to gather, record, process, and present information in order to gain knowledge. You acquire this ability as you become a more active listener, sharpen your observation, and participate in class by asking questions. You enhance this ability as you improve your reading and writing skills.

On page ix you will find a list of study skills that make up the first part of this book. During your study of biology, take time to learn about each skill and to practice it. The graphic organizing skills on the list are also introduced in your textbook on pages 901–903.

In the second part of this Study Guide, you will find a worksheet to go along with each section of your textbook. Completing these worksheets will help you review the vocabulary and major concepts in each section of a particular chapter. In addition, many of the study skills introduced in the first part of the Study Guide are applied to the chapter content, giving you the opportunity to practice the skills as you learn new material in biology. After the skills application pages, you will find a two-page chapter review that will help you prepare for taking tests. Your active participation in class and good use of this Study Guide can go a long way toward helping you achieve success in your study of biology.

Skills Development

Contents

Name _____ Date _____

SKILLS DEVELOPMENT

Using Your Textbook

Your textbook contains a wealth of detailed information about the science of biology. You will find it easier to learn this information if you know how and when to use the other features contained in your textbook.

Features That Help You Locate Information in Your Text

The **Table of Contents** is located at the beginning of your book. It lists all the units, chapters, and sections in the book and the page where each one begins. Instead of flipping haphazardly through the text until you find the passage you want, use the Table of Contents to locate it. Once you turn to the first page, use the **boldfaced** headings and subheadings to zero in on the passage you want. If you want a list of all the pages in the text where a particular subject is discussed, look that subject up in the **Index** at the end of the book.

Practice Locating Information

Use the Table of Contents to find the number of the page where each of the following sections begins.

1. Section 4–3 _____

2. Section 32–2 _____

Use the Index to find the first pages on which each of the following topics is discussed.

3. enzymes _____

4. translocation _____

Features That Help You Get Started

The first two pages of each unit contain a list of all the chapters in that unit, a brief introduction to the subject they have in common, and a photograph related to that subject.

   The first two pages of each chapter contain a brief introduction to the material and a photograph that illustrates some aspect of chapter content. A Guide for Reading identifies key words introduced in the chapter and raises questions for you to think about as you read.

   Within a chapter, each section begins with a list of **Objectives** that tell you what specific information to look for as you read.

Practice Getting Started

5. What is pictured on the first two pages of Unit 4? _____

_____

6. What is the first question in the Guide for Reading for Chapter 27? _____

_____

7. How many objectives are there for Section 29–3? _____

SKILLS DEVELOPMENT
Using Your Textbook   (continued)

Features That Help You Review What You Have Learned

Your textbook contains Section and Chapter Reviews that focus your attention on important facts and concepts. **Section Reviews** appear every few pages in the text. Each one contains several content questions and a Critical Thinking question that asks you to interpret what you have read. **Chapter Reviews** review what you have learned in a variety of ways.

- The statements in the Study Outline help you review the main concepts introduced in the chapter.
- The Vocabulary Review contains a list of the terms introduced in the chapter and the pages where they are defined. You can find out whether you know how to use these terms correctly by completing the sentences following the list.
- You can test your understanding of the main ideas discussed in the chapter by answering the questions in the Content Review section.

Chapter Reviews also contain sections on **Graphic Organizing, Critical Thinking, Creative Thinking, Problem Solving,** and **Projects.** Each section will help you review one or more important concepts introduced in the chapter.

Practice Using the Section and Chapter Reviews

8. How many content questions are there in the review of Section 27–2? _____

9. How many statements are in the Study Outline for Chapter 7? _____

10. What is the fourth Vocabulary Review word in Chapter 1? _____

11. On what page in the text is this word defined? _____

Features That Enhance Your Understanding of the Material

Your textbook contains a number of other features that help you understand chapter content.

- Photographs and diagrams help you visualize what is described in the text.
- Tables, graphs, and charts present data clearly and concisely.
- Articles in the margin raise issues related to chapter content. Titles include "Can You Explain This?," "Biology and You," and "Science, Technology, and Society."
- Longer feature articles entitled "Careers in Action," "Critical Thinking in Biology," and "Biology and Problem Solving" explore issues related to chapter content in greater detail.
- **Concept Laboratories** and **Laboratory Investigations** enable you to discover biological principles and relationships for yourself.

Practice Enhancing Your Understanding

12. What is the subject of "Biology and You" in Chapter 33?

_____

13. What is the subject of "Science, Technology, and Society" in Chapter 4? _____

_____

14. What is the title of the Concept Laboratory in Chapter 10?

_____

SKILLS DEVELOPMENT
Using Your Textbook   (continued)

15. What is the title of the Laboratory Investigation in Chapter 3?

_____

Glossary and Appendices

The **Glossary** lists in alphabetical order all the boldfaced terms introduced in the text. Refer to the Glossary whenever you forget a definition and you can't remember where the term was introduced. You will also find **Appendices** at the end of your textbook. Each appendix covers a single topic in detail.

Practice Using the Glossary and the Appendices

16. How many appendices are there in your textbook? _____

17. What is the subject of Appendix B? _____

_____

Use the Glossary to define each of the following terms.

18. ossification _____

_____

19. anterior _____

_____

20. inferior vena cava _____

_____

_____

SKILLS DEVELOPMENT

Reading for Understanding: The SQ3R Approach

You do not read a textbook in the same way you read a story or magazine article. Your purpose in reading a textbook is not to relax or to be entertained but to learn and understand something. Textbooks are designed to help you learn, but you have to do your part by using a more organized, careful approach to reading.

SQ3R is a simple, effective method for reading a chapter in your textbook. The initials stand for the steps in a sequence: Survey, Question, Read, Recite, and Review.

Survey

Surveying gives you a preview, a general feeling for the kind of information you will find in the chapter. A survey can take anywhere from 5 to 15 minutes, depending on the length of the chapter.

1. Read the title, the introductory paragraphs, the Guide for Reading, and the headings and subheadings throughout the chapter. (These headings are printed in bold, distinctive type.)
2. Look over the illustrations. Read the chapter summary.
3. Ask yourself the following questions: "What is this chapter all about?" "What kind of information will I learn?" "What do I already know about this subject?" Use the Guide for Reading to direct your questioning.

Practice

Pick a chapter in your biology textbook, preferably one you have not read. Survey the chapter, then answer the following questions.

1. Write down the chapter headings and subheadings.

_____

_____

_____

_____

2. In a sentence or two, explain what the chapter is all about.

_____

_____

_____

Question

The typical textbook chapter contains a variety of ideas, facts, and figures. You will find it easier to pick out the most important ideas if you first ask yourself a question and then read to find the answer.

1. Reread the first topic heading in your reading assignment—probably one section of a chapter.

SKILLS DEVELOPMENT
Reading for Understanding: The SQ3R Approach (continued)

2. Turn the heading into a question. For example, if the heading is "Phases of Human Respiration," you might ask yourself, "What are the phases of human respiration?"
3. Write the question in your notebook to guide your studying.

Practice

Turn each of the following topic headings into a question.

1. General Characteristics of the Diplopoda _____

_____

2. Development of Gametes _____

_____

3. The Heterotroph Hypothesis _____

_____

Read

Now that you have a specific question to answer, you can read the section with a specific purpose in mind.
1. Read the passage that follows the topic heading. Look for the same words and phrases that appear in the heading.
2. Read at your usual rate until you think you have found the answer to your question.
3. Slow down and read the information carefully.

Practice

Turn the topic heading for the following paragraphs into a question and write the question on the lines provided below. Then read the paragraphs, looking for the answer.

The Small Intestine

The small intestine is a coiled tube about 6.5 meters long and about 2.5 centimeters in diameter. Most chemical digestion and almost all absorption occur here. Unlike the stomach with its acid secretions, fluids in the small intestine are usually alkaline.

In the small intestine, chyme is mixed with **bile** from the liver, **pancreatic** (pan kree AT ik) **juices** from the pancreas, and **intestinal juice** from the glands in the wall of the intestine. These three secretions contain the enzymes and other substances necessary to complete digestion.

SKILLS DEVELOPMENT
Reading for Understanding: The SQ3R Approach (continued)

Recite

You will find it easier to remember the material you learn if you hear yourself recite or say aloud the important details. By expressing them in your own words, you can also find out whether you truly understand the material.
1. Say the information aloud several times.
2. Make sure you have answered the question clearly and completely.
3. Write the answer to your question in your notebook.

Practice

Recite the information you learned from your reading. Write the answer to your question here.

_____

_____

_____

_____

Before you go on to the last step in the SQ3R method, repeat the Question-Read-Recite sequence for the remaining sections of the chapter.

Review

Reviewing is an important final step in the SQ3R method. It gives you a chance to think back about what you have learned.
1. Reread the questions and answers in your notes.

2. Try to remember a few details that explain or defend each answer.

Practice

Review what you learned from your reading.

More Practice Using SQ3R

1. Survey the following paragraph.

The Effects of Peristalsis

When food is present, the small intestine is in constant motion. These peristaltic movements have four main effects: (1) they squeeze chyme through the small intestine; (2) they mix the chyme with digestive enzymes; (3) they break down food particles mechanically; and (4) they speed up absorption of digestive end products by bringing the intestinal contents into contact with the intestinal wall.

2. Turn the topic heading of the paragraph into a question and write it here.

_____

_____

3. Read the paragraph.

SKILLS DEVELOPMENT
Reading for Understanding: The SQ3R Approach (continued)

4. Recite what you have learned. Write the answer to your question here.

_____

_____

_____

_____

5. Review what you have learned.

6. Survey the following paragraph.

Locomotion in the Earthworm

The earthworm uses muscles to burrow through the soil. Within the body wall are two layers of muscles. An outer layer of circular muscles goes around the worm and an inner layer of longitudinal muscles extends the full length of the body. When the circular muscles contract, the worm lengthens and becomes thinner. When the longitudinal muscles contract, the body becomes shorter and thicker. Within the earthworm, the body cavity is filled with fluid. This fluid acts as a skeleton because it cannot be compressed. When the surrounding muscle layers contract, the fluid "skeleton" stiffens the body of the worm and allows it to push through the soil.

7. Turn the topic heading of the paragraph into a question and write it here.

_____

_____

8. Read the paragraph.

9. Recite what you have learned. Write the answer to your question here.

_____

_____

_____

_____

_____

10. Review what you have learned.

SKILLS DEVELOPMENT

Finding the Main Idea

Most of the paragraphs in your *Biology* textbook are organized around a central, or main, idea. Sometimes that main idea is stated directly in the form of a topic sentence. Often, though, the main idea is merely implied. In this case, you can usually figure out the main idea from supporting details given in the surrounding sentences.

Where to Look for the Main Idea

There are no strict rules about where to find the main idea. It can be stated or implied anywhere in a paragraph, even at the end. Sometimes a paragraph contains more than one main idea. In such cases, main thoughts usually may be found in both the first and last sentences. Sometimes a single main idea serves to organize a series of paragraphs or an entire passage.

Summary and transitional paragraphs usually do not have a main idea. Summary paragraphs may just contain a review of many facts. Transitional paragraphs help change from one subject to another.

Find the main idea in the following paragraph.

> Insects vary greatly in body form. Cockroaches have flattened bodies that are suited for living in cracks and crevices. Beetles have thick, plump bodies. Damsel flies and walking sticks have long, slender bodies. Moths are covered with hairs that may serve to protect them from cool evening temperatures. The hairs or bristles on bees help in the collection of pollen.

This paragraph is organized around the idea that there are a great variety of insect body forms. The main idea is contained in the first sentence. All the other sentences in the paragraph support this idea by giving examples.

Practice

The main idea of the following paragraph is contained in the first sentence. Read the paragraph. Underline the main idea. In the space provided, explain why it is the main idea.

> Recent research indicates that there are two basic mechanisms of hormone action. One of these, called the *one-messenger model*, applies mainly to steroid hormones. The other, called the *two-messenger model*, applies to protein hormones.

_____

_____

_____

_____

_____

SKILLS DEVELOPMENT
Finding the Main Idea (continued)

Now find the main idea in this paragraph:

> A flatworm moves by the beating of cilia located on the lower body surface and also by rippling and crawling motions of the body. This animal's nervous system includes enlarged ganglia at the forward end of paired nerve cords. Removal of these ganglia, or simple brain, stops the crawling activity. Crawling requires the coordination of muscles, with the brain acting as a center for coordination. The rudimentary brain in flatworms represents the simple form of this structure. In higher animals, the brain is more complex. In all animals with brains, the brain coordinates complicated behavioral sequences.

This paragraph discusses the essential role that the brain plays in stimulating and coordinating the movements of the body, an idea stated in the last sentence. The discussion about the flatworm serves to illustrate this concept.

Practice

The main idea of the following paragraph is contained in the last sentence. Read the paragraph. Underline the main idea. In the space provided, explain why it is the main idea.

> Magnification refers to enlargement in one direction, such as length, and not a change in area or "size." If a microscope has a magnification of 100×, the image of a line 1 millimeter long will appear to be 100 millimeters long. The area of an image is increased by the square of the magnification. For example, the image of a square 1 millimeter × 1 millimeter will be 100 millimeters × 100 millimeters. The square has an area of 1 square millimeter. Its image has an area of 10,000 square millimeters. Students are sometimes confused by this difference between the enlargement of a line and the enlargement of an area.

_____

_____

_____

_____

_____

Now find the main idea of this paragraph:

> The warmest average temperatures on the earth's surface occur around the equator. Traveling north or south of the equator, the average temperatures drop. The North and South poles are the coldest regions on earth. Temperatures also drop with increasing altitude. Thus, the tops of high mountains may be snow-covered even at the equator.

This paragraph does not contain a topic sentence. The main idea—that average temperatures on the earth's surface drop either as altitude increases or as distance from the equator increases—is implied by the paragraph as a whole.

SKILLS DEVELOPMENT
Finding the Main Idea   (continued)

Practice

The main idea of the following paragraph is implied rather than stated in the
form of a topic sentence. Read the paragraph. In the space provided, express
the main idea in your own words.

> In modern biology, each kind of organism has a two-word
> Latin name that is its scientific name. The first word is its genus
> name; the second identifies the species within that genus. Most
> large plants and animals also have common names. However, for
> several reasons, these names are not suitable for scientific use.
> For one thing, common names are often confusing and inexact. A
> starfish, for example, is not a fish. Also, one species may have
> several different common names. The blue jay, *Cyanocitta
> christata*, is also known as the blue coat, the corn thief, and the
> nest robber. In other cases, the same common name is used for
> two or more different species. More than a dozen different
> species of plants are commonly known as raspberries. Finally,
> common names differ from language to language. An English
> "dog" is a Spanish "perro" and a Japanese "inu." However, the
> scientific name *Canis familiaris* is understood by biologists
> everywhere.

_____

_____

More Practice Finding the Main Idea

Look for the main idea in each of the following paragraphs. If the main idea is
stated as part of a topic sentence, underline it. If it is merely implied, express it
in your own words in the space provided.

1. The amount of energy available in a food web decreases with each higher feeding level. The reason for
this is that only a small fraction of the energy taken in as food becomes absorbed as new tissue. Much
of the food ingested is not digested and absorbed. Furthermore, a large part of the energy in the food
is used for respiration and maintenance. This energy is lost as heat. As a result, only about 10 percent
of the energy taken in at any feeding level is passed upward to the next feeding level.

_____

_____

2. In 1902, W. S. Sutton, a graduate student at Columbia University, was studying the formation of sperm
in the grasshopper. He observed the pairs of homologous chromosomes in diploid cells and the
separation of the homologous chromosomes during spermatogenesis. He realized that the
chromosomes that separated during meiosis were the same as the chromosomes that had united
during the fertilization process that originally produced the animal.

_____

_____

SKILLS DEVELOPMENT

Building Vocabulary

Learning about a new subject, such as biology, means learning some unfamiliar words and terms. There are several ways to add these new words to your vocabulary.

Learning Vocabulary from Your Textbook

In your textbook, important terms that may be unfamiliar to you are printed in **boldfaced** type when they are used for the first time. Boldfaced terms are defined in the same sentence or in the following one. In some cases, the textbook tells you how to pronounce them. Boldfaced terms are also listed in the chapter review.

Practice Defining Boldfaced Terms

Read each of the following sentences and underline the phrase that defines the boldfaced term. Practice using the pronunciation key by saying the word aloud.

1. Small, saclike structures surrounded by a single membrane and containing strong digestive, or hydrolytic, enzymes are **lysosomes** (LY suh sohmz).

2. The process of breaking down the glucose molecule into 23-carbon pyruvic acid molecules is called **glycolysis** (gly KAHL uh sis).

3. Ray defined a species as a group of organisms that were structurally similar and that passed these similarities to their offspring. Closely related species were included in a broader group called a **genus** (JEE nus).

4. A tough membrane, the **pericardium** (per uh KARD ee um), covers the heart and protects it.

Pay close attention to boldfaced terms when you encounter them. Keep a list of new terms in your notebook so you can refer to it during class discussions and when you prepare for a test. If you forget a definition, you can look it up in the **Glossary** at the end of the textbook. The glossary contains an alphabetical list of all the boldfaced terms used in the text.

Getting Meaning from Context Clues

Sometimes in your reading you come across an unfamiliar word that has not been defined or explained. You can either look up this word in a dictionary or figure out its meaning from *context clues*. Look for clues in the surrounding words and phrases whose meanings you already know. These words and phrases make up the unfamiliar word's context.

The following sentence contains at least one context clue to the meaning of the word in *italics*. The underlined words point out these context clues.

There are special structures in the aorta and several other large arteries that are sensitive to the concentrations of oxygen and carbon dioxide in the blood. These *chemoreceptors* send messages to the respiratory center.

SKILLS DEVELOPMENT
Building Vocabulary   (continued)

Practice Using Context Clues

Each of the following sentences contains an italicized word that you may not recognize, along with context clues to its meaning. Underline the context clues in the first sentence. Then write your own definition for the italicized word. Do the same for the other three sentences.

1. Organisms that reproduce asexually produce *clones,* since each offspring receives an exact copy of the genes of the parent.

_____

_____

_____

2. Scientists wanted to know how resistance to antibiotics developed. One possibility was that exposure to an antibiotic caused certain bacterial cells to develop resistance to it. This would be similar to the *immunity* an individual acquires to a disease organism after recovery from the disease.

_____

_____

_____

3. To stay alive, an organism must respond to external and internal changes. The organism must maintain *homeostasis.* It must keep all factors of the internal environment within certain limits.

_____

_____

_____

4. During the summer, one large tree can give off as much as 250 liters of water each day. The evaporation of water from the leaves removes heat. This *transpiration* also has a cooling effect on the plant.

_____

_____

_____

SKILLS DEVELOPMENT

Using Greek and Latin Word Parts

Some techniques discussed in *Biology: The Science of Life* are centrifugation, microdissection, tissue culture, chromatography, and electrophoresis. In your first encounter with words like these, you may not understand them. Knowing some Greek and Latin terms, however, will help you understand parts of the words. Then you can make an educated guess about their meanings.

Figuring out the meanings of words by looking at their parts will help you understand scientific material. Take the word "centrifugation," for example. This word has its roots in two Latin words: *centrum*, which means "center," and *fugere*, which means "to flee." Knowing that, you might guess that "centrifugation" has something to do with fleeing from the center—and you would be right. Centrifugation separates substances by whirling them in a circle at high speed. The heavier substances are separated from the lighter ones in the process.

Below is a list of some common Greek and Latin roots, prefixes, and suffixes that you may find useful when you read your textbook. Use the list for the exercise that follows.

Greek and Latin Word Parts

anti-	against
arterio-	having to do with arteries
bio-	life
calor-	heat
chromo-	color
dissect	cut
electro-	referring to electricity
endo-	within, inside
exo-	without, outside
-graph	write or draw
hemi-	half
hyper-	over, above, excessive
hypo-	under, beneath, below, less than
inter-	between, among
-itis	inflammation
kilo-	one thousand
-lysis	dissolution, destruction
micro-	small, minute; one-millionth
mono-	one, single
period	a regularly occurring event
-phoresis	transmission, carrying
photo-	light
-plasm	the fluid substance of a cell
sclero-	hard
-scope	an instrument for seeing or observing
stereo-	solid, firm, three-dimensional
synthesis	a putting together

SKILLS DEVELOPMENT
Using Greek and Latin Word Parts   (continued)

Practice Using Greek and Latin Word Parts

Follow these steps for each italicized word in the sentences below. The first one is done for you so you can use it as a model.

- Underline the part or parts of the italicized word that resemble a root, prefix, or suffix on the Greek and Latin Word Parts list.
- Write down the Greek and Latin word parts that you recognize, followed by their definitions.
- If the italicized word contains more than one Greek or Latin word part, try to combine their definitions into a single phrase.
- Make an educated guess about the meaning of the italicized word.

1. One frequent cause of high blood pressure is *arteriosclerosis*.

   arterio- (having to do with arteries) / sclero- (hard) / having to do with hard arteries /

   hardening of the arteries

2. *Intercellular* fluid serves as a medium for the exchange of materials between the capillaries and the body cells.

   _____

   _____

3. Not all flowering plants exhibit the same *photoperiodic* response.

   _____

   _____

4. The magnifying power of *stereomicroscopes* varies from about 6× to about 50×.

   _____

   _____

   _____

   _____

5. In *chromatography,* the mixture to be separated is placed on a solid material to which it adheres.

   _____

   _____

   _____

6. *Electrophoresis* is a technique used to separate substances whose particles have an electrical charge.

   _____

   _____

   _____

   _____

SKILLS DEVELOPMENT
Using Greek and Latin Word Parts   (continued)

7. The organs of a vertebrate animal, such as a cat, that has an *endoskeleton* are more susceptible to injury than those of an invertebrate animal, such as a crab.

_____

_____

8. The chloroplasts are the site of *photosynthesis*, the food-making process of plants.

_____

_____

9. The preferred unit used in measuring the energy content of food is the *kilocalorie.*

_____

_____

SKILLS DEVELOPMENT

Taking Notes

As a student, you draw on your note-taking skills in many learning situations—when you listen to a lecture, when you read your textbook, and when you gather information for a report, to name only a few. The more skillful you become at taking notes, the more useful your notes will be.

In Class

When you take notes in class, you are recording either what you hear your teacher say or what you see written on the blackboard or projected on the screen. Words and ideas that your teacher writes down are almost always important, but that is not true for everything your teacher says. If you want to be sure you include only important ideas in your notes, you need to be an active listener.

An active listener participates in what the speaker is saying. Here's how.

- An active listener tries to anticipate what the speaker is going to say before he or she says it.
- An active listener asks himself or herself questions about the speaker's topic and tries to answer them before the speaker does.
- An active listener tries to connect what the speaker says with what he or she already knows.

Try to be an active listener the next time your teacher gives a lecture. Your notes will be more accurate and useful if you do.

Here are some more tips on taking notes in class.

- Take notes in a notebook, not on separate pieces of paper that can get damaged or lost.
- Begin each day's notes with the date.
- Concentrate on the main ideas and supporting details.
- Limit your notes to the key words and phrases.
- Avoid writing complete sentences.
- Use symbols and abbreviations to save space.
- Pay special attention when your teacher emphasizes or repeats something or bends forward slightly. These mannerisms are often clues as to what your teacher considers important.
- Revise and reorganize your notes later the same day to clean them up and eliminate confusion.
- Review your notes regularly, not just the night before a test.

From Your Textbook

It is easier to take notes from a textbook than from a speaker because you are not so limited by time. This means your initial textbook notes are likely to be better organized than your initial lecture notes. Nevertheless, they will be even more useful if you make an effort to identify and eliminate errors and fill in the gaps in logic. Toward this end, include questions about the material that occur to you as you read. Leave room to insert the answers when you find them.

SKILLS DEVELOPMENT
Taking Notes   (continued)

As with lecture notes, limit the notes you take from your textbook to only the most significant information. Stick to the topic sentences, the supporting details, and the key words and phrases (use the SQ3R method to find them). Include the boldfaced and italicized terms, as well as their definitions. Use the boldfaced headings that divide up your textbook into sections to organize your notes.

Practice Taking Notes from Your Textbook

Read the following passage from your textbook. The topic sentences, supporting details, and the key words and phrases are underlined. On the lines below the passage and on the next page, organize the underlined words into a useful set of notes. Your notes need not include every underlined word. Substitute your own words if you prefer.

Stimuli and Behavior

An organism's environment continually changes. These changes may involve one or more external factors, including heat, light, carbon dioxide, oxygen, moisture, and the activities of other organisms. Environmental changes also may involve internal factors, such as thirst or hunger. Any change in the external or internal environment is called a **stimulus** (plural, stimuli).

In living organisms, metabolic processes run best when internal conditions remain constant. Living things maintain constant internal conditions by psychological or behavioral responses to stimuli. When a hungry dog smells food, it salivates. Secreting saliva is a psychological response. The dog may then actively hunt for food. That response is behavioral. A person sweats when hot. If that response is not sufficient to cool the body, the individual may then remove outer clothing. Sweating is a psychological response. Removing outer clothing is a form of behavior. **Behavior** is the series of activities performed by an organism in response to stimuli. While stimuli also may result in psychological responses within an organism, such responses usually are not considered to be behavior.

_____

_____

_____

_____

_____

_____

_____

_____

_____

_____

SKILLS DEVELOPMENT

Taking Notes   (continued)

_____
_____
_____
_____
_____
_____
_____
_____

More Practice

Take notes on the rest of the passage on stimuli and behavior. This time, decide
for yourself which words and phrases to include in your notes.

> The behavior of each species is different from that of others.
> In flight, a robin usually does not respond to the sight of a rabbit.
> But another bird, such as a hawk, may respond by capturing and
> eating the rabbit.
>
> Behavior aids in the survival of the individual and of the
> species. When a rabbit sees an attacking hawk, it runs first in one
> direction and then abruptly in another. This behavior may
> confuse the attacker and allow the rabbit to escape.

_____
_____
_____
_____
_____
_____
_____
_____
_____
_____
_____
_____
_____
_____
_____

SKILLS DEVELOPMENT

Interpreting Diagrams and Tables

Science textbooks often include diagrams, tables, and charts that present a large amount of information in a small amount of space. They can help you understand the written material if you know how to interpret them.

Diagrams

A diagram is a line drawing or a photograph that illustrates something described in the text. It includes labels that pinpoint the location of important details. It may include arrows that indicate the direction of some action, such as blood flow through the circulatory system. It may also include symbols, shadings, or colors that highlight similarities and differences between various parts of the diagram. Your textbook often uses a cross-sectional diagram to show something hard to see, such as the interior of an organ. Sometimes it uses a series of diagrams to illustrate a sequence of events, such as the stages of embryo development.

Practice Interpreting a Diagram

Familiarize yourself with the following diagram.

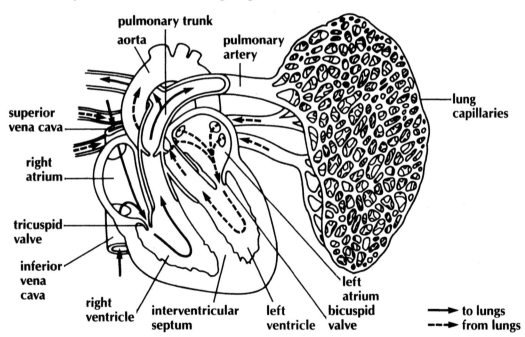

Now answer the following questions.

1. What is pictured in the diagram?

_____

2. What action is illustrated in the diagram? How can you tell?

_____

SKILLS DEVELOPMENT
Interpreting Diagrams and Tables   (continued)

3. What do the two different kinds of arrows in the diagram signify? How can you tell?

_____

_____

_____

4. With a pen or pencil, shade in the right atrium, the aorta, and the left ventricle.

Tables

A table packs a large number of facts, figures, and statistics into a small amount of space by displaying the information in rows and columns. The categories of information contained in a table are usually listed in the left-hand column. The subjects to which each category applies are usually listed as column headings across the top row. Each fact, figure, and statistic occupies its own compartment in the table. You find the one you want by looking where the category (row) and the subject (column) that interest you meet.

Practice Interpreting a Table

Familiarize yourself with the following table.

CONCENTRATIONS OF IONS IN SEAWATER AND IN BODY FLUIDS
(MILLIMOLES/LITER)

Fluid	Concentration (millimoles/liter)				
	Na^+	K^+	Ca^{2+}	Mg^{2+}	Cl^-
Seawater	459.0	9.8	10.1	52.5	538.0
Cockroach	161.0	7.9	4.0	5.6	4.0
Chicken	154.0	6.0	5.6	2.3	122.0
Human	145.0	5.1	2.5	1.2	103.0

Now answer the following questions.

1. Read the title at the top of the table. What do the numbers in the table measure?

_____

In what units are the quantities in the table expressed?

_____

2. Read the list of categories (fluids) in the left-hand column.

3. Read the names of the ions listed as column headings in the top row.

4. Read the information in the first row (seawater) from left to right.
Refer to the list of ions each time you move to a new column.

Which ion is most concentrated in seawater? _____

Which ion is least concentrated in seawater? _____

5. Repeat Step 4 for each of the remaining fluids.

SKILLS DEVELOPMENT
Interpreting Diagrams and Tables (continued)

6. Read the information in the first column (Na^+) from top to bottom. Refer to the list of fluids each time you move to a new row.

   Which fluid has the highest concentration of Na^+? _____

   Which fluid has the lowest concentration of Na^+? _____

7. Repeat Step 6 for each of the remaining ions.

8. Which fluids are the most similar in their Cl^- concentrations?

   _____

9. Which fluids differ the most in their Ca^{2+} concentrations?

   _____

SKILLS DEVELOPMENT

Graphic Organizing: Circle Graph

Textbooks often use a circle graph to portray a set of related data in picture form. Sometimes called a pie chart because it looks like a pie cut up into wedges, a circle graph represents 100%, or all of the categories of data that comprise a particular subject. Each triangular section of the graph, or slice of the "pie," represents one of these categories. The bigger the slice, the larger the quantity it represents.

Practice Interpreting Circle Graphs

Familiarize yourself with the following circle graph.

USE OF FILLED WETLANDS, MAINE TO DELAWARE
1955–1964

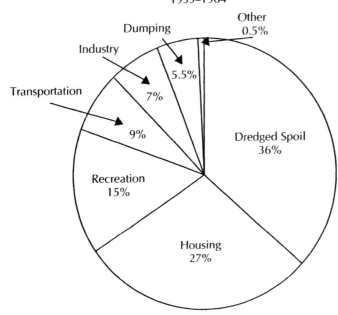

Now answer the following questions.

1. What information does the circle graph contain? _____

_____

2. What does the number in each wedge-shaped section signify? _____

_____

3. What is the fourth largest land use category in the graph? (Don't rely on size alone. Circle graph sections are sometimes drawn out of proportion, especially when they represent small quantities.)

_____

4. What is the second largest category? _____

5. What quantity is represented by the graph as a whole? _____

SKILLS DEVELOPMENT
Graphic Organizing: Circle Graph   (continued)

How to Construct a Circle Graph

1. Draw a circle.
2. Divide the circle into wedge-shaped sections, one for each category of data. The larger the category, the larger you should make the section. If you want the proportions to be precise, figure out the percentage of data represented by each category and multiply by 360. For example, if a category represents 25% of all the data, multiply 0.25 by 360. The section of the graph that represents this category should form a 90-degree angle. Use a protractor to construct the angle.
3. Identify each section and the quantity it represents. Be sure to include the units. If there is enough room, enter this information in the section. If not, record the information outside the circle and use an arrow to indicate which section it identifies.
4. Fill in the remainder of each section of the graph with a different pattern or color.
5. Give the graph a title.

Practice Constructing a Circle Graph

1. Look over the following data:

   VETEBRATE SPECIES AND MAJOR SUBSPECIES IN THE U.S., 1970s

Mammals: 408	Birds: 904	Reptiles: 349
Amphibians: 199	Fish: 1067	Total: 2927

2. Decide which section of the graph below should represent each category of data.
3. Indicate the category and the quantity represented by each section.
4. Fill in each section with a different pattern or color.
5. Give the graph a title. Include the total quantity represented by the graph.

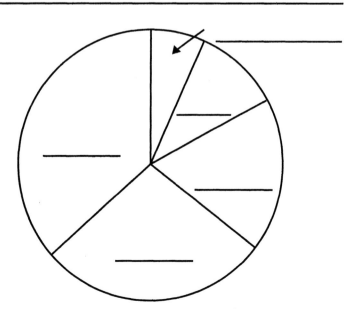

SKILLS DEVELOPMENT

Graphic Organizing: Circle Graph   (continued)

More Practice

1. Look over the following data:

DISTRIBUTION OF FISH SPECIES AND MAJOR SUBSPECIES IN U.S.
BY TYPE OF ENVIRONMENT, 1970s

Marsh: 289   Lake: 475   River: 720
Estuary: 449   Ocean: 460   Total: 2393

2. Construct and label a circle graph based on the data.

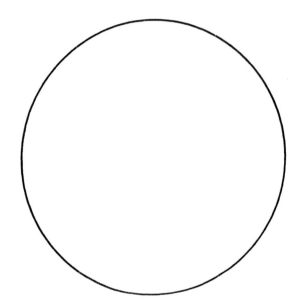

SKILLS DEVELOPMENT

Graphic Organizing: Bar Graph

Textbooks often use a bar graph to present related data side by side so you can compare them. Each bar represents a different category of data. Sometimes the bars are divided into an upper and a lower segment, each of which represents a different subcategory of data. When the bars are displayed vertically, the categories are listed on the x-axis. You measure the bars using a scale on the y-axis. When the bars are displayed horizontally, the categories are listed on the y-axis and you measure the bars using a scale on the x-axis. When neither axis contains a scale, you interpret the graph by comparing the bars with one another. The taller or longer the bar, the larger the quantity it represents.

   A bar graph can also track multiple categories of data over time by displaying the bars in groups, each of which represents a different year's worth of data. Such a graph includes a legend so you can tell apart the bars within each group.

Practice Interpreting a Bar Graph

The following bar graph compares the behaviors exhibited by eight different groups of animals.

BEHAVIOR EXHIBITED BY VARIOUS GROUPS OF ANIMALS

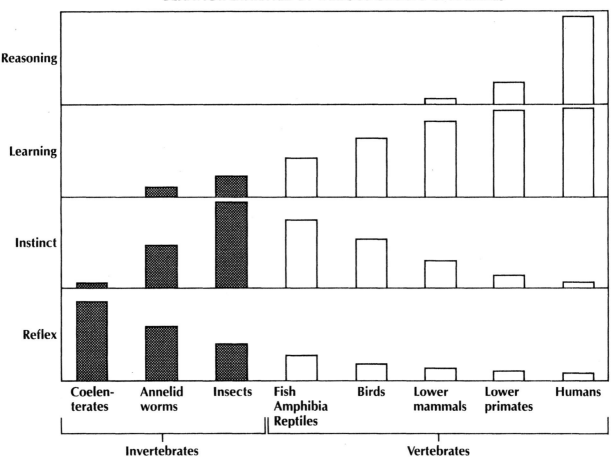

Familiarize yourself with the bar graph, and then answer the following questions.

SKILLS DEVELOPMENT
Graphic Organizing: Bar Graph (continued)

1. List the kinds of behavior that are compared in the graph. _____

_____

2. Why are some of the bars shaded while others are not? _____

_____

3. This graph does not contain a numerical scale on either the x- or the y-axis. How can you interpret the

meaning of the bars? _____

_____

4. Which group of animals exhibits the most instinctual behavior? _____

5. Which group of animals exhibits the least learning behavior? _____

6. Which group of animals exhibits the most reasoning behavior? _____

7. What pattern do you observe in the categories of behavior listed on the y-axis? _____

_____

_____

8. What differences do you observe between the vertebrate and the invertebrate animal groups? _____

_____

_____

_____

9. What pattern do you observe as you look from left to right across the graph? _____

_____

_____

How to Construct a Bar Graph

1. Create the horizontal x-axis and the vertical y-axis that define the bottom and the left side of the graph.
2. If you want the bars to be vertical, create a scale on the y-axis. If you want them to be horizontal, create a scale on the x-axis. Make sure the scale will accommodate all of your data. For example, if the largest quantity you plan to represent with a bar is 52 units, consider creating a scale with 11 divisions, each of which is 5 units long. You could also create a scale with 6 divisions, each of which is 10 units long.
3. Number the divisions of the scale.
4. Label the scale. For example, if each bar on the graph will represent the mass of an organism measured in grams, label the scale *Mass (grams)*.
5. Draw and label the bars. If appropriate, fill in each bar with a pattern or color. Create a legend that identifies the category of data represented by each pattern or color.
6. Title the graph.

SKILLS DEVELOPMENT
Graphic Organizing: Bar Graph (continued)

Practice Constructing a Bar Graph

1. Look over the following data:

ENDANGERED ANIMAL SPECIES IN THE UNITED STATES, 1979

Mammals	35
Birds	66
Reptiles	11
Amphibians	6
Fishes	28

2. Label the scale on the vertical axis of the graph below.
3. Decide which bar represents each endangered animal species and label it accordingly on the horizontal axis.
4. Give the graph a title.

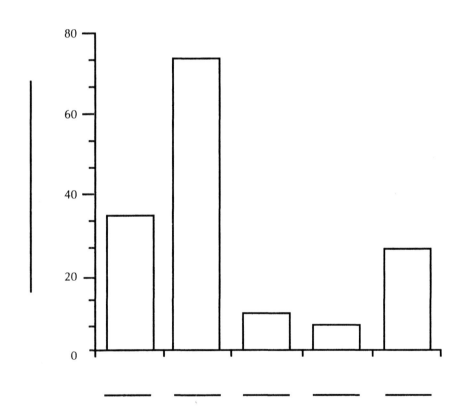

SKILLS DEVELOPMENT
Graphic Organizing: Bar Graph (continued)

5. Look over the following data.

MILLIONS OF DUCKS HARVESTED BY FLYWAY, 1968 AND 1975

Flyway	1968	1975
Mississippi	3.2	7.5
Pacific	3.7	4.3
Central	1.8	3.0

6. On the graph below, construct a set of bars for the 1975 data. The 1968 bars are already in place. Be sure you display the 1975 bars in the same order.

7. Use the legend to fill in each 1975 bar with the appropriate pattern.

8. Label the 1975 group of bars.

9. Label the vertical scale. Be sure to include the units.

10. Give the graph a title.

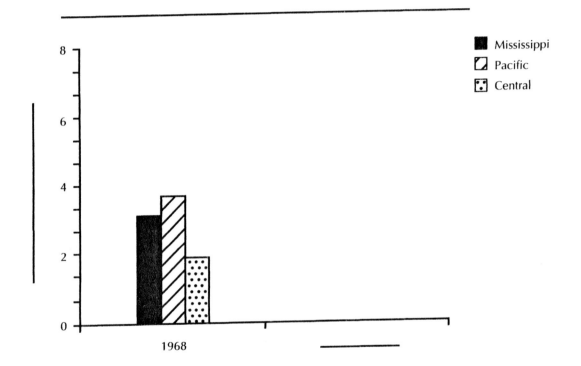

SKILLS DEVELOPMENT
Graphic Organizing: Bar Graph (continued)

More Practice

1. Look over the following data.

MOST FREQUENTLY OBSERVED BREEDING BIRD SPECIES, 1977

Species	Mean Number Observed Per Route
Red-Winged Blackbird	80
Starling	60
American Robin	37
Common Crow	31

2. Construct a bar graph using this data.

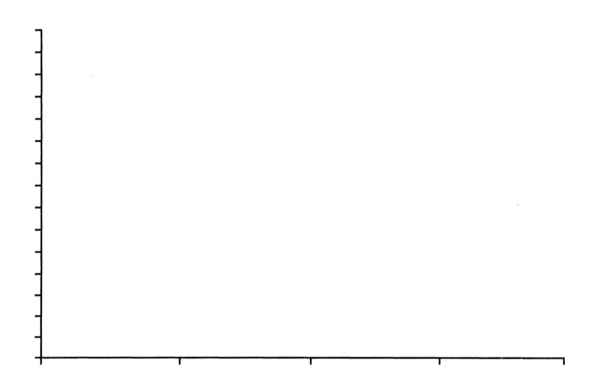

SKILLS DEVELOPMENT

Graphic Organizing: Line Graph

A line graph is the perfect tool to use when you want to illustrate the changes that take place in one quantity over time or when you want to show how one quantity changes in response to change in another quantity. The data that describe these interactions appear on the graph as dots, connected to form a line or curve. Each dot, or plot, signifies that a relationship exists between a specific measurement on the horizontal scale at the bottom of the graph and a specific measurement on the vertical scale at the left edge of the graph. The line that connects all the dots together graphically illustrates the pattern of these relationships. When more than one line appears on the same graph, each one illustrates the pattern of relationships for a different category of data.

It's easy to obtain data from a line graph. When you want to know the corresponding quantity on the vertical scale for a specific quantity on the horizontal scale, use a straightedge to mark the data line directly above the quantity on the horizontal scale that interests you. Then use the straightedge to find the quantity on the vertical scale directly to the left of your mark. Follow these steps in reverse order when you want to find the quantity on the horizontal scale that corresponds to a specific quantity on the vertical scale.

Practice Interpreting a Line Graph

The following line graph shows how the size of a bacteria population changed over an eight-hour period.

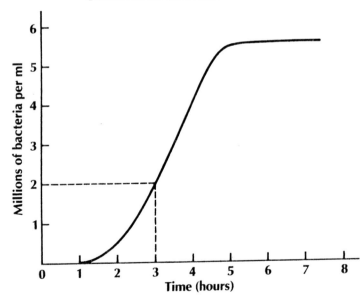

GROWTH OF BACTERIAL POPULATION

Familiarize yourself with the graph, and then answer the following questions.

1. What does the scale on the horizontal axis of the graph measure? _____

_____

2. What quantity does one unit on the horizontal scale equal? _____

SKILLS DEVELOPMENT
Graphic Organizing: Line Graph (continued)

3. What does the scale on the vertical axis measure? _____

_____

4. What quantity does one unit on the vertical scale equal? _____

_____

5. What specific information can you learn from the graph? _____

_____

6. How large was the bacteria population at the end of the fifth hour? _____

_____

7. At what point were there 3 million bacteria per milliliter? _____

How to Construct a Line Graph

1. Create the horizontal x-axis and the vertical y-axis of the graph.
2. Create scales on both the x- and y-axes. Make sure they will accommodate all of your data. For example, if the largest quantity you plan to measure on the x-axis scale is 42 units, consider creating an x-axis scale with 9 divisions, each of which is 5 units long.
3. Number the divisions of the scales.
4. Label the scales. For example, if the line on the graph will illustrate changes in the length of an organism measured in millimeters over a period of three years, label the x-axis scale *Time (years)* and the y-axis scale *Length (millimeters)*.

    Raw data for a line graph usually appear in data table form. Quantities measured on the horizontal scale usually appear in the left-hand column. Quantities measured on the vertical scale usually appear in the right-hand column.
5. Locate the first quantity in the left-hand column of the table on the horizontal scale of the graph. Using a straightedge and a pencil, draw a faint vertical line from that point across the field of the graph.
6. Locate the first quantity in the right-hand column of the table on the vertical scale of the graph. Starting at that point, draw a faint horizontal line across the field of the graph.
7. Draw a small dot, or plot, where the two lines cross.
8. Repeat steps 5–7 for the remaining pairs of data in the table.
9. Connect the plots to form a smooth line or curve. (In some cases, the plots may not fall on the line or curve. You may need to draw the line or curve so that it passes near or between plots.)
10. If the graph will contain more than one line of data, label the line you just created.
11. Repeat steps 5–10 for each additional line of data.
12. Give the graph a title.

SKILLS DEVELOPMENT
Graphic Organizing: Line Graph   (continued)

Practice Constructing a Line Graph

1. Look over the following data:

IRISH ELK

Antler Size (mm)	Skull Length (mm)
320	450
330	465
350	480
365	485
390	490

2. Number the remainder of the x-axis scale on the graph below.
3. Label the x-axis scale.
4. Number the remainder of the y-axis scale.
5. Label the y-axis scale.
6. Plot the remaining data in the table.
7. Connect the plots to form a curve.
8. Give the graph a title.

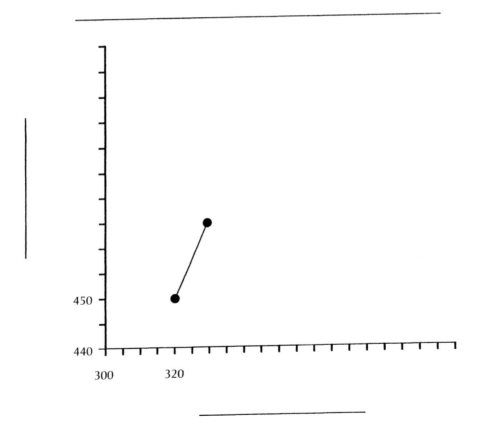

SKILLS DEVELOPMENT
Graphic Organizing: Line Graph   (continued)

More Practice

1. Look over the following data:

POPULATION OF SELECTED THREATENED AND ENDANGERED SPECIES

Species	1950	1960	1970
Whooping Crane	24	41	78
California Condor	56	43	46

2. Construct a line graph using this data. Keep track of the year on the x-axis. Keep track of the number of animals on the y-axis.

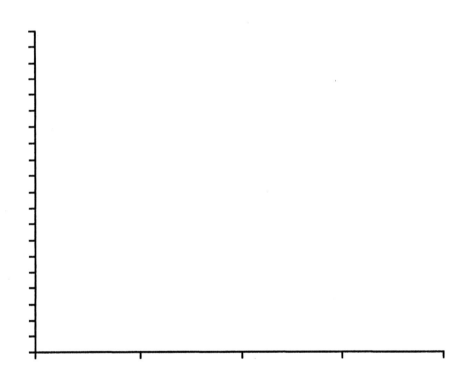

SKILLS DEVELOPMENT

Graphic Organizing: Flow Chart

Terms like *photosynthesis* and *reproduction* refer to biological processes that involve a number of steps. Sometimes there are so many steps in a process that it's difficult to remember all of them, let alone the order in which they occur. You can minimize your confusion, however, by using a flow chart to diagram such terms. The same flow chart will also help you understand how each step in the process builds on the preceding one and lays the groundwork for the next.

Lab procedures are easier to implement if you summarize them in a flow chart before you begin. The instructions in your textbook and in your lab manual include a wealth of detail designed to help you prepare for the lab. However, these same details can distract you when you are in the middle of an experiment and you want to know what to do next. If you have diagramed the experiment with a flow chart, you can ignore the details and focus instead on the procedure itself.

A flow chart consists of a series of boxes strung out in a line across the page. When necessary, the line of boxes continues on the next line. An arrow points from the first box to the second, another points from the second to the third, and so on, all the way across the chart. Each box contains a word or a phrase that summarizes one step in a sequence of steps. The arrows indicate the order of events. Details that explain and elaborate are not included in the chart. A title identifies the process or procedure diagramed in the chart. These characteristics are all illustrated in the following example.

CHANGING A FLAT TIRE

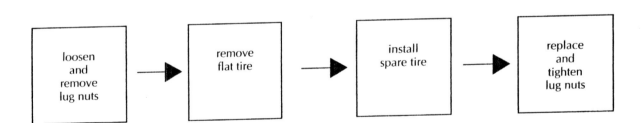

How to Construct a Flow Chart

1. List the steps in the process or procedure you want to diagram. Do not include details that explain or elaborate.
2. Number the steps.
3. Construct a series of boxes equal in length to the number of steps in the process or procedure.
4. In the first box, summarize the first step in the process or procedure with a word or a phrase.
5. Insert a right arrow following the box.
6. Repeat Steps 4 and 5 until all the boxes are full. Omit the arrow following the last box in the series.
7. Add a title that identifies the process or procedure.

SKILLS DEVELOPMENT
Graphic Organizing: Flow Chart (continued)

Practice Constructing a Flow Chart

1. The items in the following list describe the process of taking a bath. Number them in sequential order.

____ rinse off ____ fill tub

____ empty tub ____ dry off

____ dress ____ undress

____ wash with soap

2. The items in the following list describe the process of making a peanut butter and jelly sandwich. Eliminate details that explain or clarify, then number the remaining items in sequential order.

____ spread peanut butter on one slice ____ put away ingredients

____ screw jar lids on tightly ____ avoid using chunky peanut butter

____ combine slices ____ lay out two slices of bread

____ gather ingredients ____ spread jelly on the other slice

3. The items in the following list describe the process of planting a vegetable garden. Eliminate details that explain or clarify, then number the remaining items in sequential order. Construct a line of boxes for a flow chart, insert the steps and arrows, and create a title.

____ plant seeds ____ pull weeds

____ check supply of fertilizer ____ mend fence

____ plan layout ____ loosen soil

____ decide what to plant ____ water garden

SKILLS DEVELOPMENT

Graphic Organizing: Flow Chart   (continued)

More Practice

Read the following laboratory procedure, then diagram it in a flow chart. Do not include details that explain or clarify. Give the chart a title.

Procedure for Determining the Number of Stomates on a Leaf

1. Read the entire remainder of this lab before carrying out the next step in this procedure.

2. Prepare a written plan of action that describes the way you plan to proceed with the work. Get your teacher's approval of your plan before you begin any work.

3. Consider comparing the stomate density of
   - leaves of different ages from the same plant or tree
   - leaves from different types of plants
   - leaves from plants grown in different types of soil and with different water supplies
   - leaves from the same tree that ordinarily receive different amounts of sunlight

4. Familiarize yourself with the appearance of the cells that make up the outer covering of leaves by looking at the sketch in Figure 1.

5. Select one leaf to start with. Determine the stomate density of the leaf.

6. Use the result you get in Step 5 to determine the number of stomates on the entire leaf.

7. Repeat Steps 5 and 6 for one or more additional leaves, as time permits.

8. Compare your results with those obtained by other lab teams.

SKILLS DEVELOPMENT
Graphic Organizing: Flow Chart (continued)

Still More Practice

Construct a flow chart that diagrams the process of human reproduction from fertilization to birth.

SKILLS DEVELOPMENT

Graphic Organizing: Scale

Use a scale when you want to rank several items with respect to a single characteristic, such as strength or drought resistance, or when you want to place events in chronological order. In the latter case, the scale is called a timeline.

The empty framework of a scale represents the full range of possibilities for a given characteristic. The ends of the framework represent the two extremes. The item that displays the smallest amount of the characteristic appears on the left end. The item that displays the greatest amount of the characteristic appears on the right end. The remaining items are spread out on the framework between these two extremes. The more similar two items are, the closer together they appear; the more dissimilar they are, the farther apart they appear.

When a scale is used to display events in chronological order, the event that occurred first appears on the left and the one that occurred most recently appears on the right.

Scales are usually not marked off in units, so you can use them to compare items with one another but not to measure them individually. For example, you can tell which item in a pair is bigger, but not how much bigger. Scales that appear on bar and line graphs are marked off in units so you can plot and interpret data.

Practice Interpreting a Scale

1. Look over the following scale.

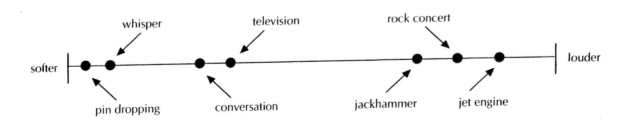

SOUNDS

2. On what characteristic does the scale focus? _____

3. How much louder is a jet engine than a whisper? _____

_____

_____

SKILLS DEVELOPMENT
Graphic Organizing: Scale   (continued)

4. Look over the following timeline of American history.

AMERICAN HISTORY

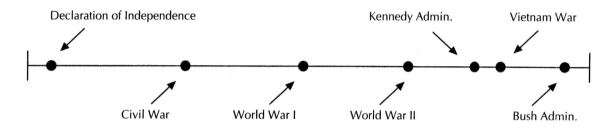

5. Which event took place most recently? _____

6. Which event took place longest ago? _____

7. Which two events occurred closest together in time? _____

_____

8. How many years separate the first and last events on the timeline? _____

_____

How to Construct a Scale or Timeline

1. Determine the number of items you want to include.
2. Determine the order in which the items should appear.
3. Draw a horizontal line across the page.
4. Place one dot on the scale or timeline for each item. The greater the difference between items, the more space you should leave between the dots that represent them.
5. Label each dot.
6. If you are constructing a scale, label both ends. For example, if the scale compares weights, label the left end *lighter* and the right end *heavier*.
7. Give the scale or timeline a title that tells what kind of information it contains.

Practice Constructing a Scale

1. Construct a scale that compares the maximum speeds of the following items: space shuttle, snail, race horse, jet, gazelle, jogger, stalking lion.

SKILLS DEVELOPMENT

Graphic Organizing: Scale   (continued)

2. Construct a timeline using the following stages of human development: adolescence, infancy, adulthood, old age, birth, death, childhood.

3. Construct a scale that ranks everyone in your immediate family by height.

SKILLS DEVELOPMENT

Graphic Organizing: Compare/Contrast Matrix

An empty matrix looks like a wall full of mail boxes at the post office. Like the post office, each box is reserved for a specific piece of information. Unlike the post office, however, all the information pertains to the same general topic.

The rows and columns of a matrix make it an ideal tool for exploring similarities and differences among a group of related subjects. That's why this graphic organizer is often called a *compare/contrast matrix*. The subjects are listed across the top row, while the characteristics used to make the comparison are listed in the left-hand column. Each of the remaining boxes contains information about the topic of the matrix.

When a matrix contains numerical entries rather than terms that describe and explain, it is called a data table.

Practice Interpreting a Compare/Contrast Matrix

1. Look over the matrix below, then answer the questions that follow.

REPRODUCTION

Characteristic	Asexual Reproduction	Sexual Reproduction
Number of Parents	one	two
Appearance of Offspring	identical to parent	not identical to either parent
Need for Special Cells or Organs	needed	not needed

2. What subjects does the matrix compare and contrast? _____

_____

3. What categories of information does the matrix use to make the comparison? _____

_____

4. How do sexual and asexual reproduction compare with regard to number of parents? _____

_____

_____

5. How do sexual and asexual reproduction compare with regard to appearance of offspring? _____

_____

_____

6. How do sexual and asexual reproduction compare with regard to the need for special reproductive

cells or organs? _____

_____

_____

SKILLS DEVELOPMENT
Graphic Organizing: Compare/Contrast Matrix (continued)

How to Construct a Compare/Contrast Matrix

1. Decide how many subjects you want to compare and contrast.
2. Decide how many characteristics or categories of information you want to use.
3. Construct the framework for the matrix with one row for the names of the subjects, one row for each characteristic or category, one column for the names of the characteristics or categories, and one column for each subject.
4. Enter the names of the categories in the left-hand column, starting with the second row.
5. Enter the names of the subjects in the top row, starting with the second column.
6. Fill in each empty box with the appropriate information. Use key words and phrases rather than complete sentences whenever possible.
7. Create a title for the matrix.

Practice Constructing a Compare/Contrast Matrix

1. Construct the framework for a matrix that will use three categories of information to compare and contrast four different subjects.

2. The following passage uses three categories of information to compare and contrast two different subjects. Read the passage, then identify the subjects and categories discussed there by labeling the boxes in the top row and in the left-hand column of the matrix on the next page.

There are two basic types of nutrition. In one kind, the organism produces its own complex nutrients using simple substances in the environment. All the green plants and some bacteria and other one-celled organisms are able to make their own nutrients in this way. Organisms that cannot make their own nutrients must obtain them by breaking down complex foods they find in the environment.

SKILLS DEVELOPMENT
Graphic Organizing: Compare/Contrast Matrix (continued)

3. Use the information contained in the following passage to complete the matrix below. Create a title for the matrix.

Transport is the process by which substances taken into the organism or produced within the organism are distributed throughout the organism. Nutrients, wastes, and other products of the life processes are distributed from one place to another within the organism. In the smallest organisms there is no real transport system. Usable materials are absorbed directly into the organism from the environment. Wastes pass from the organism directly back to the environment. In most animals there is a specialized circulatory system for carrying needed materials to all parts of the organism and for carrying wastes away. In plants, there are specialized conducting structures that carry substances from the roots and leaves to all parts of the plant.

	Smallest Organisms	Plants	Most Animals
Method of Transport			
How Useful Substances Reach All Parts of Organism			
How Wastes Are Eliminated			

SKILLS DEVELOPMENT
Graphic Organizing: Compare/Contrast Matrix (continued)

More Practice

Construct a matrix based on the information contained in the following passage. Be sure to include a title.

Regulation is the process by which an organism maintains a stable internal environment in a constantly changing external environment. The condition of a stable internal environment is called homeostasis.

In animals, regulation is accomplished primarily by the nervous system, the endocrine system, and the excretory system. The nervous system consists of a network of specialized cells that carry messages, or impulses, throughout the organism. The endocrine system consists of a number of glands that secrete chemicals called hormones. Hormones act as chemical messengers. Both nerve impulses and hormones can bring about changes in the organism in response to changes in either the internal or the external environment.

SKILLS DEVELOPMENT

Graphic Organizing: Word Map

As the saying goes, "A picture is worth a thousand words." This is especially true of a word map, a compact drawing that defines a word in much more detail than would be possible with a brief definition. A word map includes not only a definition of a word, but also the category the word belongs in and one or more examples or components of the word. These elements are included in the following structural diagram of a word map.

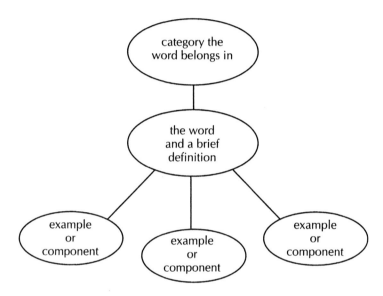

The following map of the word "dog" is typical. The word appears in the center of the map, along with a brief definition. Three examples of "dog" appear at the bottom. The category (*mammal*) in which "dog" belongs appears at the top of the map.

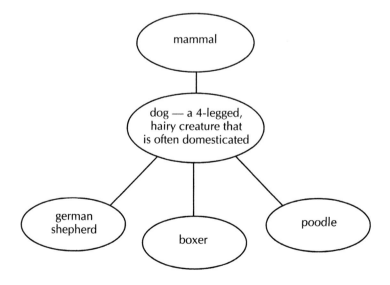

SKILLS DEVELOPMENT
Graphic Organizing: Word Map   (continued)

How to Construct a Word Map

A word map is easier to construct if you think in terms of a clock face.
1. In the center of the clock face, draw an oval. Inside this oval, write the word you want to map. Include a brief definition.
2. At the twelve o'clock position on the clock face, draw another oval. In its center, write the name of the general category that contains the word you are mapping.
3. Connect these two circles with a straight line.
4. Along the arc that extends from the four o'clock position to the eight o'clock position, draw one oval for each example or component of the word in the center of the clock face. Write one example in each of these ovals.
5. Connect each example oval to the one in the center of the clock face with a straight line.

Practice Constructing a Word Map

1. Read the following passage. On the lines below, identify the words and phrases you would use to construct a map of the term "flatworm."

> Flatworms are the simplest animals showing bilateral symmetry. They are also the simplest invertebrate group showing definite head and tail regions. They differ in both respects from the members of another invertebrate group, the coelenterates, which show radial symmetry and have no definite head or tail region. There are three major groups of flatworms: free-living flatworms such as planaria, parasitic flukes, and parasitic tapeworms. Free-living flatworms are usually aquatic and are found in both fresh and salt water.

subject of the word map _____   general category _____

definition _____

_____

example(s) _____

component(s) of the word _____

2. Insert the words and phrases you identified above into the following word map framework.

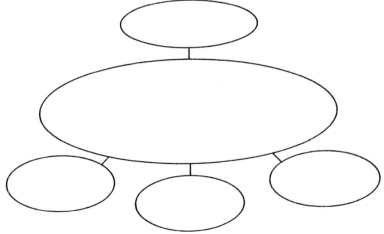

SKILLS DEVELOPMENT
Graphic Organizing: Word Map   (continued)

3. Read the following passage. On the lines below, identify the words and phrases you would use to construct a map of the term "insect."

> Biologically, insects are the most successful class of arthropods. There are nearly 900,000 known species. Nearly all insects are land animals, although a few live in fresh water and a few in salt water. Insects range in size from tiny beetles 0.25 millimeters long to some large tropical moths with a wingspan of 30 centimeters. Most insects, however, are less than 2.5 centimeters long.
>
> All insects have three separate body regions—the head, thorax, and abdomen. On the head are one pair of antennae, several mouthparts, and, in most insects, compound eyes. On the thorax are three pairs of walking legs. In flying insects, the wings are also located on the thorax. The abdomen has as many as 11 segments, with no leglike appendages.

subject of the word map _____

general category _____

definition _____

_____

example(s) _____

component(s) of the word _____

4. Construct the framework for a map based on the words and phrases you identified above. Use those words and phrases to fill in the map.

SKILLS DEVELOPMENT
Graphic Organizing: Word Map   (continued)

More Practice

Read the following passage. Underline the words and phrases you would use to
construct a map of the word.

> The mollusks are a highly successful animal group. They are the
> second largest animal phylum, after the arthropods. Oysters,
> clams, snails, squids, and octopuses are familiar mollusks. Mol-
> lusks are found in salt water, in fresh water, and on land.
> Members of this group vary greatly in size and shape. Mollusks
> range from tiny snails 1 millimeter long to giant squids, which
> can reach 16 meters in length and weigh 2 tons. The giant clam
> of the South Pacific ocean can be 1.5 meters long and weigh 250
> kilograms.

Construct the framework for a map based on the words and phrases you
identified above. Use those words and phrases to fill in the map.

SKILLS DEVELOPMENT

Graphic Organizing: Concept Map

Biological concepts are easier to understand and remember if you use both words and pictures to explain them. A concept map is well-suited for this purpose because it uses a combination of words, phrases, circles, and lines to emphasize relationships among concepts.

A concept map is constructed by placing concept words (usually nouns) in ovals and connecting them with linking words, which are written along lines extending between the ovals. The most general concept word is placed in an oval at the top of the map, and the words become more specific as you move downward.

An Example

The following passage uses ten key terms to explain how growth takes place in several different kinds of organisms.

> Growth is the process by which living organisms increase in size. It is one result of assimilation of nutrients. In one-celled organisms, growth is simply an increase in the size of the cell. In organisms made up of many cells, growth is usually the result of an increase in both the number and size of cells. Growth in multicellular organisms is accompanied by differentiation, the process whereby initially similar and unspecialized cells become specialized for specific functions.

Here's one way to map the passage.

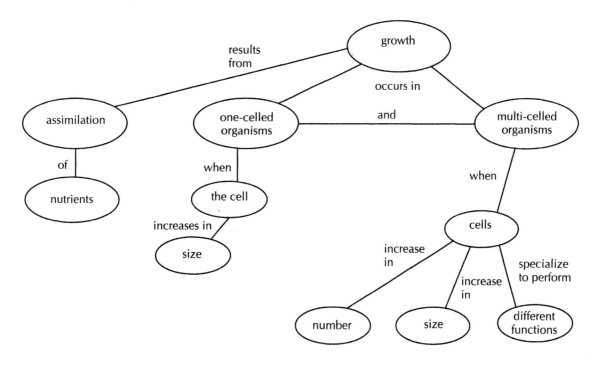

SKILLS DEVELOPMENT
Graphic Organizing: Concept Map   (continued)

The following characteristics apply to most concept maps, including the one on the previous page.
- The concept words flow from general to specific as you read down the map.
- Each encircled term plays a key role in explaining the general concept at the top of the map.
- The encircled terms in the second row or tier of the map zero-in on a specific example of the general concept.
- Each encircled term is linked to at least one other encircled term.
- Each encircled term appears only once.
- Encircled terms are usually either nouns or noun phrases, but they can be verbs or adjectives.
- The words and phrases that link encircled terms together are verbs, verb phrases, prepositions, and prepositional phrases.
- Each string of terms and linking words reads like a sentence.

Guidelines for Constructing a Concept Map

1. Read the entire passage before you attempt to map it.
2. Make a list of the concepts you want the map to contain.
3. Pick out the main concept and place it at the top of the map. (The first key term in the passage may not belong at the top of the map.)
4. Rank the remaining concepts from most general to most specific. Group together related concepts.
5. Arrange the concepts in a downward, branching structure. Map all the terms in one sentence before you go on to the next sentence. One term can follow another without a linking word or phrase between them.
6. To find out whether a string of key terms and linking words expresses a complete thought, read it out loud, beginning with the first term in the map.
7. Eliminate unnecessary repetition. When two or more sentences in a passage contain or refer to the same term, try joining their maps together.
8. Look for ways to simplify and refine the map. Move terms from one spot to another if doing so will clarify what you mean. If necessary, move an entire string of terms and the words that link them.
9. Look for ways to link different parts of the map together. Such cross-linkages demonstrate increased understanding.

   Remember that there is usually more than one way to map a passage. As a general rule, the longer the passage you are mapping, the more versions you will have to produce before you are satisfied.

STUDY GUIDE
50   BIOLOGY: The Study of Life

SKILLS DEVELOPMENT
Graphic Organizing: Concept Map (continued)

Practice Constructing a Concept Map

1. Read the following passage.

> In some animals, each individual contains both testes and
> ovaries. Such organisms are called hermaphrodites. Herma-
> phroditism is generally found among slow-moving or sessile
> animals such as earthworms, snails, and hydra.

2. List the concepts you want to include in a map of the passage.

_____

_____

3. Insert the concepts you selected into the following map.

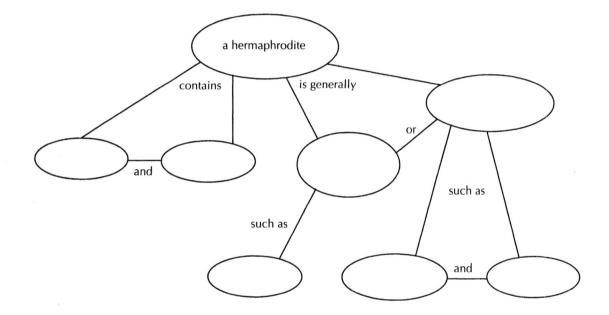

SKILLS DEVELOPMENT
Graphic Organizing: Concept Map (continued)

4. Read the following passage.

> Within the nucleus of the fertilized egg is the hereditary material, which contains all the information necessary for the development of the organism. The hereditary information is encoded within the chemical structure of DNA in the chromosomes. DNA controls the chemical processes of the cell and determines which proteins are synthesized by the cell.

5. List the concepts you want to include in a map of the passage.

_____

_____

_____

6. Insert the concepts you selected into the following map.

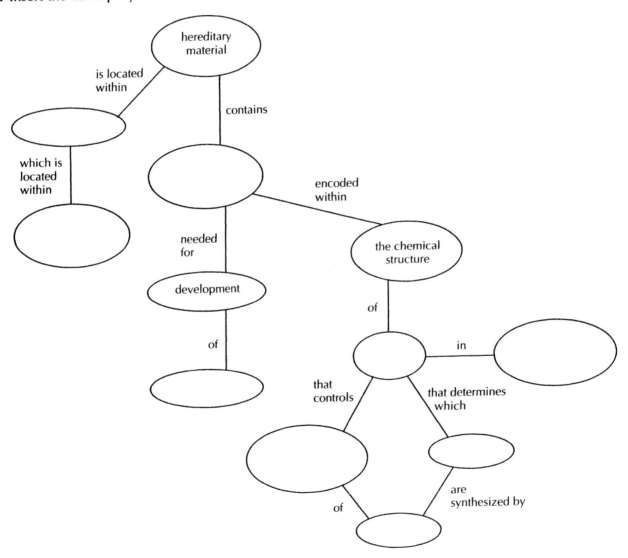

SKILLS DEVELOPMENT
Graphic Organizing: Concept Map (continued)

7. Read the following passage.

> Every organism takes materials from its environment and changes them into forms it can use. This activity is called nutrition. Substances that an organism needs for energy, growth, repair, and maintenance are called nutrients.

8. List the concepts you want to include in a map of the passage.

_____

_____

_____

9. Construct the framework for a concept map of the passage.

10. Insert the concepts you selected into the framework.

SKILLS DEVELOPMENT
Graphic Organizing: Concept Map (continued)

11. Read the following passage.

> Skates and rays have flattened, winglike bodies with whiplike tails. The rippling motion of their pectoral fins gracefully propels them through the water. They live on the ocean floor and feed on worms, mollusks, and crustaceans. Stingrays have poison stingers in their tails, which they use for defense. Electric rays produce a large electric charge, which they use to stun their prey.

12. List the concepts you want to include in a map of the passage.

_____

_____

_____

_____

13. Construct the framework for a concept map of the passage.

14. Insert the concepts you selected into the framework.

SKILLS DEVELOPMENT
Graphic Organizing: Concept Map (continued)

More Practice

1. Read the following passage.

> All the chemical reactions occurring within the cells of an organism are called its metabolism. Metabolism includes processes that build complex substances from simpler ones and processes that break down complex substances into simpler ones. Metabolism also involves the continuous release and use of energy. Many biologists consider metabolic activity to be the single most important characteristic of life.

2. Construct a concept map of the passage.

SKILLS DEVELOPMENT

Designing a Controlled Experiment

When scientists want to find out why something is the way it is or why something happens the way it does, they conduct an experiment. Since they want the results of the experiment to be taken seriously by other scientists, they employ a universal approach to solving problems called the *scientific method*.

The Scientific Method

Scientists generally follow three steps when they use the scientific method. First, they pose the question that they want to answer. Next, they form a hypothesis, their best explanation or guess as to what the answer will be. Then they design and conduct an experiment that will either prove or disprove their hypothesis.

Step 1: Define the Problem

Begin by posing your question very carefully and specifically so you can carry out a proper investigation. Then conduct a thorough search of all the relevant information available to you, including books, reports, and scientific journals. For example, if you were to pose the question, "Does a plant grow faster when light intensity is increased?", you would look for books about the biology of plants in the card catalogs of both your school and local libraries. You would also check the *Reader's Guide to Periodic Literature* for articles on plant growth in recent horticulture magazines. Finally, you would look through the book section in your local gardening store.

If you were a professional researcher, you would also write letters and make phone calls to other scientists in your field to find out what they have already learned about your subject. This would help you avoid duplicating their work.

Step 2: Formulate a Hypothesis

Based on your observations and your experience, you probably already have a sense of what the answer to your question will be. Turn this possible answer into a statement. For example, you might answer the question about the relationship between plant growth and light intensity by formulating the following hypothesis: "The rate of plant growth increases as light intensity increases."

Step 3: Design and Conduct a Controlled Experiment

In order to find out whether your hypothesis is true or false, you must test it by conducting a controlled experiment. A controlled experiment actually consists of two experiments run side by side. The original experiment is called the *control*. The second experiment duplicates the first, except for a single factor called the *experimental variable*, which you purposely change. If you take great care to ensure that only one factor differs between the two experiments, you can be confident that any difference in the results is due to this experimental variable.

SKILLS DEVELOPMENT
Designing a Controlled Experiment (continued)

Practice Designing a Controlled Experiment

Suppose you want to test the following hypothesis: "The rate of plant growth increases as light intensity increases." You want to conduct a controlled experiment to find out whether your hypothesis is true or false, so you raise two sets of plants.

1. What influences on plant growth would you keep identical for the two sets of plants?

_____

_____

_____

_____

_____

_____

2. What influence on plant growth would you allow to vary?

_____

More Practice

Design a controlled experiment to find out whether adding a teaspoon of sugar to the water in which you have placed freshly cut flowers will make the flowers last longer.

1. State the hypothesis.

_____

_____

2. What factors that might affect the freshness of the flowers should remain constant during the experiment?

_____

_____

_____

3. What factor would you allow to vary during the experiment?

_____

SKILLS DEVELOPMENT

Reading Laboratory Procedures

Your biology program includes several different kinds of lab experiments. The Concept Laboratories and the Laboratory Investigations in your textbook and the experiments in the Laboratory Manual describe in detail the procedure you should follow.

How to Read a Laboratory Procedure

Before you begin a lab, become as familiar as possible with the procedure. The following guidelines will help.

1. Read the title, the introduction, and the objective to learn the purpose of the lab and the scientific principles involved.
2. Read the experimental procedure to get a feeling for what will happen during the experiment. Look over the list of materials. Make a list of the ones you will have to supply on your own.
3. Read each step in the procedure carefully. Pay attention to details. Picture yourself performing each step. Try to imagine what could go wrong.
4. Look up the meaning of terms, abbreviations, and symbols you don't recognize in the Glossary and in the Appendix in the back of your textbook.
5. Familiarize yourself with all pictures, diagrams, and flowcharts that accompany the procedure.
6. Create a flowchart that illustrates the steps in the experiment. The Skills Development worksheet entitled "Using Graphic Organizers" will show you how.
7. Pay special attention to safety symbols, small pictures that suggest danger or the possibility of an accident. Your failure to take heed may result in someone getting hurt, in damage to expensive equipment, or in a ruined experiment. A complete list of safety symbols and their meanings is located in Appendix B of your textbook.
8. Note when the procedure tells you to measure size, mass, frequency, quantity, or temperature. Make sure you know what measuring tool and unit of measurement to use.
9. If you are unclear about any aspect of the investigation, make a list of questions to ask your teacher before the lab begins.

Practice Reading a Laboratory Procedure

Read the laboratory investigation entitled *Effect of Chemicals on Heart Rate in Daphnia* in Chapter 16 of your textbook. Then answer the following questions.

1. What is the purpose of this laboratory investigation?

_____

_____

_____

_____

SKILLS DEVELOPMENT
Reading Laboratory Procedures (continued)

2. What, in general, will you do during the experiment?

_____

_____

_____

3. List the materials you may have to supply on your own.

_____

4. At what point(s) during the procedure should you be especially careful? Why?

_____

_____

_____

_____

_____

_____

_____

5. What other critical error(s) could affect the outcome of the experiment?

_____

_____

6. What is pictured in each of the following figures?

Figure L-16A _____

_____

Figure L-16B _____

Figure L-16C _____

7. What do the three safety symbols at the beginning of the procedure mean?

_____

_____

_____

8. What will you measure during the experiment?

_____

9. What units will you use to record the data?

_____

10. What measuring tool will you use?

_____

SKILLS DEVELOPMENT

Organizing Data

When you study biology, sooner or later you will observe something that sparks your curiosity. If you form a hypothesis to explain what you have observed, you will have to perform an experiment in order to find out whether your hypothesis is correct. The experiment will produce data that you will have to organize in a manner that answers this question clearly and directly.

Data Tables

There are several techniques for organizing data. Flow charts, diagrams, graphs, and concept maps are all effective tools but when you first collect experimental data, the most useful tool is a table.

Suppose, for example, you notice one day that the stems of some of your house plants bend toward the window. You turn them away from the window, but a few days later you notice they are bent back again. You suspect that your plants are attracted by the sunlight coming in the window, so you formulate the following hypothesis: *The direction of a light source affects the direction of plant growth.*

You set up an experiment with four 25 cm-tall avocado plants labeled A, B, C, and D. You place each plant in a different closet. In the first closet, you place plant A all the way to the left and a small light source all the way to the right. In the second closet, you place plant B all the way to the right and the light source all the way to the left. In the third closet, you place plant C all the way to the left, with the light source hanging from the center of the ceiling. You place plant D in the center of the fourth closet with the light source directly above it.

The same experimental conditions are listed in the table below. Notice how much more accessible the information is in table form. You don't have to hunt through an entire paragraph to find a single piece of information. Instead, you simply find the appropriate column and read down until you find the data you want.

Plant	Location in Closet	Light Source
A	left	right
B	right	left
C	left	center
D	center	center

Practice Organizing Data

Every day you measure the stem angle of each plant. You record the following data:

On the first day the stem of plant A is bent 10 degrees to the right of vertical. Plant B is bent 10 degrees to the left of vertical. The stem of plant C is bent 5 degrees to the right of vertical, and the stem of plant D is not bent at all.

On the second day the stem of plant A is bent 20 degrees to the right. The stem of plant B is bent 20 degrees to the left. The stem of plant C is bent 10 degrees to the right, and the stem of plant D remains unchanged.

On the third day the stem of plant A is bent 45 degrees to the right. The stem of plant B is bent 45 degrees to the left. The stems of plants C and D are unchanged.

SKILLS DEVELOPMENT
Organizing Data   (continued)

On the lines below, organize the data into a table.

Day	Plant	Direction From Vertical	Angle Bending (degrees)

If you compare your data table with the paragraphs preceding it, you'll see that organizing data in table form makes it easier to read and interpret. There are no extra words to slow you down, only the essential information. The column headings make it absolutely clear what kind of information is included in the table, and the column format lets you find information quickly.

The data seem to indicate that the direction of a light source does, in fact, affect the direction of plant growth.

SKILLS DEVELOPMENT

Writing a Laboratory Report

The quality of the report you write following a laboratory session depends on how well you use a number of other science study skills.

Skills You Use Before the Lab Begins

You can lay the foundation for a successful report by thoroughly preparing yourself before you enter the laboratory. The worksheet entitled "Reading Laboratory Procedures" shows you how. A flowchart will help you rehearse what you are going to do and will provide you with a quick reference road map to follow during the lab. The Skills Development worksheet entitled "Using Graphic Organizers" shows you how to construct a flowchart.

The accuracy of your report depends on whether you can read, understand, and interpret your own notes once the lab is over. If the lab involves a comparison of two or more subjects, consider using a table to take notes. Because a table organizes information into rows and columns, you will have a separate box for each observation and measurement you make. A table will keep your notes in order and help you reconstruct what you did and what you observed when the time comes to write the report. It will also make it easier to present your data in graph form. Don't wait until the lab begins to design the table. Instead, do it when you create the flowchart. The Skills Development worksheet entitled *Organizing Data* will show you how.

Skills You Use During the Lab

Your lab report should be a complete, objective description of what happened during the lab. Think of it as a newspaper account of the experiment. Take notes as though you were a reporter. Label every piece of data. Be sure to use the correct units. Mention anything that might be important, including changes in color, texture, size, mass, physical state, and behavior. Note things you thought would happen that did not. Note your mistakes. A complete objective record of your observations and actions will help you reconstruct the experiment exactly the way it happened. It may even help you figure out what went wrong if the experiment does not turn out the way you thought it would.

Writing the Report

Write your lab report so someone who knows biology but is unfamiliar with the procedure you followed can reproduce your experiment and understand your results. Your lab notes should be the primary source of information. Try not to refer to your lab manual or to other reference materials unless absolutely necessary.
Follow these guidelines when you write the report.

1. Center the name and number of the experiment in the middle of the **title page.** Put your name, your teacher's name, and the date you submit the report in the upper or lower right-hand corner. If you do not type the report, be sure your handwriting is legible.
2. In the **introduction,** explain the purpose of the experiment and the biological principles involved. Without going into detail, summarize the steps you followed during the experiment. If you deviated in any way from

SKILLS DEVELOPMENT
Writing a Laboratory Report (continued)

the procedure set forth in the lab manual, say so. If you performed any calculations, list the formulas you used.

3. Present the **data** you collected during the experiment. If a graphic organizer such as a graph, a chart, or a diagram will clearly show trends and relationships in the data, construct one on a separate piece of paper. You can insert the graph inside the report or put it at the end. If you choose the second option, say "(See Graph 1)," "(See Table 1)," or "(See Diagram 1)" in the body of the report.

4. Show any **calculations** you performed on the data. If the same calculation applies to more than one piece of data, say so but only show the calculation once.

5. In the **conclusion,** discuss the results of the experiment and tell what you learned from them. Refer to the biological principles involved in the experiment to explain why things happened the way they did. Give reasons. Answer any questions that appear in the lab manual. Do not be afraid to guess at possible causes of error. Tell what you should have done differently.

   Be creative and original when you analyze your results. Be careful not to let your bias slant your conclusions. If you did not get the results you expected, you must determine whether your techniques or your expectations were at fault. Often you will be graded on your understanding of the procedure and the principles involved in the experiment rather than on your results. Understanding what went wrong and why is just as important as understanding what went right.

6. At the end of the report, list **references** other than your laboratory manual that you used to write the report. Include the author's name, the title of the book, journal, or periodical, the title of the article or chapter, the publication date, and the volume and page numbers.

Practice Writing a Laboratory Report

The model lab notes below were taken during the Concept Laboratory entitled *Natural Selection* in Chapter 29. Read the lab and study the notes.

Model Lab Notes
four members in group / made 64 newsprint squares, 64 color squares / mixed squares up / dumped squares onto newspaper / spread them out / no overlap / took turns grabbing squares / 5 turns each / counted squares picked up / entered totals in table / compared data with other groups / made no mistakes

	Colored Paper Animals	Newspaper Animals
Student 1	4	1
Student 2	3	2
Student 3	5	0
Student 4	4	1

Use these model lab notes to answer the following questions. If necessary, refer to the Concept Laboratory. Respond as though you had participated in the lab.

1. What was the purpose of the experiment?

_____

SKILLS DEVELOPMENT
Writing a Laboratory Report (continued)

2. Describe the biological principle involved in the experiment.

_____

_____

3. Summarize the procedure you followed during the experiment.

_____

_____

_____

_____

_____

_____

4. Add a fourth row to the data table to show how many squares of each color were not picked up.

_____

_____

_____

5. What formula did you use to figure out how many squares of each color were not picked up?

_____

_____

6. Why did more newspaper squares "survive" the experiment than colored paper squares?

_____

_____

_____

SKILLS DEVELOPMENT

Using Science Reference Materials

Science reference materials are no more difficult to use than the kinds with which you are already familiar. You already have a textbook, but you may not be aware of some of the other specialized sources available to you. You should be able to find most of the ones discussed below in your school or public library.

Other Textbooks

These science reference materials are right in your school library. You can tell whether a textbook contains the information you want by looking in the Table of Contents and in the Index. If you find the topic you want listed there, turn to the appropriate page(s) and survey the material to see if it may be of use to you. Be sure to check the end of the chapter to see if additional references are listed there. The titles you find may be just what you need.

Other Books

Your school or public library may contain other books on the same subject. You can find out by looking in the subject index of the card catalog. Use the "call number" listed there to find the book on the shelf. If it is missing, talk to a librarian. Someone may have checked it out, or it may have been put away in the wrong place.

Practice Looking for Books in the Library

Suppose you need information about the identity and function of saprobes in the ecosystem.

1. Look in your school library for textbooks that contain information about saprobes. If you find any, list their title(s) here.

   _____

   _____

   _____

2. Look in your school library for other books that contain information about saprobes. If you find any, list their title(s) here.

   _____

   _____

   _____

Specialized Magazines, Journals, and Indices

Many libraries have back issues of science magazines and journals, such as *Scholastic Science World*, *Scientific American*, *Discover*, and *Science News*. Look for articles on your subject in the cumulative journal index at the end of the last issue published each year.

   Some libraries also subscribe to more specialized journals used by doctors and scientists. For example, if you were interested in finding out about the

SKILLS DEVELOPMENT
Using Science Reference Materials   (continued)

most recent research in the use of oral insulin to treat diabetes, you could look for the journal called *Diabetes*. You could also look for articles about diabetes in the *Journal of the American Medical Association*. These articles will be difficult to understand at first, but if you look up the unfamiliar words and reread the material, the extra time and effort will be well worth it. Technical journals contain the most up-to-date information available.

If you don't have time to look in the index of every magazine or journal to see if it lists articles about your subject, try the *Reader's Guide to Periodic Literature* or specialized indices such as *Biological Abstracts*, *Science Citations Index*, and *Index Medicus*. They will list all the articles dealing with your subject that were published in the year or years you specify.

Practice Looking for Articles in Specialized Magazines, Journals, and Indices

3. Look in your school and local libraries for magazines and journals that contain information about saprobes. When you find one, note the magazine or journal name and the article title here. Also note the name of the specialized index, if that's where you found the article.

_____

_____

_____

_____

_____

_____

_____

_____

_____

_____

Computer Searches

If you cannot find your subject in the card catalog or in the journal indices, your school or local reference librarian may be able to perform a computer search for you. A computer search produces a list of articles and books that contain the information you are seeking. A typical list includes authors, titles, publication names, and publication dates. You usually have to pay for a computer search, so be sure to ask how much it costs before making a request.

If you include key words and phrases when you request a computer search, the list you receive will be even more useful. Suppose, for example, that a manual search of the specialized indices produces a list of articles about diabetes, but nothing specifically about recent research on the use of oral insulin. If you ask the computer to search for articles and books about diabetes, you will receive an even longer list of titles. Only a few of them will have anything to do with oral insulin, and you won't know which ones do until you look them over. However, if you provide the reference librarian with key words such as "diabetes," "research," and "oral insulin" when you request the search, you will receive a much shorter list of articles and books on that very narrow subject published within whatever period of time you specify.

SKILLS DEVELOPMENT
Using Science Reference Materials (continued)

Practice Requesting a Computer Search

4. Suppose you want the library computer to search for information on saprobes. What key words and phrases would help the computer narrow down the topic?

_____

_____

_____

Interviews

If you have questions about a specific topic and you know someone who has specialized knowledge, call or write that person and ask for an interview. Before you do, however, prepare for the meeting by making a list of the questions you want to ask. Mention a couple of them when you make your request, so the person you plan to interview will know what you want to talk about and can be prepared.

Museums, Zoos, and Aquariums

Museums, zoos, and aquariums have a wealth of information they are willing to share with you. Often the information you need is already on display. If it is not, or if you need more details, ask for help. Someone on the staff may be willing to answer your questions, or you may be given access to the staff library.

More Practice

5. Based on what you have already learned from your research, write down two questions about saprobes that you would like to ask an expert.

_____

_____

_____

6. List two scientific institutions in your area where you might find information about saprobes.

_____

_____

_____

SKILLS DEVELOPMENT

Making an Outline

You will find it easier to organize information into main ideas, subsets of main ideas, and supporting details if you make an outline. Once your outline is complete, you can use it to refresh your memory, to write a research paper, or to answer an essay question on a test.

Familiarize yourself with the following partial outline of a research paper on blood. Look for recurring patterns in the way the topics are displayed.

   I. Introduction
      A. Definition of blood
      B. Functions of blood
         1. Regulation of chemical balance
         2. Regulation of temperature
         3. Transportation of nutrients and wastes
         4. Protection of the body from foreign invaders
         5. Protection of the body from loss of blood
  II. Composition of blood
      A. Plasma
         1. Composition and characteristics
         2. Function
      B. Red cells
         1. Description
         2. Function
      C. White cells
         1. Description
         2. Function
      D. Platelets
         1. Description
         2. Function

Guidelines to Follow When Outlining

Because we wanted this outline to be clear and orderly, we observed the following guidelines.

- We indented topics of equal importance the same distance from the left side of the page.
- When we included a subset of topics, we never listed just one.
- We avoided using complete sentences.
- We used the following hierarchy of symbols.
  — Roman numerals (I, II) to designate the major topics
  — Capital letters (A, B, C) to designate the major subtopics
  — Arabic numerals (1, 2, 3) to divide up the subtopics
- If we had wanted to divide up the subtopics still further, we would have used lower-case letters (a, b, c).

When you use an outline to take notes from a textbook, a second draft is usually unnecessary because the material in a textbook is carefully organized. When you use an outline to take notes from a less orderly source, such as a class discussion, however, you may have to reorganize the topics in order to make the outline useful.

SKILLS DEVELOPMENT
Making an Outline   (continued)

Practice Making an Outline

Outline the following passage on the lines below. Be sure to follow the guidelines on the preceding page.

Basic Characteristics of Animals

The animal kingdom, kingdom **Animalia,** is the largest of the five kingdoms. Animals are multicellular organisms that must obtain food from their environment. Most have nervous and muscular systems that allow them to move. Most animals reproduce sexually, although some of the simpler forms also reproduce asexually. In some animals, the young have the same basic features as the adult but in others, the young are very different from the adult. In these cases, the young forms are known as larvae (LAR vee). The larvae undergo a series of developmental changes that produce the adult form.

_____

_____

_____

_____

_____

_____

_____

_____

_____

_____

_____

_____

_____

_____

_____

_____

_____

_____

_____

SKILLS DEVELOPMENT

Writing a Research Report

A biology research report is one of the most time-consuming assignments you will undertake during your high school career. The typical research report takes more than 40 hours to complete and involves the following 11 steps. A rough estimate of the time required for each step appears in parentheses.

1. Scheduling Your Time (1 hour)
2. Selecting a Topic (2 hours)
3. Planning Your Research (3 hours)
4. Doing Your Research (12 hours)
5. Creating an Outline (3 hours)
6. Plugging Your Research into the Outline (4 hours)
7. Writing the First Draft (8 hours)
8. Preparing the Bibliography, Footnotes, Title Page, and Illustrations (3 hours)
9. Editing the First Draft (3 hours)
10. Writing the Final Draft (4 hours)
11. Proofreading and Correcting (1 hour)

The steps in this process draw on a variety of science study skills, including Taking Notes, Using Science Reference Materials, and Outlining. Each of these skills is covered in another worksheet. This worksheet focuses on the first three steps in the writing process: Scheduling Your Time, Selecting a Topic, and Planning Your Research.

Step 1: Scheduling Your Time

In order to satisfy themselves that you are making progress on the report and that you are still headed in the right direction, teachers often require note cards, an outline, and a rough draft at key points along the way. Many students find that a detailed schedule helps them keep up with these deadlines.

Practice Scheduling Your Time

Suppose your biology teacher has assigned a research report due five weeks from today. You must submit your research notes at the end of the second week, an outline at the end of the third week, and a rough draft of your report at the end of the fourth week.

　Use the calendar on the next page to create a schedule that will enable you to meet all four deadlines. Be sure you leave enough time each day for school, after-school activities, work, chores, sleep, and your other homework. Show when you plan to work on each step and how many hours you think it will take.

Step 2: Selecting a Topic

Whether your teacher gives you a list of approved topics or tells you to pick one on your own, look for a topic that interests you, one that has implications for you or for someone you know. If you choose a topic that is too broad, your report will not be adequately focused. Narrow the topic down as much as possible by breaking it up into its constituent parts and choosing the one that interests you the most.

Day 1	Day 2	Day 3	Day 4	Day 5	Day 6	Day 7
Day 8	Day 9	Day 10	Day 11	Day 12	Day 13	Day 14 Research notes due
Day 15	Day 16	Day 17	Day 18	Day 19	Day 20	Day 21 Outline due
Day 22	Day 23	Day 24	Day 25	Day 26	Day 27	Day 28 Rough draft due
Day 29	Day 30	Day 31	Day 32	Day 33	Day 34	Day 35 Report due

SKILLS DEVELOPMENT
Writing a Reseach Report   (continued)

Practice Selecting a Topic

List three possible ways to narrow down each of the following topics.

1. Blood _____

_____

_____

2. Sense Receptors in the Human Nervous System _____

_____

_____

3. Plant Structure _____

_____

_____

_____

Step 3: Planning Your Research

You should find out as soon as possible whether you will have access to enough research material. Go to your school or public library. The Skills Development worksheet entitled "Using Library Reference Materials" will show you what to look for. If you can't find enough research material, you will still have time to modify your topic or change it altogether. Make a list of the books, magazines, periodicals, and other resources that look like they will be useful. Be sure you write down the information you will need to find them again.

Practice Planning Your Research

Take one of the narrowed-down topics you developed in the previous exercise to your school or public library. Locate ten sources of information about that topic and list them below. Include the call number if the source is a book. Show the title of the article and the name of the publication if the source comes from a magazine or a journal.

_____

_____

_____

_____

_____

_____

_____

_____

_____

_____

SKILLS DEVELOPMENT

Preparing for and Taking a Test

A test is your opportunity to demonstrate the depth of your knowledge. No matter how much you know, however, your score will depend on how skillful you are at preparing for and taking a test.

Preparing for a Test

In addition to maintaining good study habits throughout the school year, your test preparation regimen should include the following tasks.
• Getting organized
• Preparing your mind and body

You can fulfill each of these tasks in a variety of ways. You are the best judge of whether a particular method is suited to your own learning style.

How Do You Prepare for a Test?

Circle the number of the test preparation technique in each group you find most useful. Underline the

techniques you would like to improve. _____

Maintain Good Study Habits

1. Keep your notes and assignments in chronological order.
2. Underline or highlight key words and concepts in your notes.
3. Stay up to date on reading and writing assignments.
4. Make reviewing a part of your weekly routine.

Get Organized

1. Determine how much time you need for studying. Make a schedule.
2. Distinguish between what you do and do not know.
3. Make a list of the material you find most confusing.
4. Make a list of questions you think will appear on the test.
5. Prepare a list of questions so someone else can quiz you.

Prepare Your Mind and Body

1. Get a good night's sleep.
2. Eat a nutritious breakfast.
3. Practice a relaxation technique.

SKILLS DEVELOPMENT
Preparing for and Taking a Test   (continued)

Multiple-Choice Questions

Multiple-choice questions appear frequently in biology tests, so you should learn how to answer them skillfully. Many students find the following strategy useful.

Step 1. Try to think of the correct answer before you read the choices. If the answer is there, you can select it with confidence.

Step 2. Do not select the first answer that looks correct. You want the one that best answers the question, so read all the choices before you make your selection.

Step 3. If you can't decide which answer to choose, eliminate the ones you know are wrong. Even if you don't know what the right answer is, you may be able to isolate it.

Step 4. Be shrewd when it comes to guessing. If you will not lose credit for a wrong answer, guess whenever you want. If you will lose credit for a wrong answer, play the odds. If you can eliminate all but two of the choices with confidence, you will have a 50/50 chance of guessing correctly.

Suppose you encounter the following multiple-choice question on a test.

Mitochondria, ribosomes, and vacuoles are examples of
(a) tissues   **(b)** cells   **(c)** organs   **(d)** organelles

You think the correct answer is "enzymes" (Step 1). You look for "enzymes" on the list, but it's not there. "Tissues" (choice "a") looks like it may be the right answer, but you read the other three choices anyway in case one of them looks even better (Step 2). None of them does. You are about to select "a" when you remember that a ribosome is not a tissue, so you eliminate choice "a" from consideration (Step 3). Three choices remain, none of which looks correct to you. Since you will not lose credit for a wrong answer, you consider guessing, but you know that the odds of being right are only one in three. Suddenly, you remember that a vacuole is not an organ, so you eliminate choice "c" (Step 3). Now you have a 50/50 chance of guessing correctly. You select "organelles" (choice "d"), which is the correct answer (Step 4).

Practice Answering Multiple-Choice Questions

Underline the response that best fits each question or statement.

1. Which of the following organisms possesses prokaryotic cells?
   (a) ameba   **(b)** bacteria   **(c)** fungi   **(d)** humans

2. A cell with 96% concentration of water molecules and a 4% concentration of dissolved substances is placed in a hypertonic solution. The water molecule concentration of the solution could be
   (a) 100%   **(b)** 98%   **(c)** 96%   **(d)** 94%

3. Which is not part of the cell theory?
   (a) Cells vary in size but have the same shape.
   (b) All organisms are made up of one or more cells.
   (c) All cells carry on their own life activities.
   (d) New cells only arise from other living cells.

SKILLS DEVELOPMENT
Preparing for and Taking a Test (continued)

Matching Questions

Matching questions are similar to multiple-choice questions. Both types provide you with a group of answers from which to choose. You have to pick the one that is most correct. There is one important difference, however. Whereas each multiple-choice question comes with its own group of answers, several matching questions share the same group of answers. This means you have to approach them as a group rather than one at a time. On the other hand, the number of choices that remain decreases each time you answer one of the questions in the group. This gives you an advantage because your chances of answering the next question correctly improve.

Follow these steps when you answer matching questions.
1. Read all the questions in the group.
2. Read all the answers.
3. Match questions with answers you know are correct. Cross these answers off the list.
4. Pick one of the remaining questions. Mentally eliminate any answer you know does not match.
5. If you can eliminate all but one choice, select it and cross it off the list.
6. Guess if necessary, but not if you will lose credit for a wrong answer.
7. If you do guess, cross the answer off the list.
8. Repeat Steps 4–7 as necessary.

Here is an example of how to use this strategy. First, read the following answers and the questions that go with them.

(a) osmosis   **(b)** diffusion   **(c)** pinocytosis   **(d)** phagocytosis

1. process in which liquids or small particles are taken into the cells from the surrounding medium

2. movement of water from an area of greater concentration to an area of lesser concentration

3. ingestion of large particles or even small organisms by a cell of lesser concentration

Suppose that after reading all three questions (Step 1) and all four answers (Step 2), you are confident that the answer to question #1 is "pinocytosis," so you write down "c" and cross it off the list (Step 3). You know that neither "diffusion" nor "phagocytosis" is the correct answer to question #2, so you mentally eliminate choices "b" and "d" as possibilities (Step 4). That leaves "osmosis," so you write down "a" and cross it off the list (Step 5). You do not know whether "diffusion" or "phagocytosis" is the correct answer to question #3. Since you will not lose credit for answering incorrectly, you decide to guess (Step 6). You pick "phagocytosis," which is the correct answer.

SKILLS DEVELOPMENT
Preparing for and Taking a Test (continued)

Practice Answering a Matching Question

Use the following terms to answer questions 4–6.

(a) epithelial (b) muscle (c) connective (d) blood

4. ____ tissues specialized for contraction

5. ____ lines the inner surface of the mouth in humans

6. ____ supports and binds other tissues

Short-Answer Questions

Unlike multiple-choice and matching questions, short answer questions do not offer you any answers from which to choose. You have to come up with the answer on your own. Here are a few suggestions to follow if an answer does not immediately come to mind.

1. Underline important words in the question. This will help you focus your memory.
2. Write down ideas as they occur to you, so you won't forget them.
3. When you are ready to answer the question, make every word count. Short-answer questions rarely require more than two sentences. One or two words are often sufficient.
4. Watch out for qualifying words, such as "always" and "normal," that limit the scope of your answer.
5. Answer the question completely.

Essay Questions

When you have to answer an essay question on a test, draw on the same skills you use when you write a report. These skills are all incorporated into the following five-step method.

Step 1: Take the Question Apart

It may seem as though you don't have enough time to evaluate the question and organize your response before you begin writing but you are more likely to produce a clearly-reasoned essay if you do.
• Underline the key words and phrases in the question.
• Determine whether the question focuses on similarities, differences, examples, reasons, or steps in a process.
• Determine whether the question dictates how many parts the body of the essay should contain.

Practice Step 1

Take apart the following essay question.

What are the six major structural differences between plant and animal cells?

1. Underline the key words and phrases.

2. Does the question focus on similarities, differences, examples, reasons, or steps in a process?

_____

3. How many parts should the body of your essay contain? _____

SKILLS DEVELOPMENT
Preparing for and Taking a Test (continued)

Step 2: Organize Your Essay

It's important that you see how much ground you have to cover in the essay before you start writing. An overview of your answer will also help you establish the order of ideas.
- Create an organizing table for the essay. For example, if you have to compare the diets and metabolisms of two organisms, create a table with three rows and three columns.

Practice Step 2

Create a table for the question about plant and animal cells.

Differences	Plants	Animals
1		
2		
3		
4		
5		
6		

Step 3: Brainstorm

Each box in the table corresponds to a paragraph or a group of paragraphs in your essay.
- Pick a box in the table. Enter all the information you want that paragraph or group of paragraphs to contain.
- Repeat this brainstorming technique until all the boxes are filled in.
- If you run out of time and are unable to finish the essay, you may receive partial credit for the information contained in the table.

Step 4: Compose an Introduction

- Use key words and phrases from the question.
- Answer the question as simply and as directly as possible. If you get stuck, try turning the question into a statement.
- Don't get bogged down in specifics. You will defend your assertion in the paragraphs that follow.

Step 5: Write

- Follow the organization you established in Step 2.

- If time permits, correct spelling, punctuation, and grammar.

Chapter Review and Skills Application

Contents

THE NATURE OF LIFE
1-1   Describing Life

Part I: Vocabulary Review

Write the vocabulary term that best replaces the italicized definition in each statement.

1. *The study of living things* teaches us that although there is a great diversity of life, there is also a great unity of

   life. _____

2. All *living things* have certain characteristics, such as being highly organized and containing complex chemical

   substances and being made up of one or more cells. _____

Part II: Content Review

For each statement below, decide whether it describes only living things, only nonliving things, or both. Write "L" for living things, "N" for nonliving things, "B" for both.

_____   3. use energy

_____   4. can reproduce

_____   5. can evolve

_____   6. can grow

_____   7. have no definite form

_____   8. respond to changes in the environment

_____   9. have an unlimited life span

_____ 10. lack cells

_____ 11. have unlimited size

Part III: Skills Development

Review the skill entitled "Finding the Main Idea" on pages 8–10. Then, read each paragraph below and complete the activity that follows.

The word **biology** is easy to define. It is the study of living things. But, consider for a minute or two what this means. Think about the different kinds of living things you know. You may want to jot them down under various headings, such as domestic animals, wild animals, ocean life, insects. Don't forget the plants you know—for example, trees, wildflowers, garden flowers, house plants, weeds. If you take the time to do it, you may come up with a long list—probably 100 kinds of living things, at least.

12. What is the main idea of this paragraph? _____

_____

13. On the lines, generate your own list of living things. _____

_____

THE NATURE OF LIFE
1-1   Describing Life   (continued)

It is a human trait to try to define and classify the things we find in the world. But, the world doesn't always seem to be made for this. As a result, our definitions and classifications often have fuzzy edges. There are borderline cases that fit partly into one category and partly into another. This is especially true when we attempt to define life. There are things in the world that cannot be called clearly either living or nonliving. One example is the virus—a particle that can be stored like chemicals in a bottle but, when inside a living cell, can reproduce more of itself. Although viruses can reproduce, they do not exhibit most of the other characteristics of life.

14. What is the main idea of this paragraph?

_____

15. In the space below, explain what is meant by, and give an example of, borderline cases.

_____

_____

_____

_____

Review the skill entitled "Graphic Organizing: Compare/Contrast Matrix" on pages 41–44. Then, using "yes" or "no", fill in the empty boxes in the compare/contrast matrix below.

16.

CHARACTERISTIC	DOG	WATER	TREE	BURNING CANDLE
Highly organized with many complex chemical substances				
Made up of one or more cells				
Uses energy				
Has a definite form and a limited size				
Has a limited life span				
Grows				
Responds to changes in environment				
Reproduces				

THE NATURE OF LIFE
1-2 Life Processes

Part I: Vocabulary Review

Complete the following crossword puzzle.

ACROSS

1. Process by which living organisms increase in size
4. Incorporation of materials into the organism's body
6. Substances that an organism needs for energy, growth, repair, or maintenance
7. Process that is made up of all the activities that help maintain an organism's homeostasis
9. Process of combining simple substances chemically to form more complex substances
10. Process by which substances enter and leave cells and become distributed within cells
12. Taking materials from the external environment and changing them into usable forms
13. Removal of wastes from the body of an organism
14. All the chemical reactions occurring within the cells of an organism

DOWN

2. Process of releasing chemical energy
3. Condition in which the internal environment is kept constant
5. Taking in of food from the environment
8. Process by which organisms produce new organisms of their own kind
11. Breakdown of complex food materials into simpler forms that an organism can use

Part II: Content Review

Select the best answer for each question and write the letter in the space provided.

_____ **15.** Why are life processes necessary?
a. to give structure
b. to maintain homeostasis
c. to allow excretion
d. to distribute chemicals

_____ **16.** What are the two basic types of nutrition?
a. producing complex nutrients from simple substances found in the environment and taking in nutrients ready-made from the environment
b. reproducing simple substances found in the environment and building new substances
c. assimilating substances and excreting substances from the environment
d. ingesting substances and transporting substances from the environment

_____ **17.** How do organisms obtain energy?
a. by excretion
b. by assimilation
c. by reproduction
d. by respiration

_____ **18.** What two processes allow an organism to repair or replace worn-out parts and to grow?
a. regulation and transport
b. synthesis and assimilation
c. reproduction and ingestion
d. nutrients and excretion

_____ **19.** In multicellular organisms, what process accompanies growth?
a. anaerobic respiration
b. excretion
c. reproduction
d. cellular specialization

_____ **20.** How do an organism's digestive, transport, excretory, nervous, and endocrine systems help to maintain homeostasis?
a. They play a part in the process of regulation.
b. They help with the release of chemical energy.
c. They are involved mainly with the intake of food.
d. They are necessary nutrients.

_____ **21.** What are the two main types of reproduction?
a. Single and twin
b. Growth and regulation
c. Sexual and asexual
d. Vegetative and metabolic

_____ **22.** What basic kinds of processes are included in the metabolism of an organism?
a. nutrients and excretion
b. taking in nutrients from the environment and breaking them down into simpler ones
c. interacting with the environment and reproducing young
d. building complex substances from simpler ones and breaking down complex substances into simpler ones

CHAPTER REVIEW

Know the Terms

Select the most appropriate words from the following list to complete the paragraph.

respiration	biology	aerobic
synthesis	metabolism	homeostasis
cells	energy	organism
anaerobic	nutrition	reproduction

__(1)__ is the study of living things. Anything that is living is called a/an __(2)__, which is composed of one or more __(3)__ and utilizes __(4)__ to maintain its organization and carry out normal functions. This is derived through the process of __(5)__. There are two forms of this in living organisms. One type requires the use of oxygen and is called __(6)__. __(7)__ respiration does not require oxygen. The total of all chemical reactions within an organism is called __(8)__. Some of these reactions involve building more complex molecules from less complex ones. This is called __(9)__. In all cases, however, the organism is trying to maintain a constant internal environment, called __(10)__.

1. _____
2. _____
3. _____
4. _____
5. _____
6. _____
7. _____
8. _____
9. _____
10. _____

Match the word with the correct definition.

a. nutrients	**f.** life
b. regulation	**g.** transport
c. excretion	**h.** growth
d. sexual reproduction	**i.** assimilation
e. ingestion	**j.** asexual reproduction

11. taking in food   11. _____

12. reproduction involving only one parent   12. _____

13. removal of wastes from an organism   13. _____

14. the passing of substances into or out of cells or circulation within an organism   14. _____

15. incorporation of materials into an organism   15. _____

16. reproduction involving two parents   16. _____

17. the process by which living organisms increase in size   17. _____

18. all activities that help maintain homeostasis   18. _____

19. quality distinguishing organisms from inorganic materials   19. _____

20. substances an organism takes from its environment   20. _____

CHAPTER REVIEW

Understand the Concepts

Answer the following questions in one or two sentences.

1. You dissolve sugar in water, evaporate the water, and grow a crystal of highly organized sugar molecules. Energy holds the molecules together in a definite form and size. You drop the crystal, and it breaks. You have changed it into two crystals. Eventually you eat it, and it is gone. In one sentence explain why you think it was or was not alive. _____

_____

_____

2. Why must foods be digested? _____

_____

_____

3. Why do complex organisms need transport systems? _____

_____

_____

4. What is the purpose of respiration in living organisms? _____

_____

_____

5. How are the processes of synthesis and assimilation related? _____

_____

_____

6. How do living organisms grow? _____

_____

7. Where do wastes come from? _____

_____

8. How do the nervous, endocrine, and excretory systems contribute to homeostasis in animals? _____

_____

_____

9. In what way is reproduction important to living organisms? _____

_____

10. What is metabolism? _____

_____

BIOLOGY AS A SCIENCE
2-1   The Nature of Science

Part I: Vocabulary Review

Match the terms listed in Column II with the proper definition listed in Column I. Place the answer in the space provided.

COLUMN I

_____ 1. experimental setup in which no change is made and which serves as a reference

_____ 2. universal approach to scientific problems

_____ 3. statement that describes some aspect of a scientific phenomenon that is always true

_____ 4. single factor that is changed in one experimental setup

_____ 5. possible explanation for an observed set of facts

_____ 6. explanations that apply to a broad range of phenomena

_____ 7. International System of Units used by scientists

_____ 8. research situation set up in duplicate

COLUMN II

a. variable

b. hypothesis

c. theories

d. control

e. scientific method

f. scientific law

g. controlled experiment

h. SI

Part II: Content Review

Complete each of the following sentences.

9. When a scientist announces a finding or proposes a new idea, other scientists may _____

_____

10. The main features of the scientific method are _____

_____

11. The scientific method begins when _____

_____

12. A good hypothesis will _____

_____

13. A hypothesis can never be completely proved. At any time, however, a hypothesis may be disproved by _____

_____

14. In an experiment, the scientist sets up _____

_____

15. A controlled experiment involves two experimental setups in which _____

16. The results of an original investigation cannot be considered valid unless the investigation can be _____

_____

17. Unlike a theory or a scientific law, a hypothesis is usually an idea that is limited to _____

_____

18. Scientists can state a scientific law only after they have observed that _____

_____

19. In scientific investigations, measurements need to be expressed in _____

_____

20. Biologists need to use small units of measurement because of _____

_____

Part III: Skills Development

Review the skill entitled "Using Greek and Latin Word Parts" on pages 13–15. Then, for each italicized term in the sentences below, write down its word parts and their definitions.

GREEK AND LATIN WORD PARTS

bio-	life	**-meter**	unit of length
centi-	one-hundredth	**micro-**	small or one-millionth
deca-	ten	**milli-**	one-thousandth
-gram	unit of mass	**nano-**	one-billionth
-liter	unit of volume	**-ology**	science or branch of knowledge

17. *Microbiology* is an important branch of science.

_____

18. Some computers take only *nanoseconds* to solve a problem.

_____

19. Viruses and bacteria are *microorganisms*.

_____

20. She planted the seeds 15 *centimeters* apart.

_____

21. They hadn't seen each other in over a *decade*.

_____

22. The package weighed slightly more than one *kilogram*.

_____

23. A nurse removed 5 *milliliters* of blood from a patient.

_____

BIOLOGY AS A SCIENCE
2-2 Tools of the Biologist

Part I: Vocabulary Review

Identify the term that fits each of the definitions below. Then, to reveal the biological concept below, transfer the letters that have numbers beneath them to the corresponding blank spaces shown below.

1. technique that separates substances based on chemical or physical properties

‗‗ ‗‗ ‗‗ ‗‗ ‗‗ ‗‗ ‗‗ ‗‗ ‗‗ ‗‗ ‗‗ ‗‗ ‗‗ ‗‗
  2   31 15 38 17 27   6   36 25 34   41

2. device that uses light to produce an enlarged view of an object

‗‗ ‗‗ ‗‗ ‗‗ ‗‗ ‗‗ ‗‗ ‗‗ ‗‗ ‗‗ ‗‗ ‗‗ ‗‗
      3   43 14   45   7   10 33   1   24   4

3. the structural parts of a compound microscope that hold the specimen and lenses and permit focusing of the image

‗‗ ‗‗ ‗‗ ‗‗ ‗‗ ‗‗ ‗‗ ‗‗ ‗‗ ‗‗ ‗‗ ‗‗ ‗‗ ‗‗
      18   5   9   13   21 20 26

4. the enlargement of an image

‗‗ ‗‗ ‗‗ ‗‗ ‗‗ ‗‗ ‗‗ ‗‗ ‗‗ ‗‗ ‗‗
          12 11   8   22   46 30   19

5. process by which materials of different densities suspended in a liquid can be separated

‗‗ ‗‗ ‗‗ ‗‗ ‗‗ ‗‗ ‗‗ ‗‗ ‗‗ ‗‗ ‗‗ ‗‗
      32 35 40   39

6. technique of maintaining living cells or tissues in a culture medium outside of the body

‗‗ ‗‗ ‗‗ ‗‗ ‗‗ ‗‗ ‗‗ ‗‗ ‗‗ ‗‗ ‗‗ ‗‗
      48 51 44 42   16   49

7. microscope that can magnify images more than 250 000 times

‗‗ ‗‗ ‗‗ ‗‗ ‗‗ ‗‗ ‗‗ ‗‗ ‗‗ ‗‗ ‗‗ ‗‗ ‗‗ ‗‗ ‗‗ ‗‗ ‗‗
          47   28   50 52   29   23

‗‗ ‗‗ ‗‗ ‗‗ ‗‗ ‗‗ ‗‗ ‗‗ ‗‗
          53

CONCEPT:

‗‗ ‗‗ ‗‗ ‗‗ ‗‗ ‗‗ ‗‗ ‗‗ ‗‗ ‗‗   ‗‗ ‗‗ ‗‗ ‗‗ ‗‗ ‗‗ ‗‗ ‗‗ ‗‗ ‗‗ ‗‗
 1   2   3   4   5   6   7   8   9 10   11 12 13 14 15 16 17 18 19 20 21

‗‗ ‗‗ ‗‗ ‗‗ ‗‗ ‗‗ ‗‗ ‗‗   ‗‗ ‗‗ ‗‗   ‗‗ ‗‗ ‗‗ ‗‗ ‗‗   ‗‗ ‗‗
22 23 24 25 26 27 28 29   30 31 32   33 34 35 36 37   38 39

‗‗ ‗‗ ‗‗   ‗‗ ‗‗ ‗‗ ‗‗ ‗‗   ‗‗ ‗‗ ‗‗ ‗‗ ‗‗ ‗‗
40 41 42   43 44 45 46 47   48 49 50 51 52 53

BIOLOGY AS A SCIENCE
2-2 Tools of the Biologist (continued)

Part II: Content Review

Select the best answer for each question and write the letter in the space provided.

_____ 8. What technique involves tiny instruments to perform operations on living cells under a microscope?
   a. spectrophotometry
   b. microdissection
   c. tissue culture
   d. electrophoresis

_____ 9. The magnifying glass is an example of a
   a. stereomicroscope
   b. phase-contrast microscope
   c. compound microscope
   d. simple microscope

_____ 10. Which instrument passes a finely focused electron beam over the surface of a specimen?
   a. scanning electron microscope
   b. transmission electron microscope
   c. stereomicroscope
   d. phase-contrast microscope

_____ 11. The three systems that make up a compound microscope are
   a. magnification, light, and specimen
   b. simple, complex, and light
   c. optical, mechanical, and light
   d. stereo, mechanical, and optical

_____ 12. The ability of a microscope to show two points that are close together as separate images is known as:
   a. absorption
   b. magnification
   c. resolution
   d. phase-contrast

_____ 13. What method is used to determine the substances in a sample from the kind of light it absorbs?
   a. magnification
   b. resolution
   c. electrophoresis
   d. spectrophotometry

_____ 14. To separate the components in a sample of blood, what laboratory technique would you use?
   a. magnification
   b. microdissection
   c. centrifugation
   d. tissue culture

_____ 15. What type of light microscope is used to study the surface structure of specimens?
   a. simple microscope
   b. stereomicroscope
   c. transmission electron microscope
   d. phase-contrast microscope

_____ 16. To prepare a specimen to be viewed with an electron microscope, it is
   a. placed in a water drop on a slide and stained
   b. separated by centrifugation, dried, and stained
   c. placed in a vacuum chamber and embedded in plastic
   d. dried, embedded in plastic, sliced thin, and stained

Part III: Skills Development

Review the skill entitled "Graphic Organizing: Flow Chart" on pages 34–37. Then complete the flow chart below to show the sequence of steps in preparing a specimen to be observed under a compound microscope.

17.

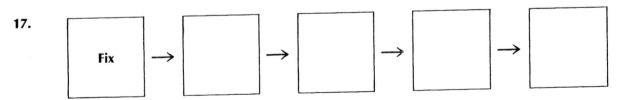

Fix → □ → □ → □ → □

Name _____ Date _____

CHAPTER REVIEW

Know the Terms

Match the metric prefix with the proper unit.

a. mega   **d.** milli
b. kilo   **e.** micro
c. centi   **f.** deci

  1. one-thousandth   **1.** _____

  2. one-millionth   **2.** _____

  3. one million   **3.** _____

  4. one-hundredth   **4.** _____

  5. one thousand   **5.** _____

Match the microscope part with its function.

a. diaphragm   **d.** high power objective
b. coarse adjustment   **e.** low power objective
c. fine adjustment   **f.** stage

  6. regulates the amount of light   **6.** _____

  7. used to locate the specimen   **7.** _____

  8. used for approximate focusing   **8.** _____

  9. used for final focusing   **9.** _____

10. allows further magnification   **10.** _____

Select the most appropriate words from the list to complete the following paragraphs.

problem	scientific law	kilometer
meter	scientific method	milligram
experiment	theory	observation
hypothesis	gram	
liter	variable	

                                                      11. _____

Scientists universally use the __(11)__ to solve problems. The approach begins with defining the __(12)__. Then they formulate a/an __(13)__ that they test using a/an __(14)__ where only one single factor, called a/an __(15)__, is changed. If the process verifies their thoughts on the problem they may propose a/an __(16)__, which may become a/an __(17)__ if it is always true.

12. _____

13. _____

14. _____

15. _____

16. _____

17. _____

    In scientific investigations, the SI or metric system is used. __(18)__ is the basic unit of length; __(19)__ is the unit of mass; and __(20)__ is the unit of volume.

18. _____

19. _____

20. _____

CHAPTER REVIEW

Understanding the Concepts

Answer each of the following questions in one or two sentences.

1. What is the difference between a hypothesis and a theory? _____

_____

_____

_____

2. The objective lens of a compound microscope magnifies an image 25 times. The eyepiece (ocular) magnifies it 10 times. What is the total magnification of the microscope? _____

_____

3. Why do biologists stain specimens? _____

_____

4. Of what value is the electron microscope to scientists? _____

_____

_____

5. How do the scanning and transmission electron microscopes differ in the images they produce? _____

_____

_____

6. Why do scientists use the metric system? _____

7. List, in their usual order, the steps of the scientific method. _____

_____

_____

_____

8. Why do optical microscopes lose their resolution as magnification increases? _____

_____

_____

9. Explain how a centrifuge separates materials. _____

_____

_____

BASIC CHEMISTRY
3-1   Atomic Theory of Matter

Part I: Vocabulary Review

Complete the paragraphs by filling in each blank with the correct vocabulary term.

In spite of the large number of different substances, there are only about 100 kinds of basic building blocks of matter called **(1)**_____ . Substances made up of only one kind of atom are called **(2)**_____ . Substances made up of two or more atoms that are combined in definite proportions are known as **(3)**_____ .

Each atom has a small central part called the **(4)**_____ . Inside this central part are found positively charged **(5)**_____ and neutral **(6)**_____ . In the space outside the central part, there are tiny, negatively charged **(7)**_____ .

The number of protons that an atom has determines its **(8)**_____ . The **(9)**_____ is equal to the sum of the atom's protons and neutrons. Varieties of atoms that differ only in the number of neutrons in their atomic nuclei are called **(10)**_____ .

An unstable nucleus gives off charged particles and radiation. This property, called **(11)**_____ , causes the atom to change to another isotope. Radioactive isotopes are called **(12)**_____ .

Part II: Content Review

The sentences below are incorrect statements. Rewrite the underlined part of the sentences to make them correct.

13. <u>Compounds</u> cannot be subdivided any further by any ordinary chemical means. _____

14. Most substances are <u>elements</u>. _____

15. Scientists use <u>microscopes</u> to decide whether a substance is an element or a compound. _____

16. Atoms are <u>hard, solid balls</u>. _____

17. Protons are <u>negatively</u> charged, neutrons are <u>positively charged</u> and electrons are <u>neutral</u>. _____

18. The number of <u>neutrons</u> determines the atomic number of an element. _____

_____

_____

19. The mass number of an atom is equal to <u>its atomic number.</u> _____

_____

_____

20. Normally, atoms have the same number of <u>protons</u> as <u>neutrons.</u> _____

_____

_____

21. Atoms with unfilled outer energy levels <u>cannot</u> form compounds. _____

_____

_____

22. When atoms combine to form compounds, their <u>protons are exchanged.</u> _____

_____

_____

_____

23. Isotopes are varieties of an element that differ only in the number of <u>electrons.</u> _____

_____

_____

24. <u>All</u> nuclei emit charged particles and radiation at times that cannot be predicted. _____

_____

25. Radioactivity is a <u>chemical</u> process that changes the <u>electron</u> structure of an atom. _____

_____

_____

BASIC CHEMISTRY
3-2 Chemical Bonding and Chemical Reactions

Part I: Vocabulary Review

Fill in the vocabulary term that best completes each statement.

1. The force of attraction that holds atoms together is called a _____ .

2. New substances produced by a chemical change are known as _____ .

3. A _____ is made up of two or more atoms that act as a single particle.

4. The force of attraction between two charged atoms is called an _____ .

5. When chemical bonds are broken and atoms form new bonds in new combinations, a _____ _____ has taken place.

6. In a _____ , each element is represented by a chemical symbol and the proportions in which the atoms combine are shown by subscripts.

7. In one molecule of water, two _____ hold the molecule together.

8. Most elements that form _____ are gases under ordinary conditions.

9. _____ are the substances present before a chemical reaction starts.

10. A _____ shows the number and kind of atoms in a molecule as well as how the atoms are bonded to one another.

11. The _____ states that mass can be neither created nor destroyed in a chemical reaction.

12. An atom with an excess charge is called an _____ .

Part II: Content Review

Read each "Cause" and fill in an appropriate "Effect" in the space provided. An example is given below.

CAUSE	EFFECT
13. When 2 hydrogen atoms bond with 1 oxygen atom,	*a water molecule forms.*
14. When a hydrogen atom reacts with another hydrogen atom,	_____
15. After a chlorine atom receives an electron from a sodium atom,	_____
16. When two ions with opposite charges attract each other,	_____
17. If the bonds that hold together a water molecule are broken,	_____
18. If an atom has 6 electrons in its outer energy level,	_____

CAUSE	EFFECT
19. When a chlorine atom shares 1 electron with an atom of hydrogen,	_____ _____ _____
20. When sodium ions and chloride ions come in contact,	_____

Part III: Skills Development

Review the skill entitled "Interpreting Diagrams and Tables" on pages 19–21. Then, use the following diagram to answer the questions below.

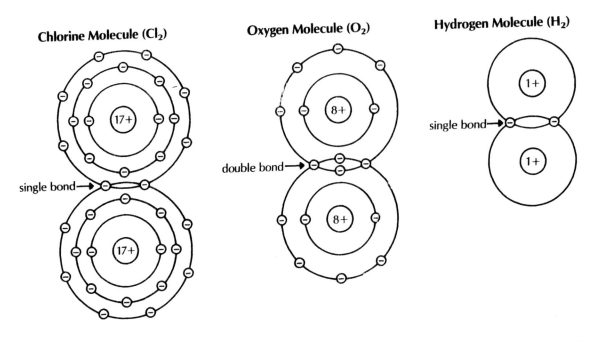

Chlorine Molecule (Cl_2)   Oxygen Molecule (O_2)   Hydrogen Molecule (H_2)

21. What are pictured in the diagram? _____

22. What holds each molecule together? _____

23. How many electrons are shared by the two chlorine atoms in the chlorine molecule? _____

24. How many electrons are shared by the two oxygen atoms in the oxygen molecule? _____

25. How many electrons are shared by the two hydrogen atoms in the hydrogen molecule? _____

26. What do the chemical formulas, Cl_2, O_2, and H_2 mean? _____

_____

_____

BASIC CHEMISTRY
3-3   Mixtures

Part I: Vocabulary Review

If a statement below is true, write TRUE in the space at the left. If a statement is false, correct the statement by writing in the space at the left the term(s) to replace the underlined word(s).

_____   1. Any homogeneous mixture can be called a <u>solute</u>, although the term is usually used for mixtures that are liquids.

_____   2. A mixture that separates on standing is called a <u>solution</u>.

_____   3. In a <u>suspension</u>, the particles of the solute are larger than molecules or ions, but they are too small to settle out.

_____   4. The air around you is an example of a <u>suspension</u>.

_____   5. The liquid substance that makes up the bulk of a solution is called the <u>solute</u>.

_____   6. The medium in which a <u>colloidal dispersion</u> forms can be either a liquid, a gas, or a solid.

_____   7. In a true solution, the particles of the <u>solute</u> remain spread throughout the solvent indefinitely.

_____   8. The substances dissolved in a solvent are called <u>suspensions</u>.

_____   9. The force of gravity causes particles to gradually settle out of a <u>solution</u>.

_____   10. Sand mixed with water is an example of a <u>colloidal dispersion</u>.

_____   11. The substances in a <u>mixture</u> retain their usual properties.

_____   12. Smoke is an example of a <u>solution</u> of carbon particles in air.

Part II: Content Review

For each statement below, decide whether it relates to a solution (liquid-based homogeneous mixture), suspension, or colloidal dispersion. Write "SO" for solution, "SU" for suspension, or "C" for colloidal dispersion.

_____   13. If you let this mixture stand, particles will slowly settle to the bottom.

_____   14. This mixture contains particles that are larger than molecules or ions, but are still too small to settle out.

_____   15. In this kind of mixture the particles are molecules or ions that remain dissolved indefinitely.

_____   16. A teaspoon of table salt mixed with a cup of water is an example of this type of mixture.

_____   17. This type of mixture usually has water as a solvent.

_____   18. In this kind of mixture, you would find solutes.

_____   19. In this mixture, dissolved substances are in the form of molecules or ions.

_____   20. In this kind of mixture dissociation of ionic substances occurs.

_____   21. A cloudy mixture of clay particles in water would be an example of this kind of mixture.

Part III: Skills Development

Review the skill entitled "Taking Notes" on pages 16–18. Then, read the following passage from your textbook and take notes on it.

In every compound, the atoms or ions are joined by chemical bonds. The atoms or ions are present in fixed proportions and in a definite arrangement in space. It is possible, however, for many substances to be physically mixed without forming new chemical bonds. The result is called a **mixture.** The substances in a mixture may be present in any proportions. In fact, the proportions can change as one substance is added to or removed from the mixture. No matter what their proportions, however, the different substances in the mixture retain their usual properties.

For example, consider a mixture of table salt (sodium chloride) and iron filings. If this mixture is placed in water, the salt will dissolve, as it normally does. The iron filings will remain undissolved. On the other hand, a magnet will attract the iron filings in the mixture and leave the salt behind. See Figure 3–17.

The substances in a mixture may be spread evenly throughout the mixture. Such a mixture is said to be *homogeneous* (hoh muh JEE nee us). Air, for example, is a homogeneous mixture of several different gases. The gases in air include nitrogen, oxygen, carbon dioxide, water vapor, and a few others.

22. _____

_____

_____

_____

_____

_____

_____

_____

_____

_____

_____

_____

_____

_____

_____

_____

_____

_____

_____

_____

BASIC CHEMISTRY
3-4 Acids, Bases, and Salts

Part I: Vocabulary Review

Complete the following sentences with a phrase that correctly uses the word in parentheses. An example is given below.

1. A salt is an ionic compound that is produced when _a neutralization reaction occurs between an_ _acid and a base_____. (neutralization)

2. Acid solutions, which have high concentrations of H^+, have _____ _____. (pH)

3. When hydrochloric acid reacts with sodium hydroxide, and water is evaporated from the resulting solution of ions, then _____ _____. (salt)

4. Acid rain occurs when oxides of sulfur and nitrogen in the air _____ _____. (acids)

5. When dissolved in water, a compound that produces _____ _____. (base)

6. A substance, such as phenolphthalein, that changes color when _____ _____. (indicator)

Part II: Content Review

Answer each of the following questions in one or two sentences.

7. If a lake had a pH of 4, how might you bring the pH level closer to neutral? _____
_____

8. What indicator would you use to find out if a solution has a pH of about 4? Explain. _____
_____
_____

9. What happens when sodium hydroxide is dissolved in water? _____
_____
_____

10. How does the kind of ion produced by acids in solution differ from the kind produced by bases in solution?
_____
_____

11. What happens to the ions of acids and bases during neutralization? _____

_____

_____

_____

12. How would you neutralize a base? _____

_____

_____

13. Why is the pH of pure water considered to be neutral? _____

_____

_____

14. Why is the H^+ concentration in basic solutions less than the H^+ concentration in water? _____

_____

_____

_____

Part III: Skills Development

Review the skill entitled "Graphic Organizing: Scale" on pages 38–40. Then, complete the pH scale below by adding the following substances: lemon juice (pH 2); molasses (pH 5); blood (pH 7); apple juice (pH 3); borax solution (pH 9) and ammonia water (pH 11).

15.

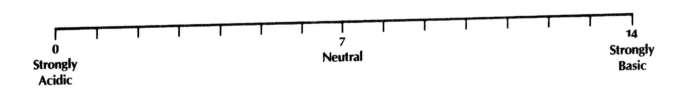

0
Strongly
Acidic

7
Neutral

14
Strongly
Basic

CHAPTER REVIEW

Know the Terms

Complete the following crossword puzzle.

ACROSS

1. Negatively charged particle in an atom
3. Substance made up of one kind of atom
5. Atom with an altered number of neutrons
7. Compound that produces an excess of hydrogen ions in water
9. Attracting force between atoms

DOWN

2. Substance made of two or more kinds of atoms
4. Electrically neutral particle in the nucleus of an atom
6. Compound that produces an excess of hydroxyl ions in water
8. One or more atoms with an electrical charge

Define or describe each of the following words.

10. atom: _____

_____

11. chemical bond: _____

_____

12. molecule: _____

_____

13. reactant: _____

_____

14. solution: _____

_____

CHAPTER REVIEW

Understand the Concepts

Answer the following questions in one or two sentences.

1. Distinguish between a solute and a solvent. _____

2. Balance the following equation: $CO_2 + H_2O \longrightarrow C_6H_{12}O_6 + O_2$

3. Distinguish between a structural formula and a molecular formula. _____

4. How is a suspension different from a solution? _____

5. What might be the result of mixing two solutions of equal volume, one of which has a pH of 9 and the other, a pH of 5? _____

6. Why do atoms share electrons? _____

7. Name the three types of atomic particles and describe where each is found in the atom. _____

8. Why do you suppose we use symbols to represent elements? _____

9. What do you think a "double" covalent bond is? _____

10. How could you separate a mixture of gravel and sand? _____

11. How would you separate the solute and solvent of a solution? _____

12. Why do scientists use radioisotopes? _____

CHEMICAL COMPOUNDS OF LIFE
4-1   Biologically Important Compounds

Part I: Vocabulary Review

Compare and contrast the following pairs of terms. First list their similarities, then their differences.

1. organic compounds and inorganic compounds: _____

_____

_____

_____

_____

_____

2. cohesion and adhesion: _____

_____

_____

_____

_____

Part II: Content Review

Explain why each of the following is important for living organisms. An example is given below.

3. organic compounds: *Organisms and their products contain organic compounds. Organic compounds*

provide the basis for the enormously complex structures and reactions of living things.

4. inorganic compounds: _____

_____

_____

5. water: _____

_____

6. adhesion: _____

_____

_____

7. carbon: _____

_____

_____

Part III: Skills Development

Review the skill "Finding the Main Idea" on pages 8–10. Then, find the main idea in each of the following paragraphs from your text. Underline the main idea and, in the space provided, explain why it is a main idea.

A carbon atom has 6 electrons. As you can see in Figure 4–4, 2 of these electrons occupy the first energy level, which leaves 4 electrons for the second level. This means that the carbon atom can fill its outer energy level by forming 4 covalent bonds with other atoms. One electron in each bond comes from the carbon atom. The other electron comes from another atom bonded to the carbon. The atoms bonded to a carbon atom can be other carbon atoms. These atoms may be bonded into long chains. A long chain may have other groups of chains of atoms branching from it. Carbon atoms may also be bonded into rings with side branches or bonded with other rings. The possible size and variety of these arrangements is unlimited.

8. _____

_____

_____

_____

_____

Of all the inorganic compounds found in living things, water is the most important. All living organisms need water to survive, and most organisms contain water. About 65 percent of your body weight is water. People have been known to survive for weeks without food but only a few days without water. Water is essential because many biological processes can take place only in water solutions. the properties of water, which are discussed below, will help you to understand the way living things function.

9. _____

_____

_____

_____

_____

CHEMICAL COMPOUNDS OF LIFE
4-2   Carbohydrates and Lipids

Part I: Vocabulary Review

Complete the following crossword puzzle.

ACROSS

2. Process by which sugar molecules can be bonded together
3. Simple sugars
4. Compounds with more than two simple sugars joined together
6. Compound that plays a part in the hardening and narrowing of arteries
8. Large molecules made up of repeating units
11. Compounds of carbon, hydrogen, and oxygen
12. Process by which disaccharides and polysaccharides can be broken apart

DOWN

1. Two simple sugars joined together
5. Kind of fat made up of fatty acids with single carbon-to-carbon bonds
6. Part of a fatty acid molecule that consists of 1 carbon atom joined to an OH group by a single bond and to an oxygen atom by a double bond
7. Kind of molecule made up of a chain of carbons to which hydrogens are bonded, and having a carboxyl group at one end
9. Substances commonly called fats, oils, and waxes
10. Form of stored sugar found in plants

CHEMICAL COMPOUNDS OF LIFE

4-2 Carbohydrates and Lipids   (continued)

Part II: Content Review

For each statement below, decide whether it relates to carbohydrates, lipids, or both. Write "C" for carbohydrates, "L" for lipids, or "B" for both.

_____ 13. are formed by the dehydration synthesis of 3 fatty acid molecules and 1 glycerol molecule

_____ 14. used as a source of energy by living organisms

_____ 15. consist of carbon, hydrogen, and oxygen

_____ 16. may be saturated or unsaturated

_____ 17. have the same ratio of hydrogen to oxygen as water

_____ 18. include monosaccharides, disaccharides, and polysaccharides

_____ 19. may be stored by an organism

_____ 20. contain carboxyl groups

_____ 21. affect levels of cholesterol in the body

_____ 22. are part of cell structures

Part III: Skills Development

Review the skill entitled "Interpreting Diagrams and Tables" on pages 19–21. Then, use the diagram to answer the questions below.

Maltose (a disaccharide)   + Water ⟶   Glucose   +   Glucose

23. What process does this diagram illustrate? _____

_____

24. What are the reactants? The products? _____

_____

25. Are the products more complex or less complex than the reactants? _____

_____

26. Where are the new OH groups formed on each glucose molecule? _____

_____

CHEMICAL COMPOUNDS OF LIFE
4-3 Nucleic Acids and Proteins

Part I: Vocabulary Review

Write the correct vocabulary term that best replaces the italicized definition in each statement.

1. *Compounds that contain phosphorous and nitrogen in addition to carbon, hydrogen, and oxygen* were first found in the cell's nucleus. _____

2. One kind of nucleic acid is *the hereditary material that is passed on from one generation to the next during reproduction.* _____

3. *A second kind of nucleic acid* along with DNA plays an important role in the activities of all the cells in an organism. _____

4. Each long chain of the DNA molecule is made up of *repeating units, each of which consists of a 5-carbon sugar bonded to a phosphate group and a nitrogenous base.* _____

5. *Compounds that contain nitrogen as well as carbon, hydrogen, and oxygen* make up many cell structures as well as hormones, antibodies, and enzymes. _____

6. Proteins are made up of many *smaller structural units, each of which has the general formula*

$$NH_2-\underset{\underset{H}{|}}{\overset{\overset{R}{|}}{C}}-COOH.$$ _____

7. The dehydration synthesis of 2 amino acids results in a *bond between the amino group (NH$_2$) of one amino acid and the carboxyl group (COOH) of the other,* and the loss of 1 water molecule. _____

8. The product of the dehydration synthesis of 2 amino acid molecules is a *molecule that consists of two amino acids bonded together.* _____

9. *A long chain of amino acids* can be formed by adding amino acids to either end of a dipeptide. _____

Part II: Content Review

Complete each of the sentences below.

10. The two kinds of nucleic acids are called _____

11. A DNA molecule contains 4 different kinds of nitrogenous bases, which are _____

_____

12. The DNA molecule usually takes the shape of a coiled ladder called a _____

13. The number of different amino acids commonly found in proteins is _____

14. The structure of RNA molecules is different from DNA molecules in three main ways, which are _____

_____

_____

15. Amino acids may be bonded together to form polypeptides by the process of _____

_____

16. All proteins are made up of one or more _____

_____

17. Typical shapes of protein molecules are _____

_____

18. The enormous variety of proteins is made possible by _____

_____

_____

19. The first protein structure to be determined was that of _____

_____

Part III: Skills Development

Review the skill entitled "Graphic Organizing: Compare/Contrast Matrix" on pages 41–44. Then, complete the matrix below by filling in the empty boxes.

20.

CHARACTERISTIC	DNA	RNA
Number of strands		
Kind of sugar		
4 kinds of nitrogenous bases		
Function		

CHEMICAL COMPOUNDS OF LIFE
4-4 Enzymes

Part I: Vocabulary Review

Match the terms listed in Column II with the proper definition listed in Column I. Place the answer in the space provided.

COLUMN I   **COLUMN II**

_____ **1.** substance that enzymes act upon   **a.** enzyme

_____ **2.** surface region of an enzyme into which substrate molecule fits   **b.** catalyst

_____ **3.** protein substance necessary for chemical reactions in cells   **c.** substrate

_____ **4.** organic substances that are not proteins and allow an enzyme to   **d.** active site
          perform its catalytic function

_____ **5.** substance that brings about reactions without being changed itself   **e.** coenzymes

Part II: Content Review

Read each "Cause" and fill in an appropriate "Effect" in the space provided. An example is given below.

CAUSE   **EFFECT**

6. When gasoline is burned in an automobile engine,   *a small explosion that helps drives*

                                                                    the engine is produced.

7. When maltase acts upon a molecule of maltose,   _____

8. When pepsin mixes with food in the stomach,   _____

                                                                    _____

9. When a substrate molecule comes in contact with the active   _____
site of an enzyme,
                                                                    _____

10. When an enzyme brings together 2 substrate molecules,   _____

                                                                    _____

11. According to the induced-fit model, when a substrate enters _____
an enzyme's active site,
                                                                    _____

12. As an enzyme binds to a substrate,   _____

                                                                    _____

13. When there are small amounts of enzyme in the presence of a _____
substrate,
                                                                    _____

14. If the temperature is low,   _____

                                                                    _____

                                                                    _____

15. When temperatures are too high, _____

_____

_____

16. When there is a very small amount of enzyme and a great
deal of substrate, the rate of the reaction _____

_____

_____

17. When all substrate molecules are occupied continuously by
enzymes, then the reaction rate _____

_____

Part III: Skills Development

Review the skill entitled "Graphic Organizing: Line Graph" on pages 30–33. Then, use the following graph to
answer the questions below.

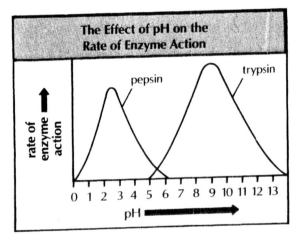

18. Does pepsin work best in acidic or basic surroundings? _____

19. At about what pH is the rate of pepsin's action the highest? _____

20. Moving up the pH scale, at what pH does pepsin stop working? _____

21. Does trypsin work best in acidic or basic surroundings? _____

22. At about what pH is the rate of trypsin's action the highest? _____

23. Moving down the pH scale when does trypsin stop working? _____

24. Between what pH readings do the actions of pepsin and trypsin overlap? _____

CHAPTER REVIEW

Know the Terms

Select the most appropriate words from the list to complete the following paragraphs.

nucleic acids	amino acids	peptide bond	adenine
thymine	polysaccharide	saturated	glycerol
DNA	lipids	enzymes	RNA
ribose	cytosine	carbohydrates	monosaccharides
hydrolysis	proteins	oxygen	disaccharide
hydrogen	fatty acids	guanine	carbon
dehydration synthesis	deoxyribose	organic compounds	unsaturated

Living organisms are composed of a special category of molecules called __(1)__. Molecules must have both __(2)__ and __(3)__ atoms in them to be in this category. In addition they usually contain __(4)__ atoms as well.

Sugars and starches are __(5)__, which always have a carbon to hydrogen ratio of 2:1. They are composed of building blocks called __(6)__. Two of these units can be attached to each other through a process called __(7)__, which results in a __(8)__. If more subunits are hooked on, we get a __(9)__. This type of molecule can be broken into its building blocks again through the reverse reaction, called __(10)__.

__(11)__ have a hydrogen to oxygen ratio greater than 2:1 and include fats, oils, and waxes. If the carbon-to-carbon bonds in these molecules are all single bonds, they are said to be __(12)__. If there are any double bonded carbons, the molecule is said to be __(13)__. The building blocks of these molecules are __(14)__ and __(15)__.

The group of organic molecules that contain nitrogen are called __(16)__. They have __(17)__ as their building blocks. The bond connecting two of these together is called a __(18)__. Some of these molecules function as __(19)__, which catalyze chemical reactions within cells.

The group of organic molecules that were first discovered in the nucleus of the cell are called __(20)__. There are two kinds of these molecules. They are __(21)__ and __(22)__. One of these is described as a double helix. Its subunits are composed of a five-carbon sugar, called __(23)__, and one of four bases.

1. _____
2. _____
3. _____
4. _____
5. _____
6. _____
7. _____
8. _____
9. _____
10. _____
11. _____
12. _____
13. _____
14. _____
15. _____
16. _____
17. _____
18. _____
19. _____
20. _____
21. _____
22. _____
23. _____

CHAPTER REVIEW

Understand the Concepts

Answer the following questions in one or two sentences.

1. Why are a hydrogen and hydroxyl removed during a dehydration synthesis reaction? _____

_____

_____

2. Why are a hydrogen and hydroxyl necessary for hydrolysis? _____

_____

_____

3. Why can organic molecules get so large? _____

_____

_____

4. How is a peptide bond formed? _____

_____

_____

5. How are the two chains of a double helix held together? _____

_____

_____

6. Why are small amounts of enzymes sufficient to catalyze a large number of chemical reactions? _____

_____

_____

7. Explain how glucose, fructose, and galactose can be different molecules even though they all have the

same molecular formula ($C_6H_{12}O_6$). _____

_____

_____

8. Why is the polar nature of a water molecule important to living organisms? _____

_____

_____

_____

THE CELL
5-1 What Is a Cell?

Part I: Vocabulary Review

Complete the following sentences with a phrase that correctly uses the word(s) in parentheses. An example is provided below.

1. Whether one-celled or many-celled, the life processes of an organism *are carried on by its cells*

_____ . (cells)

2. Cells that usually are between 1 and 10 micrometers in diameter and that lack _____

_____ . (prokaryotic cells)

3. Cells that usually are between 10 and 100 micrometers in diameter and that have _____

_____ . (eukaryotic cells)

4. In eukaryotic cells, the cell's hereditary material _____

_____ . (nucleus)

Part II: Content Review

Explain why each of the following is important to our understanding of the cell.

5. microscopes: _____

_____

6. Robert Hooke: _____

_____

7. Anton van Leeuwenhoek: _____

_____

8. Henry Dutrochet: _____

_____

9. Robert Brown: _____

_____

10. Matthias Schleiden: _____

_____

11. Theodor Schwann: _____

_____

12. Johannes Purkinje: _____

_____

13. Rudolph Virchow: _____

_____

14. Max Schultze: _____

_____

15. Felix Dujardin: _____

_____

16. the cell theory: _____

_____

_____

17. prokaryotic cells and eukaryotic cells: _____

_____

18. surface area-to-volume ratio: _____

_____

Part III: Skills Development

Review the skill entitled "Graphic Organizing: Scale" on pages 38–40. Then, complete the time line below by writing in the names of the scientists whose discoveries led up to the cell theory. Be sure to write the scientists' names at the appropriate points on the time line.

19.

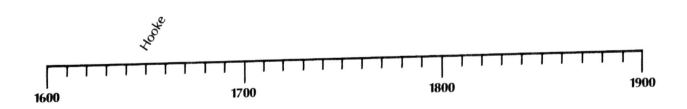

THE CELL
5-2 Cell Structure

Part I: Vocabulary Review

Below are groups of terms related to the study of this section. Cross out the one word that does not belong and explain the relationship of the remaining four terms.

1. cell wall
   central vacuole
   leucoplasts
   centrioles
   chloroplasts

   _____
   _____
   _____
   _____
   _____

2. nucleus
   vacuoles
   cytoplasm
   mitochondria
   lysosomes

   _____
   _____
   _____
   _____
   _____

3. endoplasmic reticulum
   nucleoli
   ribosomes
   Golgi bodies
   microtubules

   _____
   _____
   _____
   _____
   _____

4. cell membrane
   nuclear envelope
   chromatin
   chromosomes
   nucleoli

   _____
   _____
   _____
   _____
   _____

Part II: Content Review

Select the best answer for each question and write the letter in the space provided.

_____ 5. The cells of most bacteria, various other microorganisms, and all plants are surrounded by
   a. a cell wall
   b. an endoplasmic reticulum
   c. a nuclear envelope
   d. a plastid

_____ 6. The cell membrane can regulate the chemical makeup of the cell because
   a. the cell membrane is a solid barrier
   b. the ell brane is an impassable wall
   c. the cell membrane is selectively permeable
   d. the cell membrane is metabolically active

_____ 7. The control center for cell metabolism and reproduction is
   a. the nucleoli
   b. the cytoplasm
   c. the ribosomes
   d. the nucleus

_____ 8. The sites of protein synthesis in the cell are
   a. the lysosomes
   b. the ribosomes
   c. the centrioles
   d. the plastids

_____ 9. Which organelles process, package, and store products that are secreted by cells?
   a. lysosomes
   b. ribosomes
   c. microtubules
   d. Golgi bodies

_____ 10. Small, saclike structures that are surrounded by a single membrane and contain strong digestive enzymes are called
   a. lysosomes
   b. ribosomes
   c. microfilaments
   d. cilia

_____ 11. Cells that require large amounts of energy have large numbers of energy-releasing organelles called
   a. vacuoles
   b. flagella
   c. mitochondria
   d. Golgi bodies

_____ 12. Which cell structures are composed of the protein actin and are involved in muscle contraction in muscle cells?
   a. microfilaments
   b. microtubules
   c. vacuoles
   d. mitochondria

_____ 13. What are the hairlike organelles that are capable of movement and extend from the surface of many kinds of cells?
   a. vacuoles and plastids
   b. cilia and flagella
   c. microtubules and microfilaments
   d. nuclei and nucleoli

_____ 14. What organelles are found in plant cells and are filled with a fluid called cell sap?
   a. Golgi bodies
   b. nucleoli
   c. microtubules
   d. vacuoles

_____ 15. Membrane-enclosed organelles that are found only in the cells of photosynthetic, eukaryotic organisms include
   a. cilia, flagella, and basal bodies
   b. leucoplasts, chromoplasts, and chloroplasts
   c. centrioles, ribosomes, and lysosomes
   d. microtubules, microfilaments, and flagella

THE CELL
5-3   Maintaining a Constant Cell Environment

Part I: Vocabulary Review

Compare and contrast the following pairs of terms. First list their similarities, then their differences.

1. diffusion and facilitated diffusion: _____

_____

_____

_____

2. osmosis and osmotic pressure: _____

_____

_____

_____

3. isotonic solution and hypotonic solution: _____

_____

_____

_____

_____

4. passive transport and active transport: _____

_____

_____

5. pinocytosis and phagocytosis: _____

_____

6. endocytosis and exocytosis: _____

_____

_____

Part II: Content Review

Answer each of the following questions in one or two sentences.

7. Which kinds of molecules pass easily through cell membranes and which kinds do not pass through easily?

_____

_____

_____

8. What are the conditions under which diffusion occurs and what is the final result of diffusion? _____

_____

_____

_____

9. What happens to a plant cell in a hypotonic solution? In a hypertonic solution? _____

_____

_____

_____

_____

Part III: Skills Development

Review the skill entitled "Graphic Organizing: Concept Map" on pages 49–55. Then, complete the concept map below.

10.

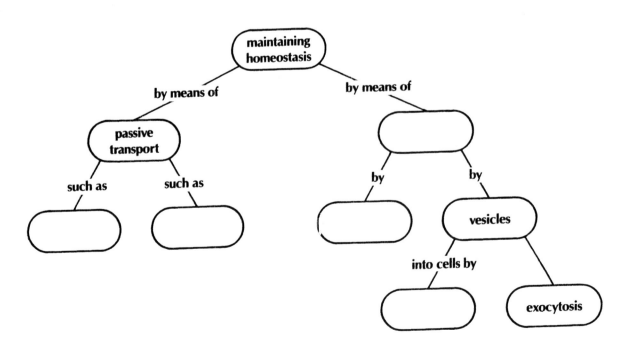

THE CELL
5-4 Organization of Cells in Living Things

Part I: Vocabulary Review

Replace the italicized definition with the correct vocabulary term.

1. In plants, there are *groups of cells that are structurally similar and perform the same function*, which transport water and nutrients throughout the plant. _____

2. *Tissues that support other body tissues and bind tissues and organs together* give the body form. _____ _____

3. *Tissues that cover body surfaces and line body cavities and organs* are in the form of sheets of closely packed cells that may be one or several cell layers thick. _____

4. *Tissues that are specialized for contraction* may be found in the heart, may be attached to the bones of the skeleton, or may line various organs. _____

5. The stomach, which has nerves, muscles, and blood vessels, is a(n) *group of tissues that work together to perform a specific function.* _____

6. The digestive system, which includes the mouth, esophagus, stomach, intestines, pancreas, and liver, is a(n) *group of organs that work together to perform a specific function.* _____

Part II: Content Review

For each statement below, decide whether it relates to a colonial organism, a multicellular organism, or both. Write "C" for colonial, "M" for multicellular, or "B" for both.

_____ 7. These organisms have tissues.

_____ 8. These organisms consist of more than one cell.

_____ 9. These organisms consist of a few or many cells that are loosely attached to each other and that show little or no specialization among themselves.

_____ 10. These organisms may contain organ systems.

_____ 11. *Volvox* is an example of this kind of organism.

_____ 12. Usually, any one of the cells of this kind of organism has the capacity to produce a new organism.

_____ 13. In these kinds of organisms, the cells cannot function as independent, single-celled organisms, each performing all life functions.

_____ 14. These organisms may have groups of tissues that work together to perform specific functions.

_____ 15. This kind of organism includes humans.

_____ 16. All the separate cells, tissues, organs, and organ systems must function together for this kind of organism to carry on its life processes.

Part III: Skills Development

Review the skill entitled "Graphic Organizing: Word Map" on pages 45–48. Then, complete the word maps below.

17.

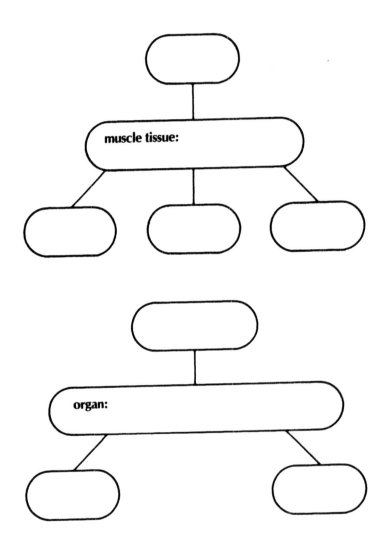

CHAPTER REVIEW

Know the Terms

Select the most appropriate words from the list to complete the following paragraphs.

organism	Hooke	system
Virchow	organ	tissue
Dutrochet	van Leeuwenhoek	Brown

Our knowledge of cells is an accumulation of work by a number of biologists over a period of time. It began in the 1600s when __(1)__ and __(2)__ used the first microscopes to study cells. By the 1800s, microscopes were so improved that more cell detail could be seen by the user. __(3)__ observed that all cells had a nucleus and __(4)__ theorized that all living things were made of cells. Schleiden and Schwann generally are credited with the cell theory, but it was __(5)__ who determined that living cells come from existing cells.

Cells are the basic structural and functional units of all living organisms. A group of cells with a common function constitutes a/an __(6)__. Several types of these with a common function make up a/an __(7)__, and these, working together, constitute a __(8)__. A group of these working together make up the entire __(9)__.

1. _____
2. _____
3. _____
4. _____
5. _____

6. _____
7. _____
8. _____
9. _____

Place the following labels on the diagram of an animal cell below:

nucleus	mitochondrion	cell membrane
Golgi body	nucleolus	lysosome
endoplasmic reticulum	vacuole	chloroplast

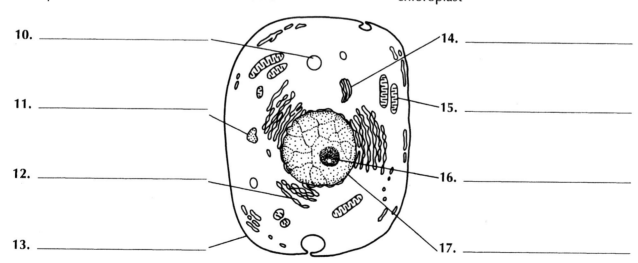

10. _____

11. _____

12. _____

13. _____

14. _____

15. _____

16. _____

17. _____

CHAPTER REVIEW

Understand the Concepts

Answer each of the following questions in one or two sentences.

1. Name two structures found in plant cells that are not found in animal cells. _____
_____

2. Distinguish between pinocytosis and phagocytosis. _____
_____
_____

3. Compare active and passive transport. _____
_____
_____
_____
_____

4. What is the role of the nucleus in the cell? _____
_____

5. If a plant cell lost its plastids, what would go wrong with it? _____
_____

6. How are osmosis and diffusion related? _____
_____
_____
_____

7. Put the following levels of complexity in an order from least complex to most complex: tissue, system,
organ, cell, organism. _____
_____

8. How does the prokaryotic cell differ from the eukaryotic cell? _____
_____
_____
_____

9. What would happen to a cell placed in an isotonic solution? _____
_____
_____

CELLULAR RESPIRATION
6-1   Energy for Life

Part I: Vocabulary Review

Compare and contrast the following pairs of terms. First list their similarities, then their differences.

1. ATP and ADP: _____

_____

_____

_____

_____

_____

2. oxidation and reduction: _____

_____

_____

_____

3. cellular respiration and oxidation-reduction reactions: _____

_____

_____

_____

Part II: Content Review

Complete each of the sentences below.

4. Burning a fuel releases energy in the form of _____ and _____ .

5. Living things use _____ to carry out their life functions.

6. The energy stored in food is released through the process of _____ .

7. When a phosphate group is bonded to the end of an ADP molecule, _____ is formed.

8. When the third phosphate of ATP is removed and bonded to another compound, it transfers energy to the other compound in a process called _____ .

9. When one substance in a reaction is oxidized, another substance must be _____ .

10. The loss of hydrogen atoms is a form of _____ .

11. As hydrogen atoms are transferred to NAD or FAD, these coenzyme molecules _____ .

Part III: Skills Development

Review the skill entitled "Interpreting Diagrams and Tables" on pages 19–21. Then review the diagram below and answer the questions.

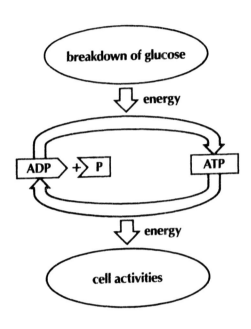

12. What process provides the cell with the energy needed to carry out its activities? _____

_____

13. How does the cell first use the energy released when glucose is broken down? _____

_____

14. What happens to ATP when energy is released for cell activities? _____

_____

15. Why might the process shown in the diagram be called the ATP-ADP cycle? _____

_____

_____

CELLULAR RESPIRATION
6-2 Anaerobic Respiration

Part I: Vocabulary Review

Complete the following crossword puzzle.

ACROSS

3. The splitting of glucose followed by the conversion of pyruvic acid to some end product with no further release of energy
4. Process of breaking down a glucose molecule into two 3-carbon pyruvic acid molecules

DOWN

1. Kind of cellular respiration that requires free oxygen
2. Kind of cellular respiration that can occur without oxygen

Part II: Content Review

Answer each of the following questions in one or two sentences.

5. Which kind of cellular respiration releases the maximum amount of energy from a molecule of glucose?

_____

_____

6. Give some examples of organisms that carry on anaerobic respiration. _____

_____

7. In what part of the cell do the first steps in respiration occur? _____

_____

8. Into what 3-carbon compound is the energized glucose molecule split during the first part of glycolysis?

_____

CELLULAR RESPIRATION

6-2 Anaerobic Respiration (continued)

9. How is phosphoglyceraldehyde changed into pyruvic acid during glycolysis? _____

_____

10. What step in glycolysis produces chemical energy that the cell can use? _____

_____

11. In anaerobic respiration, what process provides the cell with all its energy? _____

_____

12. Name some possible end products of anaerobic respiration in yeast and bacteria. _____

_____

_____

13. Name two industrial processes that make use of fermentation. _____

_____

Part III: Skills Development

Review the skill entitled "Interpreting Diagrams and Tables" on pages 19–21. Then, use the following diagram to answer the questions.

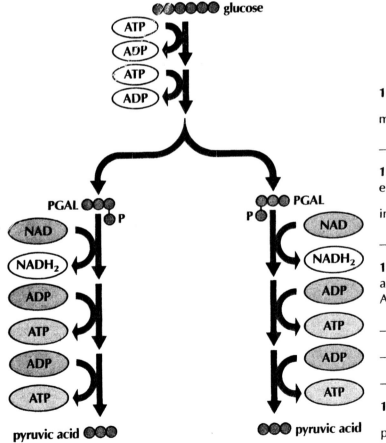

KEY
- carbon atom
- ADP, NAD (low energy)
- ATP, NADH₂ (high energy)

14. How many carbon atoms does a molecule of glucose have? _____

15. How many ATP are needed to provide energy for 1 molecule of glucose to be split into two PGAL? _____

16. How many high-energy ATP molecules are formed during glycolysis and how many ATP are changed back to low-energy ADP?

_____

_____

17. How many carbon atoms does each pyruvic acid molecule have? _____

CELLULAR RESPIRATION
6-3 Aerobic Respiration

Part I: Vocabulary Review

Fill in the vocabulary term that best completes each statement.

1. Inside the mitochondrion, pyruvic acid breaks down into carbon dioxide, $NADH_2$, and an acetyl group that combines with coenzyme A to form _____ .

2. Only 1 ATP molecule is produced by each turn of the _____ .

3. A highly organized system of enzymes and coenzymes that carries out energy-releasing reactions and is located in the inner mitochondrial membrane is known as the _____ .

4. During periods of strenuous activity, extra supplies of oxygen are delivered to the muscles to pay back the

_____ .

Part II: Content Review

Explain why each of the following is important to the process of aerobic respiration. The first answer has been written for you.

5. mitochondria: *This is where the steps of aerobic respiration that follow glycolysis take place.*

_____

6. inner membrane of the mitochondrion: _____

_____

_____

7. acetyl CoA: _____

_____

_____

8. Krebs cycle: _____

_____

_____

9. electron transport system: _____

_____

_____

_____

10. free oxygen: _____

_____

CELLULAR RESPIRATION

6-3   Aerobic Respiration   (continued)

11. water of metabolism: _____

_____

_____

12. 36 ATP molecules: _____

_____

_____

13. muscle fatigue: _____

_____

_____

14. oxygen debt: _____

_____

_____

15. proteins, carbohydrates, and fats: _____

_____

Part III: Skills Development

Review the skill entitled "Graphic Organizing: Flow Chart" on pages 34–37. Then complete the flow chart of aerobic respiration by filling in the following terms in the correct order: Krebs cycle; electron transport chain; glycolysis; and pyruvic acid breakdown.

16.

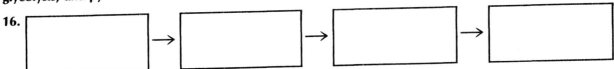

Next, complete the flow chart of anaerobic respiration by filling in the following terms in the correct order: lactic acid; pyruvic acid breakdown; glycolysis; and alcoholic fermentation.

17.

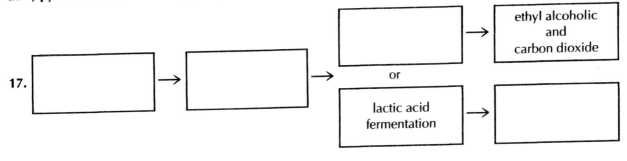

CHAPTER REVIEW

Know the Terms

Complete the following paragraphs using the list of words below.

anaerobic	chemical energy	aerobic	FAD
coenzymes	NAD	glycolysis	glucose
oxygen	reduction	ATP	mitochondria
fermentation	Krebs cycle	water	ADP
chemical bonds	oxidation	cellular respiration	carbon dioxide

All things require __(1)__ to maintain life. This is contained within __(2)__ in nutrient molecules. It is released within cells through the process of __(3)__. There are two types of the process. The first requires the presence of __(4)__ and is called __(5)__. The second does not require this and is called __(6)__. Both of these processes result in the release of energy that can be used to change __(7)__ into __(8)__, which is a temporary energy storage molecule.

1. _____
2. _____
3. _____
4. _____
5. _____
6. _____
7. _____
8. _____

The organic compound from which cells obtain most of their energy is __(9)__. One molecule of this can yield up to 36 molecules of ATP. This occurs through a series of reactions involving the transfer of electrons between atoms. If an atom gains electrons, it is called __(10)__. If it loses electrons, it is called __(11)__. These reactions are controlled by enzymes. Working along with these enzymes are __(12)__, which act as hydrogen acceptors. Two examples of these, involved with cellular respiration, are __(13)__ and __(14)__.

9. _____
10. _____
11. _____
12. _____
13. _____
14. _____

The initial step in this entire process involves the splitting of glucose. This is called __(15)__. This process, followed by the conversion of pyruvic acid to ethyl alcohol, is called __(16)__. Cells that can use environmental oxygen during respiration can extract more energy from the molecules and do so by running the end products of the previous process through the __(17)__, which occurs in the __(18)__ in the cell. The products of this process go to the electron transport chain where more energy is extracted. The final end product of this process is __(19)__.

15. _____
16. _____
17. _____
18. _____
19. _____

CHAPTER REVIEW

Understand the Concepts

Answer the following questions in one or two sentences.

1. What is the role of oxygen in aerobic respiration? _____

_____

_____

2. What happens to the energy released during cellular respiration? _____

_____

_____

3. Explain the ADP-ATP cycle. _____

_____

_____

4. Compare the energy release of aerobic respiration with that of anaerobic respiration. _____

_____

_____

_____

5. What is the role of enzymes in cellular respiration? _____

_____

_____

6. Explain the importance of phosphorylation in biochemical reactions. _____

_____

_____

_____

7. Explain the function of FAD and NAD in aerobic respiration. _____

_____

_____

_____

8. What role does the Krebs cycle play in cellular respiration? _____

_____

_____

9. Compare the efficiencies of aerobic and anaerobic respiration. _____

_____

_____

CLASSIFICATION OF LIVING THINGS
7-1 Classification

CHAPTER 7

Part I: Vocabulary Review

Identify the term that fits each of the definitions below. Then, to reveal the biological concept, transfer the letters that have numbers beneath them to the corresponding blank spaces shown below.

1. branch of biology that deals with the classification of living things

 __ __ __ __ __ __ __
 17   26   19

2. taxonomic category that includes closely related species

 __ __ __ __ __
 32 35   1

3. broadest taxonomic category that includes related phyla or divisions

 __ __ __ __ __ __
    37   13

4. taxonomic category that includes related classes   __ __ __ __ __ __
 2   24

5. taxonomic category that includes related orders   __ __ __ __ __
 4   8   28 11

6. taxonomic category that includes related families   __ __ __ __ __
 23   9   6   16

7. population of similar organisms that interbreed in nature

 __ __ __ __ __ __ __
 7   34   5   25 20

8. two-word system for identifying each kind of organism

 __ __ __ __ __ __ __   __ __ __ __ __ __ __
 10 31   18   3   36   29   22 12

9. theory that species gradually change over time

 __ __ __ __ __   __ __ __ __ __ __ __ __ __
    38   15 14   27

10. preserved evidence of an organism

 __ __ __ __ __ __
 21   33 39 30

CONCEPT:

 __ __ __ __ __ __ __   __ __ __ __ __   __ __ __ __   __ __ __ __
 1 2 3 4 5 6 7   8 9 10 11 12   13 14 15 16   17 18 19 20

 __ __ __ __   __ __ __ __ __ __ __ __   __ __ __ __ __ __ __
 21 22 23 24   25 26 27 28 29 30 31 32   33 34 35 36 37 38 39

CLASSIFICATION OF LIVING THINGS

7-1   Classification   (continued)

Part II: Content Review

The sentences below are incorrect statements. Rewrite the sentences to make them correct.

11. Taxonomy is a branch of biology that preserves living organisms by stuffing them. _____

_____

_____

12. Aristotle grouped animals according to the structure of their bodies. _____

_____

13. The first scientist to use the term *species* was Theophrastus. _____

_____

14. Closely related species are included in a broader group called a kingdom. _____

_____

15. The founder of modern taxonomy was the English naturalist John Ray. _____

_____

16. The broadest taxonomic category is the species. _____

_____

17. In modern biology, each kind of organism has an 8 to 10 word Latin name—its scientific name. _____

_____

18. According to the theory of evolution, new species never arise. _____

_____

19. A phylogenetic tree indicates when related groups of organisms were given scientific names. _____

_____

20. Taxonomists use only fossil information to classify organisms. _____

_____

_____

CLASSIFICATION OF LIVING THINGS
7-2   Major Taxonomic Groups

Part I: Vocabulary Review

Complete the following crossword puzzle.

ACROSS

5. Tool used to identify organisms already classified by taxonomists
6. Phylum to which humans and other mammals belong
7. Plants and certain other organisms that make their own food
8. Kingdom that includes all prokaryotic organisms
10. Phylum to which grasshoppers and other insects belong
12. Phylum to which earthworms belong

DOWN

1. Kingdom to which eukaryotic organisms that are mostly unicellular belong
2. Kingdom to which mosses, liverworts, ferns, and seed plants belong
3. Organisms that obtain their food from the environment
4. Phylum to which the hydra belongs
9. Kingdom that includes multicellular eukaryotic organisms that usually can move from place to place on their own during some part of their life cycle
11. Kingdom to which molds, yeasts, mushrooms, rusts, and smuts belong

CLASSIFICATION OF LIVING THINGS
7-2   Major Taxonomic Groups   (continued)

Part II: Content Review

Select the best answer for each question and write the letter in the space provided.

_____ 13. The five-kingdom system of classification that is used by most scientists includes the following kingdoms:
  a. ameba, hydra, earthworm, grasshopper, human
  b. Monera, Protista, Fungi, Plantae, Animalia
  c. protozoa, Coelenterata, Annelida, Arthropoda, Chordata
  d. heterotrophs, autotrophs, producers, consumers, predators

_____ 14. Members of this kingdom live either as parasites on other living things or as decomposers of dead matter.
  a. Monera   c. Fungi
  b. Protista   d. Plantae

_____ 15. Nearly all members of this kingdom carry on photosynthesis and most live on land.
  a. Monera   c. Fungi
  b. Protista   d. Plantae

_____ 16. This kingdom includes invertebrates and vertebrates.
  a. Animalia   c. Arthropoda
  b. autotrophs   d. Annelida

_____ 17. What is the term for organisms, such as green plants, that make their own food?
  a. heterotrophs   c. Fungi
  b. autotrophs   d. predators

_____ 18. Insects are included in this phylum.
  a. Coelenterata   c. Annelida
  b. Arthropoda   d. Chordata

Part III: Skills Development

Review the skill entitled "Graphic Organizing: Word Map" on pages 45–48. Then, complete the word map below.

19.

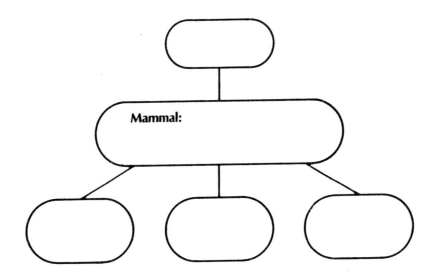

CHAPTER REVIEW

Know the Terms

Complete the following paragraphs, using the list of words below. You may use a word more than once.

species	Aristotle	genus	phylum
Theophrastus	kingdom	John Ray	order
Linnaeus	family	class	taxonomy

Several early attempts at classification were made by different individuals. __(1)__ attempted to classify living organisms according to the environment in which they lived. __(2)__ grouped plants according to the type of stem they had. In the 1600s __(3)__ grouped organisms according to similar structures and coined the word, __(4)__. Groups of these then were included in a broader group called __(5)__. Finally, the Swedish botanist __(6)__, now called the father of taxonomy, devised our modern system of taxonomy.

Our modern system of taxonomy is based upon grouping living organisms according to structural characteristics. It proceeds from the general to the specific. The categories, from the most general to the most specific, are __(7)__, __(8)__, __(9)__, __(10)__, __(11)__, __(12)__, and __(13)__.

1. _____
2. _____
3. _____
4. _____
5. _____
6. _____
7. _____
8. _____
9. _____
10. _____
11. _____
12. _____
13. _____

Supply the defined term.

14. _____ is the most specific part of the scientific name of an organism.

15. _____ is the classification of living things.

16. A _____ _____ is used to identify and classify a living organism.

17. A _____ is the largest group within a kingdom.

18. _____ is the kingdom in which organisms are mostly unicellular and have no defined nucleus.

14. _____
15. _____
16. _____
17. _____
18. _____

CHAPTER REVIEW

Understand the Concepts

Answer the following questions in one or two sentences.

1. Why was Linnaeus' system of taxonomy selected over previous systems? _____

_____

_____

2. What does the scientific name of an organism tell you about it? _____

_____

_____

3. List the taxonomic categories from the broadest to the most specific. _____

_____

4. What is the purpose of a classification system? _____

_____

_____

_____

5. Why did early attempts at classification fail within a short period of time? _____

_____

_____

_____

6. Phylogeny is the evolutionary history of a group of organisms. What information do taxonomists use to produce a phylogenetic tree? _____

_____

_____

7. Describe the basic characteristics of organisms in the kingdom Fungi. _____

_____

_____

_____

8. How does a taxonomic key help to classify an unknown organism? _____

_____

NUTRITION
8-1 The Process of Nutrition

Part I: Vocabulary Review

Identify the term that fits each of the definitions below. Then, to reveal the biological concept below, transfer the letters that have numbers beneath them to the corresponding blank spaces shown below.

1. organic compounds used as coenzymes or converted to coenzymes

 __ __ __ __ __ __ __
 13   8 16   5   1

2. a unit of energy that represents one thousand calories

 __ __ __ __ __ __ __ __ __ __ __
              10 17

3. organisms that cannot synthesize their own organic nutrients from inorganic compounds

 __ __ __ __ __ __ __ __ __ __ __ __ __
   6   3   11 19 15   9

4. the process by which an organism obtains its nutrients and then breaks them down into a usable form

 __ __ __ __ __ __ __ __ __
  7   2   14

5. waste material from the digestive tract eliminated from the body through the anus __ __ __ __ __
                                                                                      18

6. substances that provide the energy and materials needed for metabolic activities

 __ __ __ __ __ __ __ __ __
        20

7. inorganic chemical elements that an organism must obtain from its environment for normal functioning

 __ __ __ __ __ __ __
       24   4   21

8. indigestible material found in fruits, vegetables, and grains __ __ __ __ __
                                                                   23 22   12

CONCEPT:

 __ __ __ __ __ __ __ __ __   __ __ __   __ __ __ __ __
  1   2   3   4   5   6   7   8   9   10 11 12   13 14 15 16 17

 __ __ __   __ __ __ __
 18 19 20   21 22 23 24

Part II: Content Review

Select the best answer for each question and write the letter in the space provided.

_____ 9. Nutrients are important for living things because
        a. they provide energy.
        b. they provide material for metabolic activities.
        c. they are needed for the growth, maintenance and repair of cells.
        d. a, b, and c answers are correct.
        e. none of the answers given are correct.

_____ 10. Which of these lists represents *all* of the nutrients?
  a. carbohydrates, proteins, fats, water, minerals, and vitamins
  b. calcium, chlorine, iodine, iron, potassium, fiber, sugar, and starch
  c. proteins, sugar, starch, fiber, and fats
  d. all foods

_____ 11. In general, how do organisms obtain their nutrients?
  a. Some synthesize their own nutrients.
  b. Some take in food that contains the nutrients.
  c. All organisms obtain their nutrients differently.
  d. Both a and b are correct.
  e. None of the answers given are correct.

_____ 12. Which kinds of organisms are autotrophs?
  a. Plants are the only autotrophs.
  b. Plants and algae are autotrophs.
  c. Plants, algae, and certain microorganisms are autotrophs.
  d. Plants, algae, most animals, and certain microorganisms are autotrophs.
  e. All living things are autotrophs.

_____ 13. Which of the following statements are true about heterotrophs?
  a. They include all animals, fungi, and certain microorganisms.
  b. They cannot synthesize their own food.
  c. They must take in "ready-made" organic nutrients.
  d. All of the above answers are correct.

_____ 14. Nutrients that release 4 kilocalories per gram are
  a. proteins and carbohydrates.
  b. carbohydrates and fats.
  c. fats and proteins.
  d. proteins, carbohydrates, and fats.

_____ 15. The daily caloric needs of an individual should be based upon
  a. height and weight.
  b. age and sex alone.
  c. lifestyle and body condition.
  d. all of the above factors.
  e. none of the above factors because caloric needs are the same for all individuals.

_____ 16. The Food Guide Pyramid includes all of these *except*
  a. the milk, yogurt, and cheese group.
  b. the protein group.
  c. the vegetable group.
  d. the fruit group.
  e. the bread, rice, cereal, and pasta group.

_____ 17. Which of the foods supplies protein, vitamins A and D, calcium, calories, and water? (Refer to Figure 8-4 in the text.)
  a. eggs
  b. most vegetables
  c. milk
  d. most fruits
  e. margarine

_____ 18. The dietary sources of carbohydrates include
  a. sugary foods.
  b. starchy foods.
  c. high-fiber foods
  d. all of the answers given.
  e. none of the answers given.

NUTRITION
8-2 Adaptations for Nutrition and Digestion

Part I: Vocabulary Review

Use the clues below to complete the crossword puzzle.

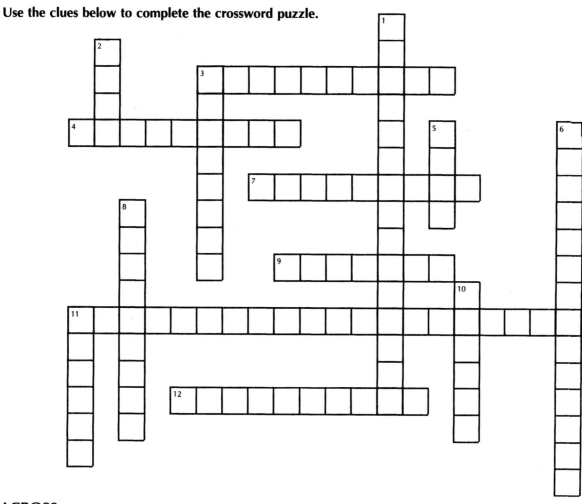

ACROSS

3. Passage of nutrients through the cell membrane into the cell
4. Structure that connects the pharynx with the crop in the earthworm
7. Process by which food molecules are broken down
9. Muscular organ in the earthworm used to take up food into the mouth
11. Place where digestion begins in the hydra
12. Fold in the intestinal wall of the earthworm that increases surface area

DOWN

1. Digestive tube
2. Structure in earthworms and grasshoppers through which waste materials leave the digestive tube
3. Opening through which indigestible matter is discharged from the paramecium
5. Thin-walled organ that acts as a storage chamber in the digestive tube of the earthworm
6. Organs that secrete saliva
8. Location in digestive tube of earthworm where chemical digestion and absorption of food occur
10. Liquid released into the mouth of grasshopper that begins the chemical breakdown of food
11. Location in the paramecium where food collects to form vacuoles

NUTRITION
8-2 Adaptations for Nutrition and Digestion (continued)

Part II: Content Review

For each statement below, decide whether it relates to the mechanical breakdown of food, the chemical breakdown of food, or to both of these processes. Write "M" for mechanical, "C" for chemical, or "B" for both.

_____ 13. requires digestive enzymes

_____ 14. increases surface area

_____ 15. involves physical change, not a chemical change

_____ 16. large particles are broken into smaller particles

_____ 17. involves teethlike plates in the grasshopper, and sand in the gizzard of the earthworm

_____ 18. produces molecules that can pass into the cell

_____ 19. involved in digestion

_____ 20. occurs in protists when food vacuole fuses with the lysosomes

Part III: Skills Development

Review the skill entitled "Graphic Organizing: Compare/Contrast Matrix" on pages 41–44. Then complete the matrix below to compare digestion in protists, hydra, earthworms, and grasshoppers.

21.

CHARACTERISTIC	PROTISTS	HYDRA	EARTHWORM	GRASSHOPPER
Description of body plan				
How food taken into organism				
Type of digestion (intracellular, extracellular)				
Digestive structures or organs				

NUTRITION
8-3 The Human Digestive System

Part I: Vocabulary Review

Match each of the terms listed in Column II with the proper definition listed in Column I. Write the letter of the answer in the space provided.

COLUMN I

_____ 1. enzyme that breaks down starch into maltose

_____ 2. wave-like contractions of the muscles in the alimentary canal

_____ 3. digestive enzyme found in gastric juice that begins the digestion of protein

_____ 4. thin, soupy liquid produced from solid foods in the stomach during digestion

_____ 5. accessory gland that secretes a substance containing sodium bicarbonate into the small intestine

_____ 6. tiny vessels of the lymphatic system located in the small intestine that absorb fatty acids and glycerol

_____ 7. organ in which bile is stored

_____ 8. acidic substance secreted by glands in the stomach wall

_____ 9. substance produced in the liver that emulsifies fats

_____ 10. fingerlike projections in the lining of the small intestine that aid in the absorption of digested food

COLUMN II

a. villi

b. gallbladder

c. pepsin

d. peristalsis

e. gastric juice

f. lacteals

g. pancreas

h. chyme

i. bile

j. salivary amylase

Part II: Content Review

Read each "Cause" and fill in an appropriate "Effect" in the space provided. An example is given below.

CAUSE

11. After food enters the mouth,

12. As the epiglottis covers the larynx,

13. When reverse peristalsis occurs,

14. When hydrochloric acid backs up into the esophagus,

15. As a result of the acidic pH in the stomach,

16. When a person thinks about, sees, smells, or tastes food,

EFFECT

saliva is secreted. _____

_____

_____

_____

_____

_____

_____

_____

_____

_____

_____

NUTRITION

8-3 The Human Digestive System (continued)

17. When the pyloric sphincter opens,

_____
_____
_____

18. If the mucous layer protecting the stomach lining breaks down,

_____
_____

19. When the large intestine absorbs too much water from digested food,

_____

20. When intestinal glands secrete intestinal juice,

_____
_____
_____

Part III: Skills Development

Review the skill entitled "Interpreting Diagrams and Tables" on pages 19–21. Then, identify each structure marked with a number in the diagram below. Complete the chart by filling in a *major* digestive function for each structure identified.

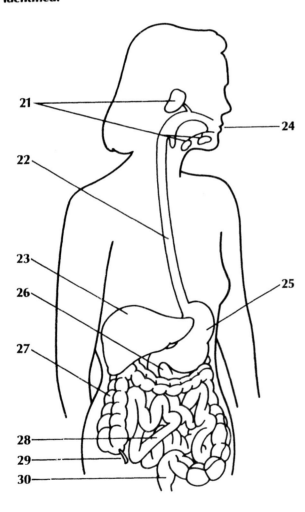

STRUCTURE	FUNCTION
21.	
22.	
23.	
24.	
25.	
26.	
27.	
28.	
29.	
30.	

CHAPTER REVIEW

Know the Terms

Complete the following crossword puzzle.

ACROSS

4. Produces gastric juice
5. The end of the digestive system
6. Part of the lymphatic system that absorbs the end products of lipid digestion.
7. Fingerlike projections in small intestine that absorbs nutrients
10. Emulsifies lipids
11. Absorption takes place here

DOWN

1. Digests carbohydrates in the mouth
2. Lower part of large intestine
3. A measure of heat energy
6. Produces bile
8. Solid wastes
9. Digestive enzyme found in gastric juice

Match the organ with its function in human digestion.

a. grinds food
b. temporarily stores food and adds gastric juice

c. connects pharynx to stomach
d. absorbs water
e. eliminates wastes

f. stores wastes
g. finishes digestion and absorbs nutrients

12. large intestine   12. _____

13. esophagus   13. _____

14. rectum   14. _____

15. small intestine   15. _____

16. mouth   16. _____

17. anus   17. _____

18. stomach   18. _____

CHAPTER REVIEW

Understand the Concepts

Answer each of the following questions in one or two sentences.

1. Trace the path of food through the alimentary canal of the grasshopper. _____
_____
_____

2. Why are nutrients needed by the body? _____
_____

3. What is the relationship between autotrophs and heterotrophs? _____
_____

4. Where does digestion take place in protozoa? _____
_____

5. List the human accessory glands, what each produces, and what the product does to food.

GLAND   PRODUCT   EFFECT
_____
_____
_____
_____

6. How is a large surface area important in digestion and absorption? _____
_____
_____
_____

7. What nutrients are required by living organisms? List them as organic and inorganic. _____
_____
_____
_____

8. What is the difference between an autotroph and a heterotroph? _____
_____

TRANSPORT
9-1 Adaptations for Transport

Part I: Vocabulary Review

Complete the paragraph below by filling in the blanks with the correct vocabulary term(s).

The process by which substances move into or out of cells or are distributed within cells is called

(1) _____ . Large or complex organisms with many cells that are far from the outside

environment need a **(2)** _____ to transport materials. In humans, the circulatory

system consists of blood, a network of blood vessels, and a **(3)** _____ that pumps the

blood. Like the circulatory system in the earthworm, the human circulatory system is an example of a

(4) _____ . Human blood and earthworm blood are red because of the iron-

containing pigment **(5)** _____ , which increases the amount of oxygen the blood can

carry. The smallest blood vessels through which blood flows in humans and earthworms are the microscopic

(6) _____ . In contrast to humans and earthworms, the grasshopper has a different kind of

circulatory system, called an **(7)** _____ , where blood is not always enclosed in vessels.

Part II: Content Review

Complete each of the following sentences.

8. Transport is necessary for moving substances _____

_____

9. The circulatory system acts as a link between _____

_____

10. In humans, the pumping of blood through the circulatory system is accomplished by _____

11. Protists, such as the ameba and the paramecium, do not need a circulatory system because _____

_____

12. Through diffusion, the ectoderm and the endoderm of hydra can exchange the following materials with the

environment: _____

13. In hydra, nutrients from the gastrovascular cavity pass into the cells of the endoderm by _____

_____

14. Within each cell of the hydra, nutrients and other substances move around by _____

_____

15. The gastrovascular cavity of the hydra serves both _____

_____

16. The five pairs of blood vessels that pump blood in the earthworm are identified as _____

_____

17. The exchange of materials between the blood and the body cells of the earthworm takes place _____

_____

18. The two main types of circulatory systems, one of which is found in the earthworm and the other in the

grasshopper, are _____

_____

19. In the grasshopper, oxygen and carbon dioxide are transported through _____

_____

20. Contraction of the grasshopper's heart, which is near the rear of the animal, forces the blood _____

_____

21. The exchange of materials between the blood and the body cells of the grasshopper takes place while _____

_____

22. Blood is kept moving through the grasshopper's body spaces by _____

_____

23. An important difference between the closed circulatory system and the open circulatory system is that _____

_____

Part III: Skills Development

**Review the skill entitled "Graphic Organizing: Compare/Contrast Matrix" on pages 41–44. Then, complete the
matrix below, comparing and contrasting transport in the earthworm with transport in the grasshopper.**

24.

CHARACTERISTIC	TRANSPORT IN EARTHWORM	TRANSPORT IN GRASSHOPPER
Type of system		
Blood color		
Substances transported by blood		
Major blood vessel(s)		
Heart(s)		
Where materials are exchanged		

TRANSPORT
9-2   The Human Circulatory System

Part I: Vocabulary Review

In each of the following word groups, cross out the one word that does not belong and explain the relationship of the four remaining terms.

1. arteries
   valves
   veins
   aorta
   pulmonary artery

   _____

   _____

   _____

2. pericardium
   diastole
   systole
   S-A node
   A-V node

   _____

   _____

   _____

3. atria
   ventricles
   pulse
   pericardium
   S-A node

   _____

   _____

   _____

Part II: Content Review

Explain why each of the following is important in the human circulatory system. The first answer is given as an example.

4. closed circulatory system: *A closed circulatory system provides the pressure needed to move blood to and from all parts of the human body.*

5. arteries: _____

_____

_____

6. veins: _____

_____

_____

7. capillaries: _____

_____

_____

_____

TRANSPORT

9-2 The Human Circulatory System   (continued)

8. heart: _____

_____

9. pericardium: _____

_____

10. atria: _____

_____

11. ventricles: _____

_____

12. septum: _____

_____

_____

13. A-V valves: _____

_____

14. semilunar valves: _____

_____

15. double pump: _____

_____

_____

16. heartbeat cycle: _____

_____

17. pulmonary artery: _____

_____

_____

18. aorta: _____

_____

19. S-A node: _____

_____

20. A-V node: _____

_____

21. pulse: _____

_____

TRANSPORT
CHAPTER **9**

9-3   Pathways of Human Circulation

Part I: Vocabulary Review

Write the vocabulary term that best replaces the italicized definition in each statement.

1. *The pathway that carries blood between the heart and lungs* is one of the two major pathways in the human circulatory system. _____

2. *The other major pathway of the human circulatory system* carries blood between the heart and the rest of the body. _____

3. Blood is returned to the heart from the head, arms, and chest through the *large vein that empties into the right atrium of the heart.* _____

4. Blood from the lower body regions is returned to the heart by the *other large vein that empties into the right atrium.* _____

5. If an artery that is part of the *branch of the systemic circulation that supplies blood to the muscle tissue of the heart* is blocked, a heart attack can occur. _____

6. *The branch of systemic circulation that carries blood from the digestive tract to the liver* helps to maintain the balance of glucose in the blood. _____

7. *The branch of the systemic circulation that carries blood to and from the kidneys* insures that certain wastes are removed from the blood and excreted by the kidneys. _____

8. All the cells of the body are bathed in a *colorless, watery fluid,* which helps move materials between the capillaries and the body cells. _____

9. Without the *system of vessels that returns excess fluid and proteins from the intercellular spaces to the blood,* the constant loss of fluid from the blood eventually would drain the circulatory system. _____

10. Muscular activity squeezes the lymph vessels and pushes the *fluid inside the lymph vessels* toward lymph ducts that eventually empty into the blood. _____

11. *The glands that are found along the lymphatic vessels* play an important role in the body's defense against disease. _____

Part II: Content Review

For each statement below, decide whether it relates to pulmonary circulation, systemic circulation, or circulation of lymph. In the space provided, write "P" for pulmonary circulation, "S" for systemic circulation, or "L" for circulation of lymph.

_____ **12.** As blood passes through the liver, any excess glucose is converted by the liver into glycogen; if the blood lacks enough glucose, the liver converts glycogen into glucose.

_____ **13.** Inside the capillaries of the lungs, blood gains oxygen and gets rid of carbon dioxide.

_____ **14.** Without this system, the body tissues would swell with excess fluid.

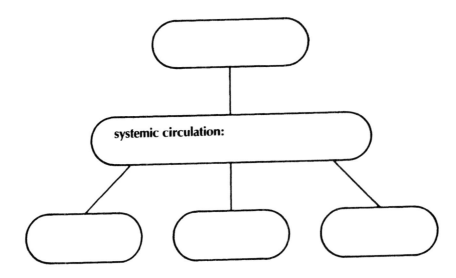
_____ **15.** Intercellular fluid and proteins pass readily into the capillaries of this system.

_____ **16.** The veins of this system carry oxygen-rich blood to the left atrium of the heart.

_____ **17.** This pathway of the human circulatory system begins in the left ventricle of the heart.

_____ **18.** The aorta is part of this system.

_____ **19.** The right duct of this system drains into a large vein on the right side of the neck.

_____ **20.** The right ventricle pumps oxygen-poor blood through arteries of this pathway.

_____ **21.** The largest veins of the body empty into the right atrium of the heart.

_____ **22.** Glands in this system produce some types of white blood cells that contain products able to destroy bacteria and other foreign substances.

_____ **23.** One branch of this system supplies blood to the muscle of the heart.

_____ **24.** This pathway adds oxygen and removes carbon dioxide from the blood.

_____ **25.** A branch of this system carries blood to and from the kidneys.

Part III: Skills Development

Review the skill entitled "Graphic Organizing: Word Map" on pages 45–48. Then, complete the word map below.

26.

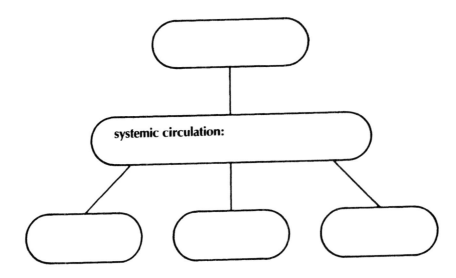

systemic circulation:

CHAPTER REVIEW

Know The Terms

Match the vocabulary word with the proper definition.

a. artery   e. vein   h. pericardium   k. hemoglobin
b. arteriole   f. systole   i. cardiac   l. pacemaker
c. capillary   g. diastole   j. atrium   m. pulse
d. venule

1. carries blood toward heart	6. small vein	1. _____ 6. _____
2. period of heart relaxation	7. period of heart contraction	2. _____ 7. _____
3. small artery	8. membrane around the heart	3. _____ 8. _____
4. referring to the heart	9. carries blood away from heart	4. _____ 9. _____
5. chamber of the heart	10. smallest blood vessel	5. _____ 10. _____

Define or describe the following words.

11. aorta: _____

_____

12. closed circulatory system: _____

_____

13. hemoglobin: _____

_____

14. lymph: _____

_____

15. open circulatory system: _____

_____

16. pulmonary circulation: _____

_____

17. pulse: _____

_____

18. systemic circulation: _____

_____

19. transport: _____

_____

20. ventricle: _____

_____

CHAPTER REVIEW

Understand the Concepts

Answer the following questions in one or two sentences.

1. What is the purpose of a circulatory system? _____

_____

2. Distinguish between an open and a closed circulatory system. _____

_____

_____

3. Starting with the right atrium, list in order the flow of blood through the human heart. _____

_____

_____

_____

4. What do the two numbers refer to in a blood pressure reading? _____

_____

_____

5. Trace the flow of blood through the blood vessels in a closed circulatory system. _____

_____

_____

_____

6. Distinguish between systemic and pulmonary circulation. _____

_____

_____

7. Explain transport in protists. _____

_____

8. What would happen if the coronary artery became blocked? _____

_____

_____

9. Why don't one-celled and simple multicellular animals need a circulatory system? _____

_____

_____

10. How do the pulmonary arteries differ from all the other arteries of the body? _____

_____

THE BLOOD AND IMMUNITY
10-1   Blood—A Multipurpose Fluid

Part I: Vocabulary Review

Use the clues below to complete the crossword puzzle.

ACROSS

1. Cell fragments involved in blood clotting
3. Condition in which a person has too few red blood cells or too little hemoglobin
7. Colorless blood cells that protect the body from disease-causing organisms
9. Blood cells that carry oxygen and carbon dioxide
10. Substance that gives blood its red color

DOWN

2. White blood cells responsible for antibody production
4. Hereditary disease in which persons lack one of the clotting factors
5. Proteins that bind to foreign substances in the body
6. Liquid part of blood
8. Solidification of blood at the site of an injured blood vessel

Part II: Content Review

The sentences below are incorrect statements. Rewrite the sentences to make them correct.

11. Blood is a liquid tissue that has three major functions: transportation, regulation, and reproduction. _____

_____

_____

12. Albumin, the most abundant of the plasma proteins, aids in blood clotting. _____

_____

_____

13. Some globulins are involved in the transport of proteins and other substances; other globulins help form

vitamins. _____

_____

_____

14. White blood cells transport oxygen from the lungs to the tissues of the body. _____

_____

_____

15. The nucleus of red blood cells is filled with an iron-containing protein known as hemoglobin. _____

_____

_____

16. Anemia results in the cells of the body receiving too much oxygen. _____

_____

_____

17. When there is an infection in the body, fibrinogen collects in the infected area and attacks the invading

organisms. _____

_____

_____

18. When a blood vessel is slightly injured, red blood cells rupture, releasing material that seals the leak. _____

_____

_____

19. In the clotting process, thrombin forms a network of strands that traps red blood cells and platelets to form a

clot. _____

_____

_____

THE BLOOD AND IMMUNITY
10-2   The Immune System

Part I: Vocabulary Review

If the statement is true, write TRUE in the space at the left. If the statement is false, make it true by replacing the italicized term.

_____ **1.** *Macrophages* are microorganisms that cause disease.

_____ **2.** An *inflammatory response* is part of the body's second line of defense.

_____ **3.** As part of the inflammatory response, *antigens* move to the place of injury and injest bacteria.

_____ **4.** When the cause of a disease is a virus, the infected cells produce *interferon*.

_____ **5.** The ability of the body to fight infection through the production of antibodies or cells that inactivate foreign substances or cells is called a *primary immune response*.

_____ **6.** The *complement system* is the production of antibodies and specialized cells that bind to and inactivate foreign substances.

_____ **7.** An *immune response* to an antigen acts to destroy the antigen.

_____ **8.** *B cells and T cells* are produced in the bone marrow and are capable of recognizing specific antigens.

_____ **9.** When an antigen is a bacterium, the *complement system* helps destroy the bacteria.

_____ **10.** In *passive immunity*, the body produces its own antibodies or killer T cells to attack a particular antigen.

_____ **11.** In *active immunity*, a person is given antibodies obtained from the blood of either another person or an animal.

_____ **12.** The four major blood types make up the *ABO blood group*.

_____ **13.** *Interferon* may present a problem during pregnancy when the mother is Rh − and her baby is Rh +.

_____ **14.** *Universal recipients* are people who have type O blood.

_____ **15.** *Universal donors* can receive a transfusion of any type blood in the ABO blood group.

Part II: Content Review

Read each "Cause" and fill in an appropriate "Effect" in the space provided. The first example has been completed for you.

CAUSE	EFFECT
16. If a pathogen gets past the body's first line of defense and starts an infection,	*parts of the body's second line of defense becomes activated.*

17. When cells that are damaged from an infection release certain chemicals,

_____
_____
_____
_____

18. When the pathogen is a virus,

_____
_____
_____

19. When the body recognizes foreign cells or molecules,

_____
_____
_____
_____
_____

20. When a T cell undergoes cell division,

_____
_____
_____
_____

21. If the chicken pox virus invades the body of a person who has had chicken pox,

_____
_____
_____

22. In a transfusion, if the wrong blood groups are mixed,

_____
_____
_____

Part III: Skills Development

Review the skill entitled "Finding the Main Idea" on pages 8–10. Then, underline the main idea in the following paragraph. In the space provided, explain why it is the main idea and describe how the rest of the paragraph is organized around it.

23. The body's first line of defense against pathogens involves several kinds of physical and chemical barriers. These include skin, sweat, tears, saliva, membranes lining body passages, mucus, stomach acid, and urine. Unbroken skin and the membranes lining body passages are effective barriers to most pathogens. Sweat, tears, and saliva contain chemicals that kill or inhibit some bacteria. Mucus that covers internal membranes entraps pathogens that are then washed away or destroyed by chemicals. Stomach acid destroys many pathogens that may be present in food.

_____
_____
_____

THE BLOOD AND IMMUNITY
10-3 AIDS and Immune System Disorders

Part I: Vocabulary Review

Match the terms listed in Column II with the correct definition listed in Column I. Place the answer in the space provided.

COLUMN I

_____ **1.** rapid overreaction to an antigen that is not normally harmful

_____ **2.** blood vessel cancer that is a common cause of death in AIDS patients

_____ **3.** fatal immune system disease caused by a virus

_____ **4.** virus that causes AIDS

_____ **5.** any disease in which the immune system produces antibodies against its own cells

COLUMN II

a. AIDS

b. HIV

c. allergy

d. autoimmune disease

e. Kaposi's sarcoma

Part II: Content Review

Complete each of the sentences below.

6. Immune deficiency means _____

_____

7. HIV attacks _____

8. The first symptoms of AIDS are _____

_____

9. Intravenous drug users who share needles and syringes are at risk for HIV infection because _____

_____

10. Since AIDS is sexually transmitted, the only no-risk sexual behavior is _____

_____

11. People can tell whether they have been exposed to HIV by having their blood tested for _____

_____

12. Examples of allergy-causing antigens include _____

_____

_____

13. When the immune system does not recognize cancer cells as "nonself," _____

_____

14. Four examples of autoimmune diseases are _____

_____

Part III: Skills Development

Review the skill entitled "Graphic Organizing: Bar Graph" on pages 25–29. Then, use the bar graph below to answer the following questions.

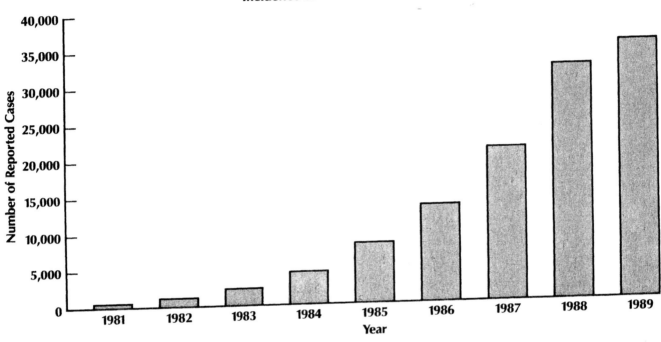

Incidence of AIDS in the United States

15. About how many cases of AIDS were reported in 1984? _____

16. How many more cases of AIDS were reported in 1989 as compared with 1984? _____

_____

17. Has the rate of increase from one year to the next increased or decreased when you compare the number of cases reported in 1988–1989 with that reported in 1986–1987? _____

_____

18. During what year did the greatest increase in the number of cases of AIDS occur, compared with the number of cases in the previous year? _____

_____

CHAPTER REVIEW

Know the Terms

Complete the paragraphs below, using the following list of words. (Some words may not be used; some may be used more than once.)

water	plasma	blood	interferon
globulin	albumin	fibrinogen	platelets
erythrocytes	formed elements	lymphocytes	macrophage
antibodies	leukocytes	pathogens	

__(1)__ is a liquid tissue that transports dissolved and suspended materials. It is composed of two parts, the __(2)__, or liquid part, and the __(3)__. The liquid part consists of 90 percent __(4)__ and 7 percent protein. The most abundant protein is __(5)__, which regulates osmosis. __(6)__ helps clot blood, while most __(7)__ is involved in fighting infection.

__(8)__ carry oxygen to the tissues of the body using a substance called __(9)__. __(10)__ are defenders of the body, while other white blood cells called __(11)__ produce antibodies. __(12)__ are small cell fragments that aid in blood clotting.

During times of infection, disease-causing organisms called __(13)__ invade the body. If they invade the body, the second line of defense includes the protein __(14)__. The third line of defense, which produces __(15)__, is called the immune system.

1. _____
2. _____
3. _____
4. _____
5. _____
6. _____
7. _____
8. _____
9. _____
10. _____
11. _____
12. _____
13. _____
14. _____
15. _____

Define or describe the following words.

16. immunity: _____

_____

17. antigen: _____

_____

18. antibody: _____

_____

19. B-cell: _____

_____

20. T-cell: _____

CHAPTER REVIEW

Understand the Concepts

Answer the following questions in one or two sentences.

1. What is indicated by an excess of white blood cells in the blood? _____

_____

2. What problems might you have if you had no platelets in your blood? _____

_____

_____

3. Compare active and passive immunity. _____

_____

_____

_____

4. What happens if someone gets a transfusion of the wrong blood type? _____

_____

_____

_____

5. How can blood clotting be bad? _____

_____

_____

_____

6. Why is it that you can't get some diseases twice? _____

_____

_____

7. What type of cell does the AIDS virus destroy? _____

_____

8. Which blood types are considered universal donors? universal recipients? _____

_____

9. Explain allergies. _____

_____

_____

GAS EXCHANGE
11-1 Adaptations for Gas Exchange

Part I: Vocabulary Review

In the space provided, write the vocabulary term that best replaces the italicized definition in each statement.

1. In protists, *the process of obtaining oxygen and removing carbon dioxide* takes place directly through the cell membrane. _____

2. In earthworms, the skin is the *boundary surface through which gas exchange takes place.* _____

3. *Colored substances, such as hemoglobin,* in the blood carry oxygen and carbon dioxide between the respiratory surface and the body cells of many multicellular animals. _____

4. In grasshoppers, gas exchange takes place through a *system of branching air tubes that carry air directly to all the cells of the body.* _____

5. Air enters and leaves the grasshopper's body through *10 pairs of openings.* _____

6. Connected to the grasshopper's tracheal tubes are several *large, collapsible, balloonlike chambers that help to pump air in and out of the tracheal system.* _____

7. *The thin layers of tissue that are richly supplied with blood vessels* provide a large surface area for gas exchange in many animals that live in the water. _____

Part II: Content Review

A. For each statement below, decide whether it relates to gas exchange in earthworms, grasshoppers, or animals with gills. Write "E" for earthworms, "G" for grasshoppers, or "A" for animals with gills.

_____ 8. The skin is the respiratory surface.

_____ 9. For gas exchange to occur, there must be a constant flow of water over the gas-exchange organs.

_____ 10. The blood of these animals does not carry oxygen or carbon dioxide.

_____ 11. The fluid-filled ends of microscopic air tubes act as a respiratory surface.

_____ 12. The gas-exchange organs of lobsters are thin layers of tissue that are richly supplied with blood vessels.

_____ 13. In these animals, oxygen diffuses from the air in the soil through the moist skin into the capillaries.

_____ 14. The blood of these soil-dwelling animals contains the respiratory pigment called hemoglobin.

_____ 15. Air is pumped into and out of the tracheal system by the contraction of muscles.

_____ 16. If water flow is stopped, these animals will die from too little oxygen.

_____ 17. When the weather is dry, these animals burrow deeper into the soil until they reach a moist area.

_____ 18. Damp soil keeps the skin of these animals moist and helps their respiratory systems to work well.

_____ 19. Thin layers of tissue, richly supplied with blood vessels, provide a large surface area for gas exchange.

_____ 20. Air enters and leaves these animals' bodies through 10 pairs of openings called spiracles.

B. Compare and contrast the following pairs of terms. First list their similarities, then their differences.

21. respiratory surface and respiratory pigments: _____

_____

_____

22. tracheal tubes and spiracles: _____

_____

_____

23. gas exchange and gills: _____

_____

_____

_____

Part III: Skills Development

Review the skill entitled "Graphic Organizing: Concept Map" on pages 49–55. Then, complete the concept map below.

24.

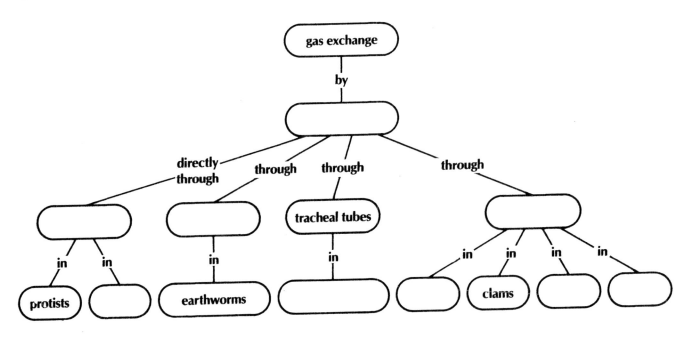

GAS EXCHANGE
11-2 The Human Respiratory System

Part I: Vocabulary Review

Complete the paragraph below by filling in each blank with the correct vocabulary term.

The gas-exchange organs in humans are the **(1)**_____ , which fill a large part of the

human chest cavity. These organs are separated from the abdominal cavity by the **(2)**_____ ,

a muscle that forms the floor of the chest cavity. Each lung is enclosed by a double-layered membrane called the

(3)_____ .

Air usually enters the human respiratory system through the nostrils, which lead into spaces in the nose called

the **(4)**_____ . Next, the air travels through the **(5)**_____ , or throat.

After leaving the throat, air passes into the voice box, or **(6)**_____ . Stretched across the

inside of the voice box are two pairs of membranes called the **(7)**_____ , which enable

humans to make sounds.

The voice box runs directly into the **(8)**_____ , or windpipe, which divides into two

cartilage-ringed tubes called **(9)**_____ . Each bronchus enters a lung and branches into

smaller tubes called **(10)**_____ . These tubes subdivide until they become a group of tiny

tubes called **(11)**_____ . Each tiny tube ends in an air chamber that contains several cup-

shaped cavities, called **(12)**_____ , where gas exchange takes place.

There are two phases of breathing. **(13)**_____ draws air into the lungs. **(14)**_____

forces air out of the lungs.

Part II: Content Review

Reorganize the four events in each group in the order in which they would be likely to occur. Write 1 next to the event that would happen first, 2 next to the event that would happen second, and so on.

15. _____ Air goes through the larynx.   _____ Air goes through the nose.

    _____ Air goes through the trachea.   _____ Air goes through the pharynx.

16. _____ Air goes into the bronchioles.   _____ Air goes into the alveoli.

    _____ Air goes into the bronchi.   _____ Air goes into the bronchial tubes.

17. _____ Air is forced out of the lungs.   _____ Gas exchange occurs in the alveoli.

    _____ Chest cavity becomes larger.   _____ Air is drawn into the lungs.

18. _____ Respiratory center of the brain is stimulated.

_____ Rate of breathing increases.

_____ During heavy exercise, lactic acid is produced by muscle cells.

_____ Acidity of the blood increases.

19. _____ Body cells take in oxygen and get rid of carbon dioxide.

_____ Carbon dioxide diffuses out of the blood into the alveoli.

_____ Blood that is rich in carbon dioxide from the body tissues is returned to the lungs.

_____ External respiration occurs.

20. _____ Smokers take in carbon monoxide in cigarette smoke.

_____ Smokers may experience shortness of breath when they are active.

_____ Hemoglobin picks up carbon monoxide more readily than oxygen.

_____ Oxygen levels drop in an active smoker's blood.

Part III: Skills Development

Review the skill entitled "Graphic Organizing: Bar Graph" on pages 25–29. Then, use the bar graph below to answer the following questions.

Incidence of Some Respiratory Diseases

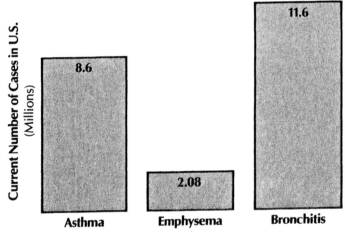

21. Which respiratory disease has the greatest number of cases in the United States? _____

22. Approximately how many times greater is the incidence of asthma than is the incidence of emphysema in the

United States? _____

23. How many more cases of bronchitis than cases of emphysema are there in the United States? _____

CHAPTER REVIEW

Know the Terms

Complete the following crossword puzzle.

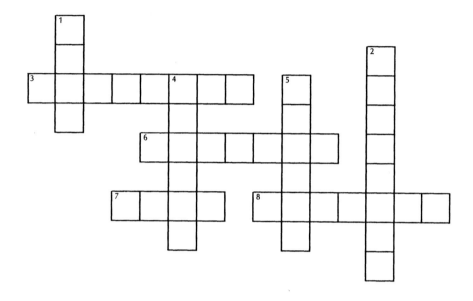

ACROSS

3. Actual gas exchange location in lungs
6. Tube from larynx to bronchi
7. Gas exchange organ in terrestrial animals
8. Air passageways between trachea and lungs

DOWN

1. Gas exchange organ in fish
2. Opening in a tracheal respiratory system
4. Voice box
5. Membrane surrounding lung

Define or describe the following words.

9. diaphragm: _____

_____

10. respiratory surface: _____

_____

11. larynx: _____

_____

12. exhalation: _____

_____

Understand the Concepts

Answer the following questions in one or two sentences.

1. Distinguish between gas exchange and cellular respiration. _____

_____

_____

2. How is surface area important to gas exchange? _____

_____

3. Why can protozoans get by without a respiratory system? _____

_____

_____

4. Why must larger animals have an efficient respiratory system? _____

_____

_____

5. What is the relationship between the respiratory system and the circulatory system in humans? _____

_____

_____

6. Why don't earthworms need lungs or gills? _____

_____

_____

7. How do humans regulate their breathing rate? _____

_____

_____

8. There is more oxygen in air than in water. Why do fish die when taken out of water? _____

_____

_____

9. How do you ''process'' the air you breathe before it gets to your lungs? _____

_____

10. Why does air enter the lungs upon inhalation? _____

_____

EXCRETION
12-1 Adaptations for Excretion

Part I: Vocabulary Review

In the space provided, write the vocabulary term that best replaces the italicized definition in each statement.

1. The process of *removing wastes and excess substances from the organism* also removes excess heat from the body. _____

2. *The excretory organs of the earthworm* are found in pairs in most segments of the earthworm's body. _____

3. The wastes in the earthworm's excretory organs leave the body through the nephridiopore as *a dilute solution made up of water, mineral salts, ammonia, and urea.* _____

4. *The waste substance that is formed from ammonia and carbon dioxide* is less poisonous to cells than ammonia. _____

5. *The excretory organs of grasshoppers and other insects* are bathed directly by the blood. _____

6. *The dry nitrogenous waste product excreted by insects, birds, and reptiles* is the least poisonous of all nitrogenous wastes. _____

Part II: Content Review

Select the best answer for each question and write the letter in the space provided.

_____ **7.** What happens to an organism that cannot remove metabolic wastes from its body?
   a. It stores the wastes in its excretory organs.
   b. It dies.
   c. It uses the wastes for energy.
   d. It recycles the wastes in its body.

_____ **8.** What are the organs of excretion in humans and other complex organisms?
   a. lungs and skin
   b. kidneys and liver
   c. a and b
   d. none of the preceding answers

_____ **9.** The excretory organs work with the circulatory, nervous, and endocrine systems to maintain
   a. metabolic wastes
   b. excess heat
   c. urea
   d. homeostasis

_____ **10.** The two wastes formed during cellular respiration are
   a. mineral salts and ammonia
   b. carbon dioxide and water
   c. urea and uric acid
   d. amino acids and potassium sulfate

_____ **11.** The breakdown of amino acids produces wastes, such as
   a. ammonia, urea, and uric acid
   b. carbon dioxide, water, and salts
   c. mineral salts
   d. feces

_____ **12.** The removal from the digestive tract of unabsorbed, undigested food in the form of feces is called
   a. excretion
   b. assimilation
   c. secretion
   d. elimination

_____ **13.** The chief nitrogenous waste of all microorganisms is
    a. ammonia
    b. urine
    c. uric acid
    d. urea

_____ **14.** To maintain homeostasis, freshwater protists must use
    a. defecation
    b. diffusion
    c. active transport
    d. osmosis

_____ **15.** Hydra get rid of metabolic wastes and excess water by
    a. respiration and metabolism
    b. diffusion and active transport
    c. defecation and urea
    d. contraction and expansion

_____ **16.** In the earthworm, wastes from the blood pass from the capillaries into the
    a. nephrostome
    b. nephridiopore
    c. bladder
    d. nephridium

_____ **17.** Useful substances pass from the body fluid in the earthworm's nephridium into the
    a. air
    b. soil
    c. nephridiopore
    d. capillary blood

_____ **18.** The waste that leaves the earthworm's body through the nephridiopore is
    a. urine
    b. carbon dioxide
    c. uric acid
    d. body fluid

_____ **19.** In the grasshopper, wastes and other substances from the blood enter the Malpighian tubules by
    a. nephridiopores
    b. digestion
    c. diffusion and active transport
    d. spiracles

_____ **20.** Uric acid passes out of the grasshopper through the
    a. Malpighian tubules
    b. anus
    c. tracheal tubes
    d. spiracles

Part III: Skills Development

Review the skill entitled "Graphic Organizing: Compare/Contrast Matrix" on pages 41–44. Then, fill in the empty boxes in the compare/contrast matrix on excretion systems shown below.

21.

CHARACTERISTIC	PROTISTS	HYDRA	EARTHWORMS	GRASSHOPPERS
Metabolic wastes				
Organs of excretion				
Method(s) of excreting wastes				

EXCRETION
12-2   The Human Excretory System

Part I: Vocabulary Review

Compare and contrast the following pairs of terms. First list their similarities, then their differences.

1. urinary system and urinary bladder: _____

_____

_____

_____

2. kidneys and nephrons: _____

_____

_____

3. ureter and urethra: _____

_____

_____

_____

4. glomerulus and Bowman's capsule: _____

_____

_____

_____

5. renal arteries and renal veins: _____

_____

_____

_____

6. epidermis and dermis: _____

_____

_____

_____

7. sebaceous glands and sweat glands: _____

_____

_____

_____

Part II: Content Review

Complete the sentences below.

8. As an excretory organ, the liver performs the following three functions: _____

_____

9. Overloading the liver with harmful materials, such as alcohol, can lead to _____

_____

10. In the small intestine, bile helps in _____

_____

11. The two reasons why the kidneys are important are _____

_____

_____

12. The three parts of the kidney are _____

_____

13. Urine is made in the nephron in two stages, which are _____

_____

14. In the nephron, filtration takes place _____

_____

15. The filtrate from the kidneys is made up of _____

_____

16. The process of reabsorption serves to _____

_____

17. People can still live after both kidneys fail by _____

_____

18. The lungs are considered a part of the excretory organs because _____

_____

_____

19. The functions of the skin include: _____

_____

_____

CHAPTER REVIEW

Know the Terms

Place the following labels correctly on the drawing of the human excretory system below.

urethra   urinary bladder   adrenal gland
ureter   kidney

1. _____

2. _____

3. _____

4. _____

5. _____

Complete the following crossword puzzle.

ACROSS

2. Removal of nitrogenous wastes
3. System composed of the kidneys, ureters, bladder, and urethra (2 words)
5. Capillary bed in Bowman's capsule that removes material from the blood
6. Structure in the nephron of the kidney where material is filtered out of the blood (2 words)
7. Gland in the skin that produces oily secretions to keep the skin pliable (2 words)

DOWN

1. Layer of skin that contains glands, nerves, blood vessels, etc.
2. Outer layer of skin
4. Individual filtering unit of the kidney

CHAPTER REVIEW

Understand the Concepts

Answer the following questions in one or two sentences.

1. Explain the need for excretion in protists. _____
_____
_____

2. Compare selective reabsorption in the earthworm with that in the grasshopper. _____
_____
_____
_____

3. Explain where nitrogenous wastes come from in humans. _____
_____
_____

4. Describe filtration and the importance of reabsorption. _____
_____
_____
_____

5. How does the excretory system relate to the proper functioning of the rest of the body? ____
_____
_____
_____

6. Why are the lungs and skin considered excretory organs? _____
_____
_____

7. Why is it an advantage to have the kidneys directly connected to the aorta and inferior vena cava? ____
_____
_____
_____

8. What would happen if the kidneys stopped filtering the blood? _____
_____
_____

SUPPORT AND LOCOMOTION
13-1 Adaptations for Locomotion

Part I: Vocabulary Review

Use the clues below to complete the crossword puzzle.

ACROSS

3. Temporary projections of cell surfaces that are used for locomotion
5. Tiny bristles that are used in earthworm locomotion
6. Short, hairlike structures that cover the paramecium
7. Tough, lightweight carbohydrate material that makes up the exoskeletons of arthropods

DOWN

1. Skeleton that is inside the body
2. Skeleton that is outside the body
4. Hairlike structures used for locomotion and limited to one or two per cell

Part II: Content Review

The sentences below are incorrect statements. Rewrite the sentences to make them correct.

8. Organisms that can move themselves from place to place are said to be sessile. _____

_____

_____

9. In multicellular animals, locomotion always involves specialized skin tissue. _____

_____

_____

10. The basis for nearly all protist and animal movement is expandable carbohydrates. _____

_____

_____

11. In all but the simplest animals, locomotion uses both muscles and an endoplasm to which the muscles are

fastened. _____

_____

12. Some protists and many invertebrates have an endoskeleton. _____

_____

13. In arthropods, the exoskeleton is covered with cilia, so that it is flexible and can move in various ways. _____

_____

14. Vertebrate skeletons are made of nonliving material and therefore, must be molted periodically as the

organisms grow. _____

_____

15. Exoskeletons are found in fish, amphibians, reptiles, birds, and mammals. _____

_____

_____

16. The paramecium uses pseudopods for locomotion. _____

_____

17. Euglena is covered with thousands of flagella. _____

_____

18. Hydras lack cells specialized for contraction. _____

_____

19. Earthworms have no muscles and rely on setae to move through the soil. _____

_____

_____

20. Fastened to the abdomen of the grasshopper are two pairs of legs. _____

_____

_____

SUPPORT AND LOCOMOTION
13-2 The Human Musculoskeletal System

Part I: Vocabulary Review

Identify the term that fits each of the definitions below. Then, to reveal the biological concept, transfer the letters that have numbers beneath them to the corresponding blank spaces shown on page 176.

1. backbone ___ ___ ___ ___ ___ ___   ___ ___ ___ ___ ___
   ₂₅   ₃₆   ₅₆   ₄

2. protein material that strengthens bone ___ ___ ___ ___ ___ ___ ___ ___ ___
   ₄₂   ₆₁   ₇₀

3. muscles used in voluntary movement ___ ___ ___ ___ ___ ___ ___ ___
   ₃₅

4. joints where bones fit tightly together ___ ___ ___ ___ ___ ___ ___ ___ ___
   ₁   ₆₈   ₆₆

5. cavity in the center of circles of bone cells

   ___ ___ ___ ___ ___ ___   ___ ___ ___
   ₁₄   ₅₅   ₃₄   ₂₀   ₅₇

6. upper part of the skull ___ ___ ___ ___ ___ ___ ___
   ₂₁   ₅₈ ₂

7. bone cells ___ ___ ___ ___ ___ ___ ___ ___ ___
   ₂₄   ₃₁   ₅₁

8. soft tissue that fills bone cavities ___ ___ ___ ___ ___ ___
   ₆₄   ₁₇   ₆₅

9. bones that make up the backbone ___ ___ ___ ___ ___ ___ ___ ___
   ₇   ₅₀   ₁₀

10. type of connective tissue that bends easily ___ ___ ___ ___ ___ ___ ___ ___ ___
    ₃₀   ₆₀   ₅₄

11. smaller fibers of a muscle fiber ___ ___ ___ ___ ___ ___ ___ ___ ___
    ₆₃ ₄₃   ₁₆ ₆₂

12. skull, vertebrae, ribs, and breastbone

    ___ ___ ___ ___   ___ ___ ___ ___ ___ ___
    ₃₉   ₅₂   ₁₅   ₃₈   ₄₈

13. process by which cartilage changes into bone

    ___ ___ ___ ___ ___ ___ ___ ___
    ₆   ₂₆   ₄₇   ₁₃   ₅₉

14. arm bones, leg bones, pectoral girdle, and pelvic girdle

    ___ ___ ___ ___ ___ ___ ___   ___ ___ ___ ___ ___
    ₁₈ ₃   ₃₃   ₃₇   ₅   ₁₁

15. point in the skeleton where bones meet ___ ___ ___ ___ ___
    ₄₄   ₂₂

16. connective tissue that holds bone together at movable joints

    ___ ___ ___ ___ ___ ___ ___
    ₅₃   ₂₈   ₆₇

17. type of muscle that bends a joint ___ ___ ___ ___ ___ ___ ___
    ₉   ₃₂

18. joint that allows bending and twisting ___ ___ ___ ___ ___ ___ ___
    ₁₉ ₄₁

19. fibers of connective tissue that fasten skeletal muscles to bones ___ ___ ___ ___ ___ ___ ___
    ₇₁   ₂₃

20. joints that allow movement in all directions

    ___ ___ ___ ___ ___ ___ ___ ___ ___ ___ ___ ___
    ₄₉   ₄₆   ₈

21. partly contracted condition of all skeletal muscles

    ___ ___ ___ ___ ___ ___ ___ ___
    ₁₂   ₂₉   ₄₀

22. type of muscle that extends a joint ___ ___ ___ ___ ___ ___ ___ ___
    ₆₉   ₂₇   ₄₅

CONCEPT:

___ ___ ___ ___ ___ ___ ___ ___ ___ ___ ___ ___ ___ ___ ___
₁ ₂ ₃ ₄ ₅ ₆ ₇ ₈ ₉ ₁₀ ₁₁ ₁₂ ₁₃ ₁₄ ₁₅

___ ___ ___ ___ ___ ___ ___ ___ ___ ___ ___ ___ ___ ___ ___ ___ ___ ___
₁₆ ₁₇ ₁₈ ₁₉ ₂₀ ₂₁ ₂₂ ₂₃ ₂₄ ₂₅ ₂₆ ₂₇ ₂₈ ₂₉ ₃₀ ₃₁ ₃₂ ₃₃

___ ___ ___ ___ ___ ___ ___ ___ ___ ___ ___ ___ ___ ___ ___ ___ ___ ___
₃₄ ₃₅ ₃₆ ₃₇ ₃₈ ₃₉ ₄₀ ₄₁ ₄₂ ₄₃ ₄₄ ₄₅ ₄₆ ₄₇ ₄₈ ₄₉ ₅₀ ₅₁

___ ___ ___ ___ ___ ___ ___ ___ ___ ___ ___ ___
₅₂ ₅₃ ₅₄ ₅₅ ₅₆ ₅₇ ₅₈ ₅₉ ₆₀ ₆₁ ₆₂ ₆₃

___ ___ ___ ___ ___ ___ ___ ___
₆₄ ₆₅ ₆₆ ₆₇ ₆₈ ₆₉ ₇₀ ₇₁

Part II: Content Review

Answer each of the following questions in one or two sentences.

23. Why is bone tissue considered an active tissue? _____

_____

_____

24. Why is the cartilage between the vertebrae important? _____

_____

25. How do antagonistic pairs of skeletal muscles affect bones? _____

_____

26. Why is it useful for involuntary muscles to control internal organs? ___

_____

_____

CHAPTER REVIEW

Know the Terms

Match the type of joint with its location in the body.

a. hinge   **c.** pivot   **e.** gliding
b. ball and socket   **d.** immovable   **f.** rotating

1. between vertebrae   **1.** _____

2. elbow   **2.** _____

3. hip   **3.** _____

4. cranium   **4.** _____

5. between skull and vertebral column   **5.** _____

Define or describe the following words.

6. ligament: _____

_____

7. tendon: _____

_____

8. cartilage: _____

_____

9. flexor: _____

_____

10. ossification: _____

_____

11. osteocyte: _____

_____

12. chitin: _____

_____

13. vertebra: _____

_____

14. flagella: _____

_____

15. collagen: _____

_____

CHAPTER REVIEW

Understand the Concepts

Answer the following questions in one or two sentences.

1. Why are the biceps and triceps an antagonistic pair? _____

_____

2. How do muscles contract? _____

_____

3. Distinguish between voluntary and involuntary muscle. _____

_____

4. How does muscle coordination enable the earthworm to move? _____

_____

_____

_____

5. Give one advantage of an endoskeleton over an exoskeleton. _____

_____

_____

6. Briefly explain how the muscular system and the skeletal system function together in locomotion. _____

_____

_____

_____

7. Distinguish between cartilage and bone. _____

_____

_____

8. What does an exoskeleton do for a grasshopper? _____

_____

_____

9. What is the difference between spongy bone and compact bone? _____

_____

_____

10. What are the two types of bone marrow and how do they differ? _____

_____

_____

NERVOUS REGULATION
14-1 The Regulatory Process

Part I: Vocabulary Review

Match the terms listed in Column II with the proper definition listed in Column I. Place the answer in the space provided.

COLUMN I

_____ 1. specialized structures that are sensitive to certain changes both inside and outside the organism

_____ 2. short, highly branched nerve fibers that receive impulses

_____ 3. place between the terminal branch of a neuron and the membrane of another cell

_____ 4. nerve cells that carry impulses from receptors to the spinal cord and brain

_____ 5. anything that causes a receptor to start impulses in a nerve pathway

_____ 6. ability of a cell to respond to its environment

_____ 7. long, thin nerve fiber that usually carries impulses away from the cell body

_____ 8. specialized group of nerve cells that controls and coordinates the activities of the nervous system

_____ 9. part of the nerve cell that contains the nucleus and the cell organelles

_____ 10. structures that surround many vertebrate axons

_____ 11. nerve cells that relay impulses from one neuron to another in the brain and spinal cord

_____ 12. white, fatty substance produced by cells that surround vertebrate axons

_____ 13. nerve cell

_____ 14. specialized structure that responds to the commands of the nervous system

_____ 15. electrochemical messages carried by nerve cells

_____ 16. bundles of nerve fibers bound together by connective tissues

_____ 17. nerve cells that carry impulses from the brain and spinal cord to effectors

COLUMN II

a. stimulus

b. Schwann cells

c. interneurons

d. effector

e. myelin

f. nerves

g. receptors

h. neuron

i. synapse

j. brain

k. axon

l. sensory neurons

m. cell body

n. motor neurons

o. irritability

p. dendrites

q. impulses

Part II: Content Review

Complete each of the following sentences.

18. In complex multicellular animals, the regulation and coordination of responses are controlled by _____

_____

_____

19. Stimulation of a receptor causes _____

_____

20. A stimulus causes _____

_____

21. Impulses reaching an effector are the result of _____

_____

_____

22. Neurons can send both _____

_____

23. Unlike other cells of the body, the nerve cells of mature animals _____

_____

_____

24. The three kinds of nerves are _____

_____

Part III: Skills Development

Review the skill entitled "Graphic Organizing: Word Map" on pages 45–48. Then, complete the word map below.

25.

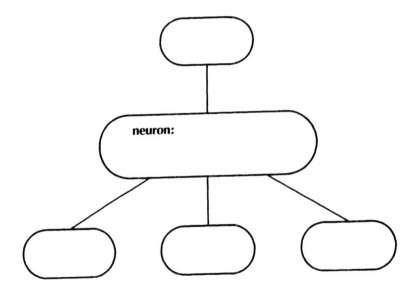

neuron:

NERVOUS REGULATION
14-2 The Nerve Impulse

Part I: Vocabulary Review

Complete the following crossword puzzle.

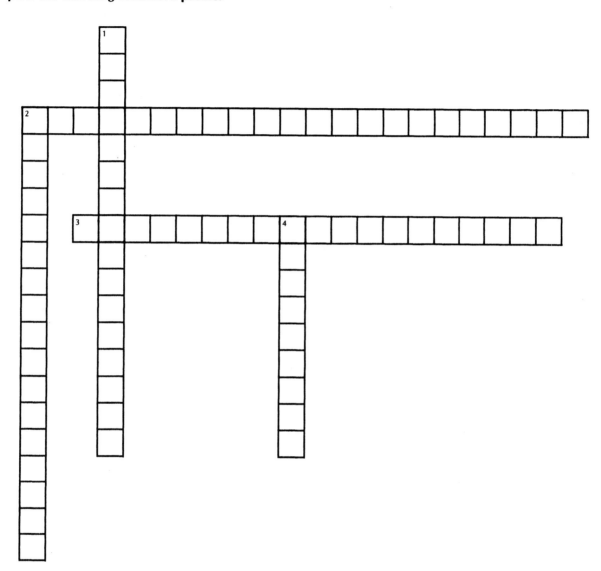

ACROSS

2. points of contact where impulses pass from motor neurons to muscles

3. active transport mechanism that pumps certain ions in and out of nerve cells, thereby changing the polarization of the membrane

DOWN

1. time during which a nerve membrane cannot be stimulated to carry impulses

2. substances that diffuse across synaptic gaps and start impulses in neighboring nerve cells

4. minimum level of sensitivity of a nerve cell

Part II: Content Review

Reorganize the four events in each group in the order in which they would be likely to occur. Write 1 next to the event that would happen first, 2 next to the event that would happen second, and so on.

5. _____ Polarization of the nerve cell membrane reverses.

   _____ Diffusion and active transport restore normal distribution of sodium and potassium ions.

   _____ Permeability of the membrane of a neuron to sodium ions suddenly increases.

   _____ Impulse from a neuron or stimulus from a receptor starts nerve impulse in the membrane of a neuron.

6. _____ Impulses from the retina travel along the optic nerve.

   _____ Light strikes light-sensitive receptors in the eye.

   _____ Brain interprets impulses as sight.

   _____ Impulses reach the brain.

7. _____ More neurotransmitter is released into synaptic gap.

   _____ Neighboring neuron carries more impulses per second.

   _____ Impulses arrive quickly.

   _____ Large amount of neurotransmitter acts as stronger stimulus on neighboring neuron.

8. _____ Acetylcholine diffuses across gap between the end of the axon and the membrane of the muscle cell.

   _____ Impulses reach motor end plates.

   _____ Acetylcholine combines with receptor molecules on the muscle cell membrane and increases permeability of the membrane to sodium.

   _____ Acetylcholine is released.

Part III: Skills Development

Review the skill entitled "Graphic Organizing: Compare/Contrast Matrix" on pages 41–44. Then, complete the compare/contrast matrix below.

9.

CHARACTERISTIC	BOTULIN TOXIN	AMPHETAMINE	BARBITURATE
Effect on neurotransmitters			
Harmful effect on the body			

NERVOUS REGULATION
14-3 Adaptations for Nervous Regulation

Part I: Vocabulary Review

Compare and contrast the following pairs of terms. First list their similarities, then their differences.

1. nerve net and ganglion: _____

_____

_____

_____

_____

_____

2. central nervous system and peripheral nervous system: _____

_____

_____

_____

_____

_____

Part II: Content Review

Read each "Cause" and fill in an appropriate "Effect" in the space provided. An example is given below.

CAUSE	EFFECT
3. If amebas are exposed to strong light or harmful chemicals,	*they move away.*
4. When a paramecium is exposed to food,	_____
	_____
5. If a paramecium is exposed to strong acids,	_____
6. When a stimulus is received by any part of the hydra's body,	_____
	_____
	_____
	_____
7. When the tentacles of the hydra touch food,	_____
	_____
	_____
	_____
8. If you touched an earthworm,	_____
	_____

9. When sensory nerve impulses reach the central nervous
   system of the earthworm,

   _____
   _____
   _____
   _____
   _____

10. Because the grasshopper has a more highly developed nervous
    system than does the earthworm,

    _____
    _____
    _____

Part III: Skills Development

Review the skill entitled "Taking Notes" on pages 16–18. Then, read the following passage from your textbook. Organize the important points into a useful set of notes.

REGULATION IN HYDRA

11. The nervous system of the hydra is in the form of a **nerve net**. See Figure 14-11.
    In this system, the nerve cells form an irregular network between the two layers
    of the body wall. This network connects special receptor cells in the body wall
    with muscle and gland cells. There is no organized center, such as a brain or
    nerve cord, to control and coordinate the nerve impulses. Instead, when a
    stimulus is received by any part of the body, impulses spread slowly from the
    stimulated area throughout the nerve net. Thus, all the muscle fibers in the
    organism respond, but the response shows coordination. For example, when a
    tentacle touches food, the impulses travel slowly through the entire organism. In
    response, the animal stretches toward the food, and the tentacles work together
    to capture the food and stuff it into the mouth.

_____
_____
_____
_____
_____
_____
_____
_____
_____
_____

CHAPTER REVIEW

Know the Terms

Complete the following paragraphs using the list of words below.

neuron	nervous system	dendrite	refractory period
axon	effector	receptors	stimulus
motor	nerve	synapse	neurotransmitter
threshold	brain	myelin	ganglion

The __(1)__ provides an organism with a means of rapid response to a __(2)__. Structures that detect these sensations are called __(3)__. If these sensations are strong enough to be above a certain level, or __(4)__, they initiate an electrical impulse that travels through a cell, called a/an __(5)__. Bundles of these cells make up a/an __(6)__. Impulses enter a nerve cell known as a/an __(7)__, proceed across the body of the cell, and travel down the __(8)__.

When an impulse gets to the end of a nerve cell it must cross a gap, or __(9)__. This is accomplished through the release of a __(10)__ such as acetylcholine. The time required for a nerve cell to set up for the next impulse is known as the __(11)__.

In most animals, the accumulation of nerve tissue that coordinates nervous activity is known as the __(12)__. After it deciphers incoming impulses, it may send impulses out to a __(13)__ neuron, which leads to a/an __(14)__. The structure, which is either a gland or a muscle, will respond to the impulse.

1. _____
2. _____
3. _____
4. _____
5. _____
6. _____
7. _____
8. _____
9. _____
10. _____
11. _____
12. _____
13. _____
14. _____

Define or describe the following words.

15. irritability: _____

_____

16. myelin: _____

_____

17. Schwann cell: _____

_____

18. synapse: _____

_____

CHAPTER REVIEW

Understand the Concepts

Answer the following questions in one or two sentences.

1. What is the purpose of a nervous system? _____

_____

_____

2. What do sensory neurons do? _____

_____

3. What are the two types of effectors and how does each respond to stimuli? _____

_____

_____

_____

4. Distinguish between a neuron and a nerve. _____

_____

_____

5. What is the role of the sodium-potassium pump in the transmission of a nerve impulse? _____

_____

_____

_____

6. How does the existence of a nerve-cell threshold make possible the all-or-none response of a neuron?

_____

_____

_____

7. What is the advantage of having a more complex nervous system? _____

_____

_____

8. How does the nervous system of the hydra differ from that of the earthworm? _____

_____

_____

_____

THE HUMAN NERVOUS SYSTEM
15-1 The Central Nervous System

Part I: Vocabulary Review

Below are groups of terms related to the study of Chapter 15. In each group, cross out one word that does not belong and explain the relationship of the remaining four terms.

1. cerebrum
   hypothalamus
   cranium
   cerebellum
   medulla oblongata

_____
_____
_____
_____
_____

2. brainstem
   pons
   medulla oblongata
   midbrain
   cerebrum

_____
_____
_____
_____
_____

3. thalamus
   hypothalamus
   spinal cord
   pons
   medulla oblongata

_____
_____
_____
_____
_____

4. corpus callosum
   cerebellum
   cerebral cortex
   cerebrum
   cerebral hemispheres

_____
_____
_____
_____
_____

5. medulla oblongata
   spinal cord
   corpus callosum
   thalamus
   pons

_____
_____
_____
_____
_____

Part II: Content Review

Select the best answer for each question and write the letter in the space provided.

_____ **6.** What subsystem of the human nervous system includes the interneurons and most motor neurons?
   a. peripheral nervous system
   b. meninges
   c. ventricles
   d. central nervous system

_____ **7.** What subsystem of the human nervous system includes the sensory neurons and the axons of all the motor neurons?
   a. peripheral nervous system
   b. cerebrospinal fluid
   c. ventricles
   d. central nervous system

_____ 8. What subsystem of the human nervous system controls most activities of the body?
   a. peripheral nervous system
   b. cerebrospinal fluid
   c. pons
   d. central nervous system

_____ 9. What protects the spinal cord?
   a. vertebrae and disks of cartilage
   b. meninges and cerebrospinal fluid
   c. both a and b
   d. none of the answers given

_____ 10. Which part of the brain receives and changes all sensory impulses, except those involved in smell?
   a. thalamus
   b. hypothalamus
   c. pons
   d. medulla oblongata

_____ 11. The forebrain is made up of
   a. pons, medulla oblongata, and midbrain.
   b. cerebrum, thalamus, and hypothalamus.
   c. cerebrum, cerebellum, and medulla oblongata.
   d. brainstem, cerebellum, and medulla oblongata.

_____ 12. What is the largest part of the human brain?
   a. pons
   b. cerebrum
   c. cerebellum
   d. medulla oblongata

_____ 13. The surface area of this layer of the brain is greatly increased by convolutions.
   a. corpus callosum
   b. pons
   c. cerebral cortex
   d. thalamus

_____ 14. What makes up the white matter of the cerebrum?
   a. sensory receptors
   b. effectors
   c. convolutions
   d. myelinated nerve fibers

_____ 15. Which part of the brain helps maintain balance?
   a. cerebellum
   b. cerebrum
   c. medulla oblongata
   d. corpus callosum

_____ 16. Which part of the brain controls many involuntary activities, such as breathing and heartbeat?
   a. cerebellum
   b. cerebrum
   c. medulla oblongata
   d. thalamus

_____ 17. When you remember a telephone number only long enough to dial it, what kind of memory are you using?
   a. short-term memory
   b. momentary memory
   c. long-term memory
   d. answers a, b, and c
   e. none of the answers given

_____ 18. What fills the spinal canal?
   a. gray matter
   b. cerebrospinal fluid
   c. white matter
   d. cartilage

_____ 19. What part of the central nervous system controls reflexes?
   a. spinal cord
   b. cerebrum
   c. cerebral cortex
   d. cerebrospinal fluid

THE HUMAN NERVOUS SYSTEM
15-2   The Peripheral Nervous System

Part I: Vocabulary Review

Compare and contrast the following pairs of terms. First list their similarities, then their differences.

1. spinal nerves and cranial nerves: _____

_____

_____

2. somatic nervous system and autonomic nervous system: _____

_____

_____

_____

3. parasympathetic nervous system and sympathetic nervous system: _____

_____

_____

_____

4. reflex and reflex arc: _____

_____

_____

_____

Part II: Content Review

Complete each of the sentences below.

5. The peripheral nervous system is made up of _____

_____

6. The neurons of the peripheral nervous system are connected to _____

_____

7. Each spinal nerve contains _____

_____

8. In spinal nerves, the cells bodies of the sensory neurons are found in ____

_____

9. As a spinal nerve gets close to the spinal cord, the sensory and motor fibers separate and the sensory fibers

enter _____

_____

10. Most of the cranial nerves serve _____

_____

11. The somatic nervous system contains both _____

_____

12. The autonomic nervous system is made up of _____

_____

_____

13. Sensory information for the autonomic nervous system is provided by _____

_____

_____

14. Organs served by the autonomic nervous system generally contain nerve endings from both _____

_____

_____

15. The effects of the nerve endings from the sympathetic and parasympathetic systems are antagonistic

because _____

_____

16. Examples of reflexes include _____

_____

_____

17. The simplest reflex arcs use only two neurons — _____

_____

18. The withdrawal reflex involves the following three neurons: _____

_____

_____

19. All voluntary behavior is controlled by the cerebrum and makes use of _____

_____

_____

THE HUMAN NERVOUS SYSTEM
15-3 Sense Receptors

Part I: Vocabulary Review

If the statement is true, write TRUE in the space at the left. If the statement is false, make it true by replacing the italicized word(s).

_____ 1. The tough outer layer, or "white," of the eye is called the *choroid coat*.

_____ 2. Light enters the eye through the *cornea*.

_____ 3. At the front of the eye, the *sclera* forms the iris.

_____ 4. The *iris* works like the diaphragm of a camera.

_____ 5. The iris has muscles that can make the size of the *pupil* larger or smaller.

_____ 6. Ciliary muscles change the shape of the *pupil* to allow the eye to focus on objects.

_____ 7. The *lens* contains light receptors.

_____ 8. The *retina* carries impulses from light-sensitive cells to the brain.

_____ 9. People who are *farsighted* can see objects near to them more clearly than objects far from them.

_____ 10. In *nearsighted* people, the eyeball is too short.

_____ 11. Light-sensitive cells called *rods* are sensitive to weak light but not to color.

_____ 12. *Cones* are retinal cells that are sensitive to color but must have bright light to function.

_____ 13. Along the *Eustachian tube* of the ear are special glands that secrete a waxy material.

_____ 14. Stretched across the inner end of the auditory canal is the *tympanic membrane*.

_____ 15. Three tiny bones inside the ear form a chain that links the eardrum to the *auditory canal*.

_____ 16. The *tympanic membrane* makes the pressure in the middle ear equal to the pressure of the atmosphere outside the body.

_____ 17. The *oval window* is the organ of hearing that is made of coiled, liquid-filled tubes.

_____ 18. The *rods* allow the body to maintain balance.

_____ 19. The *optic nerve* carries impulses from the ear to the brain.

_____ 20. Only substances in solution can stimulate the *taste buds*.

_____ 21. The receptors for smell, called the *cones*, are found in the mucous membrane lining the upper nasal cavity.

Part II: Content Review

Read each "Cause" and fill in an appropriate "Effect" in the space provided. The first example has been completed for you.

CAUSE	EFFECT

EFFECT
the pupils of the eyes dilate, or become larger.

CAUSE

22. When a person walks into a dimly lit place,

23. When ciliary muscles change the shape of the lens, _____

24. When light rays are brought into focus in front of the retina, _____

25. If the eyeball is too short, _____

26. Since there are no rods or cones where the optic nerves leaves the eye, _____

27. Because the glands of the auditory canal secrete a waxy material, _____

28. If a person has too little vitamin A, _____

29. When fluid in the semicircular canals keeps moving and stimulating the nerve endings after you stop moving, _____

30. When olfactory cells are stimulated, _____

Part III: Skills Development

Review the skill entitled "Graphic Organizing: Compare/Contrast Matrix" on pages 41–44. Then, complete the compare/contrast matrix below, comparing the various organs of sense reception in the human nervous system.

31.

CHARACTERISTIC	EYE	EAR	SKIN	TONGUE	NASAL CAVITY
Sensory function(s)					
Kind(s) of sense receptors involved					

CHAPTER REVIEW

Know the Terms

Complete the following crossword puzzle.

ACROSS

1. Reaction to a stimulus
3. Part of the nervous system not under voluntary control
5. The largest part of the human brain
9. Bundle of neurons
10. Trunk of nerves coming from the brain

DOWN

2. Factor that causes a response
4. Part of the brain located below the rear part of the cerebrum
6. Part of the brain beneath the cerebellum and continuous with the spinal cord
7. Involuntary, automatic response
8. Individual nerve cell

Supply a definition for the word given.

11. hypothalamus: _____

_____

12. sclera: _____

_____

13. Eustachian tube: _____

_____

14. olfactory cells: _____

_____

CHAPTER REVIEW

Understand the Concepts

Answer each of the following questions in one or two sentences.

1. Explain the structure of a reflex arc. _____
_____
_____
_____

2. Distinguish between the sympathetic and parasympathetic nervous systems. _____
_____
_____
_____

3. What would happen if a nerve in the spinal cord was severed? _____
_____

4. What is the function of the autonomic nervous system? _____
_____
_____

5. What is the central nervous system and what does it control? _____
_____

6. What is the peripheral nervous system? _____
_____
_____

7. What would happen if the optic nerve was cut? _____
_____
_____

8. Why do you think the brain requires 20 percent of the body's blood supply? _____
_____
_____

9. Why may humans have a greater capacity for intelligence than other vertebrates? _____
_____
_____

CHEMICAL REGULATION
16-1 Glands and Hormones

Part I: Vocabulary Review

Fill in the vocabulary term that best completes each statement.

1. Through chemicals released into the bloodstream, the _____ of animals regulates metabolism, homeostasis, growth, and reproduction.

2. Organs made up of epithelial cells that specialize in the secretion of substances needed by the organism are called _____ .

3. _____ are glands that discharge their secretions into ducts, which then carry the secretions to where they are used.

4. Ductless glands, or _____ , release secretions directly into the bloodstream.

5. The secretions produced by the endocrine glands are called _____ .

6. An example of a protein-type hormone that cannot pass through cell membranes is_____ .

7. Local hormones that produce their effects without entering the bloodstream are known as _____ .

8. When feedback reinforces the original change, it is referred to as _____ .

9. When feedback opposes the original change, it is called _____ .

10. Thyroid stimulating hormone (TSH) stimulates the thyroid to produce the hormone _____ .

Part II: Content Review

The sentences below are incorrect statements. Rewrite each sentence to make it correct.

11. The endocrine system is faster than the nervous system in producing an effect. _____

_____

_____

12. The endocrine system produces effects that tend to last for very short periods of time. _____

_____

_____

13. Traveling through the bloodstream, neurotransmitters regulate overall metabolism, maintenance of homeostasis, growth, and reproduction as well as other body processes. _____

_____

_____

14. Each type of hormone is recognized by all body tissues. _____

_____

15. The tissue regulated by a given hormone is called the hormone tissue. _____

_____

16. Protein-type hormones cannot pass through the blood. _____

_____

17. Insulin is an example of a steroid hormone. _____

_____

18. Epithelial cells are being studied for use in the treatment of high blood pressure, stroke, asthma, and ulcers.

_____

_____

19. Most glands are regulated by positive feedback. _____

_____

20. The secretion of a hormone usually is controlled by the concentration of the blood. _____

_____

_____

21. In target cells, receptor proteins recognize a particular steroid hormone and react with it to form DNA. _____

_____

_____

_____

22. The one-messenger model describes the action of protein-type hormones. _____

_____

_____

Part III: Skills Development

Review the skill entitled "Graphic Organizing: Compare/Contrast Matrix" on pages 41–44. Then, complete the compare/contrast matrix shown below.

23.

CHARACTERISTIC	PROTEIN-TYPE HORMONES	STEROID HORMONES
Chemical makeup		
Ability to pass through cell membrane		
Model of action		

CHEMICAL REGULATION
16-2 The Human Endocrine System

Part I: Vocabulary Review

Complete the paragraphs below by filling in each blank with the correct vocabulary term.

adrenal glands	glucagon	hypothalamus	progesterone
diabetes mellitus	gonads	norepinephrine	releasing factors
corticosteroids	islets of Langerhans	parathyroid gland	testosterone
epinephrine	hypersecretion	pineal gland	thymus
estrogen	hyposecretion	pituitary gland	thyroid gland

The improper functioning of an endocrine gland may result in an excess, or **(1)** _____ , of a hormone. It also may result in a deficiency, or **(2)** _____ , of a hormone.

The "master gland" is the **(3)** _____ , which is connected to and controlled by a part of the brain called the **(4)** _____ . Hormones, known as **(5)** _____ , control the release of hormones from the anterior lobe of the pituitary.

Another important gland, the **(6)** _____ , is located in the neck just below the larynx and in front of the trachea. Imbedded in the back of this gland are four tiny, oval glands called the **(7)** _____ _____ .

Capping the kidneys are the **(8)** _____ . The inner layer, or medulla, of each of these glands secretes two hormones: **(9)** _____ and **(10)** _____ . The adrenal cortex releases other hormonal compounds called **(11)** _____ .

The endocrine part of the pancreas consists of clusters of hormone-secreting cells, called the **(12)** _____ . Alpha cells secrete the hormone **(13)** _____ , while beta cells secrete the hormone insulin. Undersecretion of insulin can result in a condition, called **(14)** _____ , which can be inherited.

The sex glands, or **(15)** _____ , are the ovaries of the female and the testes of the male. The ovaries produce the hormones **(16)** _____ and **(17)** _____ . The testes secrete androgens, the most important of which is **(18)** _____ .

Early in life, the **(19)** _____ , a gland located in the upper chest near the heart, produces the hormone thymosin, which plays a role in childhood immunity. The **(20)** _____ , a pea-sized structure attached to the base of the brain, produces the hormone melatonin, which may inhibit sexual development in human males and females.

Part II: Content Review

Read each "Cause" and fill in an appropriate "Effect" in the space provided. An example is given below.

CAUSE

EFFECT

the hormone thyroxine is produced and released by the thyroid gland.

21. When TSH is released,

22. When there is an undersecretion of growth hormone,

23. When LH is secreted by the pituitary of females,

24. When prolactin is secreted by the pituitary of a female after she gives birth,

25. When the hormone oxytoxin is released by the pituitary,

26. If the level of parathormone is low enough,

27. When epinephrine and norepinephrine are secreted in response to sudden stresses,

28. When there is an undersecretion of the hormones of the adrenal cortex,

29. When the compound cortisone is given to a person with allergies,

30. When the level of glucose in the blood is high after the ingestion of glucose,

31. When athletes use steroids,

32. When the thymus produces the hormone thymosin,

CHAPTER REVIEW

Know the Terms

Match the endocrine gland with the hormone that it produces. You may use a gland more than once.

a. adrenal   **d.** pituitary   **g.** pancreas
b. thyroid   **e.** testes
c. parathyroid   **f.** ovaries

1. follicle-stimulating hormone	6. adrenalin	1. _____	6. _____
2. glucagon	7. insulin	2. _____	7. _____
3. cortisol	8. parathormone	3. _____	8. _____
4. thyroxine	9. estrogen	4. _____	9. _____
5. luteinizing hormone	10. androgens	5. _____	10. _____

Define or describe the following words.

11. diabetes: _____

_____

12. hormone: _____

_____

13. norepinephrine: _____

_____

14. testosterone: _____

_____

15. endocrine gland: _____

_____

16. estrogen: _____

_____

17. insulin: _____

_____

18. pituitary gland: _____

_____

19. hypersecretion: _____

_____

20. exocrine gland: _____

CHAPTER REVIEW

Understand the Concepts

Answer each of the following questions in one or two sentences.

1. How are the nervous system and the endocrine system similar? _____

2. How are the nervous system and endocrine system different in the manner of functioning? _____

3. Compare the speed of response of the nervous system and the endocrine system. _____

4. Why are endocrine glands called ductless glands? _____

5. What does the fact that hormones are present in low concentrations in the bloodstream indicate to you? _____

6. Why is it important that a hormone is recognized only by a specific target tissue? _____

7. How are hormone secretions regulated? _____

8. Briefly explain the "one messenger model" of hormone action. _____

PLANT NUTRITION
17-1 Plants and Light

Part I: Vocabulary Review

Match each of the terms listed in Column II with its definition listed in Column I. Place the letter of the answer in the space provided.

COLUMN I

_____ **1.** particle of light that has a fixed amount of energy

_____ **2.** regions between the grana of a chloroplast

_____ **3.** autotrophs that use light energy to drive the reactions needed to make food

_____ **4.** stacks of thylakoids

_____ **5.** wavelengths of light absorbed by a particular pigment

_____ **6.** organelles containing photosynthetic membranes

_____ **7.** process of capturing light and transforming the energy of sunlight into chemical energy

_____ **8.** photosynthetic membranes arranged in the form of flattened sacs

_____ **9.** most abundant and important photosynthetic pigments

_____ **10.** bacteria that oxidize inorganic chemicals for the energy to drive their food-making reactions

_____ **11.** substance that absorbs light

COLUMN II

a. photosynthesis

b. photoautotrophs

c. chemoautotrophs

d. photon

e. pigment

f. absorption spectrum

g. chlorophylls

h. chloroplasts

i. thylakoids

j. grana

k. stroma

Part II: Content Review

Complete each of the following statements.

12. By the beginning of the 1800s, scientists had identified the following three basic requirements for plant growth: _____

13. When green plants carry out photosynthesis, they use carbon dioxide and water to _____

14. All green plants, many protists, and some forms of bacteria are capable of making food from _____

15. Although light travels in waves, it acts as if it were made up of _____

16. The shorter the wavelength of light, the more _____

17. In photosynthetic organisms, the absorbed energy from light is used to make _____

18. In plants, there are two types of chlorophyll, _____

_____

19. Both forms of chlorophyll absorb _____

20. Chlorophyll *b*, carotenes, and xanthophylls absorb light and transfer the energy to _____

21. In green plants, photosynthesis occurs within organelles called _____

22. Only when chlorophyll is combined with the specialized proteins and other substances in photosynthetic

membranes can light energy be _____

_____

Part III: Skills Development

Review the skill entitled "Using Greek and Latin Word Parts" on pages 13–15. Then, for each italicized term in the sentences below, write down its word parts and their definitions.

auto-	self	**photo-**	light
chemo-	chemical	**-plast**	organized particle
chloro-	green	**-synthesis**	a putting together
hetero-	other	**-troph**	nourishing

23. Most of the oxygen in the atmosphere is thought to be the result of *photosynthesis.* _____

_____

24. A *chemoautotroph* oxidizes inorganic chemicals, thereby obtaining energy to drive its food-making reactions.

_____

_____

25. In green plants, photosynthesis occurs within *chloroplasts.* _____

_____

26. An organism that uses light to drive the reactions to make food from simple inorganic substances is called a

photoautotroph. _____

_____

27. A *heterotroph* is an organism that depends on other plants and animals as its source of food. _____

_____

PLANT NUTRITION
17-2 Chemistry of Photosynthesis

Part I: Vocabulary Review

Complete the following sentences with a phrase that correctly uses the word(s) in parentheses.

1. When pigments in the photosynthetic membranes of a chloroplast absorb light, then _____
_____ . (light reactions)

2. In green plants, light reactions produce high-energy compounds that are used in _____
_____ . (dark reactions)

3. The series of enzyme-controlled reactions called the Calvin cycle _____
_____ . (carbon fixation)

Part II: Content Review

Read each "Cause" and fill in an appropriate "Effect" in the space provided. An example is given below.

CAUSE	EFFECT
	glucose, oxygen, and water are produced.
4. When carbon dioxide and water react in the presence of light,	
5. When the pigments in the photosynthetic membranes of chloroplasts absorb light,	_____
6. When photosystem II absorbs light,	_____ _____
7. When photosystem I absorbs light,	_____ _____
8. If 6 molecules of carbon dioxide react with 6 molecules of RuBP,	_____ _____
9. When ATP and $NADPH_2$ react with PGA,	_____
10. When the intensity of sunlight increases,	_____ _____
11. If photosynthesis takes place at extremes of temperature,	_____ _____
12. If there is a shortage of water during photosynthesis,	_____ _____
13. During cellular respiration,	_____ _____

Part III: Skills Development

Review the skill entitled "Finding the Main Idea" on pages 8–10. Find the main idea in the following paragraphs and write it in the space provided. Then, explain why you chose it as the main idea.

Light intensity, temperature, and water and mineral availability are only a few of the factors that affect the rate of photosynthesis. As the intensity of sunlight increases, the rate of photosynthesis increases, but only up to a point. Usually, photosynthesis takes place most rapidly at a specific temperature. At extremes of temperature—below 0°C or above 35°C—the enzymes are damaged, and the rate of photosynthesis is slowed. A shortage of water tends to slow photosynthesis. If the shortage is severe, photosynthesis may stop. Of course, many minerals play a role in photosynthesis. If these minerals are in short supply, photosynthesis, as well as other metabolic processes, is affected.

14. _____

_____

_____

_____

_____

In its effect, photosynthesis is the reverse of cellular respiration. Both processes occur simultaneously in light. Respiration, however, takes place in the cytoplasm and mitochondria. Photosynthesis occurs in the chloroplasts. In respiration, glucose and oxygen are used to produce carbon dioxide and water and to release energy. (See Chapter 6.) In photosynthesis, carbon dioxide, water, and energy are used to produce glucose and to release oxygen. Thus, photosynthesis captures light energy, storing it as chemical energy, and cellular respiration releases chemical energy. Figure 17-9 compares photosynthesis and cellular respiration.

15. _____

_____

_____

_____

_____

PLANT NUTRITION
17-3 Special Cases

Part I: Vocabulary Review

Compare and contrast the following pairs of terms. First list their similarities, then their differences.

1. C_4 pathway and the Calvin cycle: _____

_____

_____

_____

_____

2. chemosynthesis and photosynthesis: _____

_____

_____

_____

Part II: Content Review

Answer each of the following questions in one or two sentences.

3. What kinds of organisms besides green plants carry out photosynthesis? _____

_____

4. How do C_4 plants get the extra energy that is needed to fix carbon dioxide by the C_4 pathway? _____

_____

5. Give two examples of C_4 plants. _____

6. Where does photosynthesis occur in photosynthetic bacteria? _____

_____

7. How are blue-green bacteria similar to plants? _____

_____

8. Why is it that photosynthetic bacteria with bacteriochlorophyll do not release oxygen? _____

_____

_____

9. Where do chemosynthetic bacteria get the energy to make ATP and $NADPH_2$? _____

_____

10. How does mistletoe, a parasitic green plant, add to its nutrition? _____

_____

11. Of what benefit is the fungus that is associated with the roots of the Indian pipe plant? _____

_____

12. What vital nutrient do insect-eating plants, such as the Venus flytrap and the pitcher plant, obtain from their

insect prey? _____

PART III: Skills Development

Review the skill entitled "Using the SQ3R Approach" on pages 4–7. Then, follow the instructions below.

Survey the following paragraph.

HETEROTROPHIC PLANTS

Some plants have developed heterotrophic methods of nutrition in addition to, or instead of, photosynthesis. Some of these plants are parasitic. The mistletoe, for example, is parasitic on oaks and other trees. Although the mistletoe is photosynthetic, it adds to its nutrition by siphoning sap from the vascular tissue of the host tree. The dodder plant is also parasitic, but it cannot photosynthesize. The roots of the dodder plant grow into the tissues of its host, from which it draws nutrients and water. The roots of the Indian pipe, another parasitic plant, form a combination with a fungus. The Indian pipe depends on the fungus for nutrients and water. The fungus gets nutrients from decaying matter in the soil.

Turn the topic heading of the paragraph into a question.

13. Write the question in the space below.

_____

Read the paragraph.

Recite what you have learned.

14. On the lines below, answer the question that you wrote in number 13.

_____

_____

_____

_____

Review what you have learned.

CHAPTER REVIEW

Know the Terms

Complete the following crossword puzzle.

ACROSS

1. Calvin cycle
3. Process of converting light energy to chemical energy
4. Carotene or xanthophyll
5. Primary photosynthetic pigment in plants
6. Carries hydrogen from light reactions to dark reactions

DOWN

2. Organism capable of synthesizing nutrients from inorganic material
4. Particle of light

Complete the following paragraphs using the list of words below.

chemical	green plants	chlorophyll
glucose	carbon dioxide	chloroplasts
water	light	enzymes
chemoautotrophs	absorption	oxygen

Photosynthesis is the process whereby __(7)__ convert __(8)__ and __(9)__ into __(10)__, using __(11)__ energy, which is transformed into __(12)__ energy.

This process is carried out in __(13)__, which contain the pigment __(14)__. The reactions involved are catalyzed by __(15)__.

7. _____

8. _____

_____

9. _____

_____

10. _____

11. _____

12. _____

13. _____

14. _____

15. _____

Understand the Concepts

Answer the following questions in one or two sentences.

1. What is the relationship between photosynthesis and cellular respiration? _____
_____
_____

2. What is the purpose of photosynthesis? _____
_____
_____

3. The light reactions produce three molecules, two of which are needed by the dark reaction and one that is a byproduct. What are these molecules? _____
_____
_____
_____

4. What does the absorption spectrum of chlorophyll demonstrate? _____
_____
_____
_____

5. Why are the light reactions of photosynthesis essential for the dark reactions? _____
_____
_____

6. What is the C_4 pathway and why is it advantageous to plants that use it? _____
_____
_____
_____

7. What advantage do insect-eating plants have over those that cannot eat insects? _____
_____
_____
_____

8. How do chemoautotrophs differ from photoautotrophs? _____
_____

PLANT STRUCTURE
18-1 Plant Tissue

Part I: Vocabulary Review

Complete the paragraph by filling in each blank with the correct vocabulary term.

A plant is held in the soil and takes up water and minerals from the soil through its **(1)**_____ .
The **(2)**_____ of the plant hold the leaves and allow them to receive sunlight. Photosynthesis
occurs mainly in the **(3)**_____ of the plant.

There are a number of types of tissues in plants. Plant cells that frequently undergo mitosis and cell
division make up the **(4)**_____ . These are found in certain regions of the plant called
(5)_____ . In woody plants, a type of meristem, called the **(6)**_____ ,
adds tissues that increase the thickness of stems and roots. There are two types of cambia. The **(7)**_____
_____ produces tissues that transport water and nutrients. The **(8)**_____
produces **(9)**_____ , the protective tissue that covers the surface of woody stems and roots.

Another protective tissue, the **(10)**_____ , forms the outer layer on leaves, green stems, and
roots. The epidermis on above-ground parts of a plant secretes a layer of wax, the **(11)**_____ ,
which reduces water loss and protects against infection. The **(12)**_____ are tissues that conduct
materials throughout the plant. The **(13)**_____ conducts water and minerals from the roots upward through the stems and into the leaves. The **(14)**_____ conducts food and other nutrients.
Another tissue type is **(15)**_____ , which produce and store food and support the plant.

Part II: Content Review

**For each statement below, decide whether it relates to meristematic tissues, protective tissues, vascular tissues, or
fundamental tissues. Write "M" for meristematic, "P" for protective, "V" for vascular, or "F" for fundamental.**

_____ **16.** Most of the cells that form mature xylem are dead.

_____ **17.** Sclerenchyma tissue is found where support is needed.

_____ **18.** The rapidly dividing cells found at the apex of the root or stem cause the root or stem to grow longer.

_____ **19.** Sieve cells line up end to end to form sieve tubes, through which dissolved nutrients are transported.

_____ **20.** This layer is usually one cell thick and its cells fit tightly together, forming the outer layer on leaves,
green stems, and roots.

_____ **21.** In woody plants, the cambium adds tissues that increase the thickness of stems and roots.

_____ **22.** Most of the cells that make up phloem are alive and contain cytoplasm.

_____ **23.** The parenchyma cells have chloroplasts and make food by photosynthesis.

_____ **24.** Cork covers the surface of woody stems and roots and helps prevent injuries to more delicate inner tissues.

_____ **25.** In the spring, sap, containing dissolved materials, is moved upward through the phloem.

_____ **26.** Fibers are a type of sclerenchyma cell.

_____ **27.** Cells of the epidermis secrete a waxy cuticle.

_____ **28.** The phloem is made of sieve cells and companion cells.

_____ **29.** Collenchyma cells support stems and leaves and other parts of the plant.

_____ **30.** Vessel elements in xylem form conducting tubes called vessels.

Part III: Skills Development

Review the skill entitled "Graphic Organizing: Compare/Contrast Matrix" on pages 41–44. Then, complete the matrix below.

31.

CHARACTERISTIC	MERISTEMATIC TISSUES	PROTECTIVE TISSUES	VASCULAR TISSUES	FUNDAMENTAL TISSUES
Function(s)				
Cell type(s)				
Location in plant				

PLANT STRUCTURE
18-2 Roots

Part I: Vocabulary Review

Fill in the vocabulary term that best completes each statement.

1. The first structure to emerge from a sprouting seed is the _____

2. Branches of the primary root are called _____

3. A thimble-shaped group of cells that forms a protective covering for the delicate meristematic tissues of the root tip is the _____

4. The region of actively dividing cells just behind the thimble-shaped covering of the root tip is the

_____

5. Behind the actively dividing cells in the root tip are cells that enlarge and push the root tip forward, forming a region called the _____

6. Behind the region where cells enlarge and push the root tip forward are cells that mature and become specialized, forming the _____

7. The process by which unspecialized cells develop into specialized cells is called _____

8. The hairlike extensions found protruding from the epidermis in the region of the root tip are the _____

9. Just beneath the epidermis of the root tip is the _____

10. The innermost layer of the cortex is called the _____

11. The core of the root is the _____

Part II: Content Review

In the space provided, explain how each of the following relates to the structure and/or function of plant roots. A sample answer is provided in question 12.

12. taproot system: _A taproot system develops when the primary root grows rapidly and remains the largest root in the root system._

13. fibrous root system: _____

_____

_____

14. adventitious root system: _____

_____

15. prop roots: _____

_____

16. climbing roots: _____

_____

17. aerial roots: _____

_____

18. root cap: _____

_____

19. meristematic cells: _____

_____

_____

20. elongation zone: _____

_____

21. maturation zone: _____

_____

_____

22. epidermis: _____

_____

_____

23. root hairs: _____

_____

_____

24. cortex: _____

_____

_____

25. vascular cylinder: _____

_____

26. nitrogen-fixing bacteria: _____

_____

_____

27. mycorrhizal fungi: _____

_____

_____

PLANT STRUCTURE
18-3 Stems and Leaves

Part I: Vocabulary Review

Replace the italicized definition within each statement with the correct vocabulary term. An example is given in question 1.

1. Herbaceous plants usually live for one or two years and have *soft, green juicy stems.* **_herbaceous stems_**

2. Woody plants usually live for more than two years and have *stems made up of thick, tough tissue.*

_____

3. The exchange of gases between the atmosphere and tissues inside leaves and stems is made possible by *small openings in the epidermis.* _____

4. *Strands of conducting tissue that contain xylem and phloem* are scattered throughout the stem in monocots and are arranged in a ring in dicots. _____

5. *The central region of the stem* of a dicot is made of parenchyma cells that store food. _____

6. At the tip of a dormant twig is the *apical meristem enclosed by overlapping scales.* _____

7. *Structures found at nodes along a stem* may develop into new branches or may remain small and dormant.

_____

8. *Holes that pass through cork tissue* allow the exchange of oxygen and carbon dioxide between the atmosphere and the internal tissues. _____

9. Most leaves have a *stalk that joins the leaf to the stem.* _____

10. Some trees, such as the aspen and the birch, have *leaves made up of only one blade and one petiole.*

_____

11. Each stomate is surrounded by *two specialized epidermal cells.* _____

12. The *photosynthetic tissue between the upper and lower epidermis of a leaf* is where photosynthesis takes place in a leaf. _____

13. The *upper portion of the mesophyll* is made of tall, tightly packed cells that are filled with chloroplasts.

_____

14. The *lower portion of the mesophyll* is made of loosely arranged cells. _____

15. The *arrangement of veins* in the leaves of dicots appears as a network of branches. _____

Part II: Content Review

For each question, write the letter of the best answer in the space provided.

_____ 16. What does vascular tissue transport?
a. water
b. food
c. minerals
d. a and c
e. a, b and c

_____ 17. Which plants are examples of herbaceous plants?
  a. lilac and forsythia   **d.** a and b
  b. oaks and maples   **e.** b and c
  c. corn and tomatoes

_____ 18. Why do the stems of herbaceous monocots show little growth in diameter?
  a. They have no cambium.   **c.** They have no phloem.
  b. They have no pith.   **d.** They have no xylem.

_____ 19. What is a function of the cells of the pith?
  a. transport of food   **c.** photosynthesis
  b. storage of food   **d.** respiration

_____ 20. What makes woody stems tough?
  a. large amounts of cork   **c.** large amounts of mesophyll
  b. large amounts of phloem   **d.** large amounts of xylem

_____ 21. How can the age of a woody dicot stem be determined?
  a. by counting guard cells   **c.** by counting annual rings
  b. by counting vascular bundles **d.** by counting nodes

_____ 22. What makes up bark?
  a. spring wood and summer wood   **c.** phloem, cork cambium, and cork cells
  b. heartwood and sapwood   **d.** vascular bundles, cuticles, and pith

_____ 23. For what function are most leaves specialized?
  a. reproduction   **c.** storing food
  b. making food   **d.** support

_____ 24. How does water vapor pass out of leaves?
  a. through the stomates   **c.** through the lenticels
  b. through the veins   **d.** through the petiole

Part III: Skills Development

Review the skill entitled "Graphic Organizing: Compare/Contrast Matrix" on pages 41–44. Then, complete the matrix below.

25.

CHARACTERISTIC	MONOCOT	DICOT
Vascular bundles		
Venation		

PLANT FUNCTION
19-1 Transport

Part I: Vocabulary Review

Complete the following crossword puzzle.

ACROSS

3. Explanation of trans-location
5. Movement of dissolved food through a plant
6. Process that accounts for the movement of water to the tops of the tallest trees

DOWN

1. Osmotic pressure caused by a buildup of solutes in the xylem of roots
2. Formation of water drops at the tips of leaves as the result of root pressure
4. Evaporation of water vapor from plant surfaces

Part II: Content Review

Answer each of the following questions in one or two sentences.

7. What happens to most of the water that plants absorb? _____
_____

8. Name four factors that may cause the stomates to close. _____
_____
_____

9. What conditions cause stomates to open? _____
_____
_____

10. Describe the role of active transport in the opening of stomates. _____
_____
_____
_____

11. How do stomates close? _____
_____
_____

12. What powers the active transport system that pumps potassium ions into guard cells? _____
_____
_____

13. How does guttation occur? _____
_____
_____

14. By what two forces are water columns in the zylem held together? _____
_____

15. What happens to translocation if the sieve cells of a plant are killed? _____
_____
_____

16. What causes the dissolved food in the phloem to move throughout the plant? _____
_____
_____

MITOSIS AND ASEXUAL REPRODUCTION CHAPTER 20

20-1 Mitosis

Part I: Vocabulary Review

Below are groups of terms related to the study of Chapter 20. In each group, cross out one word that does not belong and explain the relationship of the remaining four terms.

1. asexual reproduction _____

   mitosis _____

   cytokinesis _____

   interphase _____

   sexual reproduction _____

2. interphase _____

   prophase _____

   metaphase _____

   anaphase _____

   telophase _____

3. chromatid _____

   centromere _____

   asters _____

   spindle _____

   chromatin _____

4. cell wall _____

   cell plate _____

   spindle _____

   chromosomes _____

   centrioles _____

Part II: Content Review

Select the best answer for each question and write the letter in the space provided.

_____ 5. What two processes occur when a cell with a distinct nucleus divides?
   a. assimilation and reproduction   c. spindles and cell walls
   b. mitosis and cytokinesis   d. centrioles and asters

_____ 6. Which form of reproduction involves special reproductive cells?
   a. mitosis   c. asexual reproduction
   b. cytokinesis   d. sexual reproduction

_____ 7. In nondividing cells, nuclear DNA exists as
   a. chromatin.   c. centrioles.
   b. chromosomes.   d. histones.

_____ 8. What phase lasts from the end of one cell division to the beginning of the next?
   a. prophase   c. interphase
   b. anaphase   d. telophase

MITOSIS AND ASEXUAL REPRODUCTION

20-1 Mitosis (continued)

_____ 9. By the end of what phase of mitosis do the nuclear membrane and the nucleolus disappear?
  a. prophase
  b. metaphase
  c. anaphase
  d. telophase

_____ 10. During what phase does each doubled chromosome give rise to two single-stranded, identical chromosomes?
  a. prophase
  b. metaphase
  c. anaphase
  d. telophase

_____ 11. What happens to the duplicate chromosomes during anaphase?
  a. They are reabsorbed.
  b. They change into chromatin.
  c. They replicate.
  d. They move to opposite poles.

_____ 12. What happens to the spindle and asters during telophase?
  a. They disappear.
  b. They replicate.
  c. They form into pairs.
  d. They become part of the nucleus.

_____ 13. In animal cells, how does division of the cytoplasm come about?
  a. by forming a cell plate
  b. by restructuring the nucleus
  c. by pinching-in of the cell membrane
  d. by pinching-in of the cell wall

_____ 14. What structures do dividing plant cells lack?
  a. centrioles and asters
  b. chromosomes
  c. spindles and centromeres
  d. nuclei

_____ 15. Where do cells tend to divide rapidly?
  a. skin epithelial cells
  b. root tip cells
  c. developing embryo
  d. a, b, and c
  e. none of the answers given

_____ 16. What happens to a cell when it reaches the largest size that is characteristic of its type?
  a. It becomes round.
  b. It migrates.
  c. It stops growing or it divides.
  d. Its nucleus stops functioning.

Part III: Skills Development

Review the skill entitled "Graphic Organizing: Compare/Contrast Matrix" on pages 41–44. Then fill in the empty boxes to show Cytokinesis in the compare/contrast matrix shown below.

17.

CHARACTERISTIC	ANIMAL CELL	PLANT CELL
Description of what happens during cytokinesis		
When cytokinesis occurs during mitosis		
Where cytokinesis occurs in the cell		

MITOSIS AND ASEXUAL REPRODUCTION CHAPTER 20
20-2 Asexual Reproduction

Part I: Vocabulary Review

In the space provided, write the vocabulary word that best replaces the italicized definition in each statement.

1. In *the simplest form of asexual reproduction*, the parent organism divides into two parts that are about equal.

_____

2. *A type of asexual reproduction in which the parent organism divides into two unequal parts* takes place in yeast, hydra, sponges, and some worms. _____

3. *Single, specialized cells that are produced by certain organisms* are often surrounded by a special thick, hard outer wall. _____

4. Relatively simple animals, such as planarians, show *the ability to regrow lost parts*. _____

5. *Asexual reproduction involving roots, stems, and leaves* can occur naturally or artificially. _____

_____

6. Tulips, onions, and lilies reproduce by *short, underground stems surrounded by thick, fleshy leaves that contain stored food*. _____

7. The crocus grows from a *short, stout underground stem that lacks fleshy leaves, but contains stored food.*

_____

8. White potatoes are *enlarged parts of underground stems that contain stored food*. _____

9. Strawberry plants reproduce quickly by means of *stems that grow sideways and have buds*. _____

10. In ferns, *enlarged portions, called nodes, occur along each stem that grows sideways underground*.

_____

11. Geraniums can reproduce vegetatively from a *stem, leaf, or root that is used to produce a new individual*.

_____

12. *A stem bent over so that part of it is covered with soil* is used to reproduce plants such as raspberries.

_____

13. *A stem or bud removed from one plant and joined permanently to the stem of a closely related plant* is used to propagate grapevines and roses. _____

Part II: Content Review

Complete each of the following sentences.

14. In binary fission, no parent is left because _____

15. In the paramecium, the micronucleus controls _____

_____

16. As budding begins in hydra, undifferentiated cells on the side of the parent undergo _____

_____

17. Three kinds of organisms that reproduce asexually by spores are _____

_____

18. If a hydra is cut in half, each half will _____

_____

19. In vegetative reproduction, undifferentiated cells _____

_____

20. Five kinds of specialized stems that are involved in natural vegetative reproduction include _____

_____

21. Three means of artificial vegetative reproduction that allow farmers and gardeners to grow plants with

desirable traits are _____

_____

22. Three advantages of artificial vegetative propagation are _____

_____

_____

Part III: Skills Development

Review the skill entitled "Graphic Organizing: Compare/Contrast Matrix" on pages 41–44. Then fill in the empty boxes in the compare/contrast matrix shown below.

23.

CHARACTERISTIC	BINARY FISSION	BUDDING	SPORE FORMATION
Kind of reproduction involved			
Description of reproductive process			
Organisms that undergo this form of reproduction			

CHAPTER REVIEW

CHAPTER **20**

Know the Terms

Complete the following crossword puzzle.

ACROSS

5. Reproduction where there is only one parent
6. Process by which a cell's nucleus divides
7. Cellular structure to which the chromosomes attach
8. Stage of mitosis when chromatids become visible
9. Stage of mitosis when chromosomes line up at the cell's equator
10. Last phase of mitosis

DOWN

1. Stage of mitosis when chromosomes move to opposite poles
2. Stage of mitosis when DNA replicates
3. Structure at which chromatids are attached
4. Specialized reproductive cell of asexual organisms
7. Reproduction usually involving two parents

Define the word given.

11. aster: _____

_____

12. budding: _____

_____

13. cytokinesis: _____

_____

CHAPTER REVIEW

Understand the Concepts

Answer each of the following questions in one or two sentences.

1. List the four stages of mitosis in their proper sequence. _____

_____

_____

2. Describe what happens in metaphase of mitosis. _____

_____

_____

3. How is mitosis in plant cells different than in animal cells? _____

_____

_____

4. How is telophase of mitosis the reversal of prophase? _____

_____

_____

_____

5. Where in the cell does most of the activity occur during mitosis? _____

_____

_____

6. What are the advantages of asexual reproduction? _____

_____

_____

7. What is the disadvantage of asexual reproduction? _____

_____

_____

8. What is the purpose of mitosis? _____

_____

_____

9. List five methods of asexual reproduction. _____

_____

MEIOSIS AND SEXUAL REPRODUCTION
21-1   Meiosis

Part I: Vocabulary Review

Complete the following crossword puzzle.

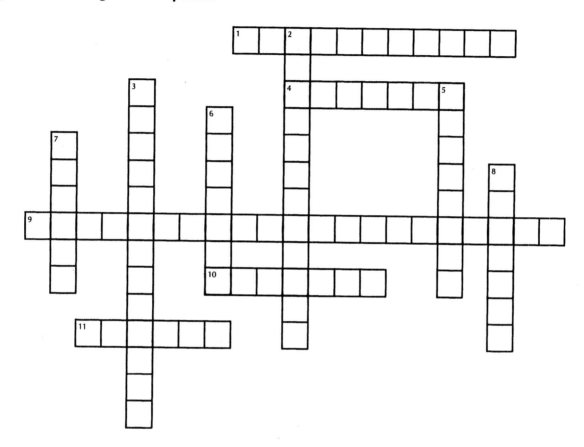

ACROSS

1. Separation of homologous chromosomes during anaphase I of meiosis
4. Kind of cell division that produces gametes
9. Chromosomes that make up each pair of similar chromosomes
10. Cells that have all the homologous chromosomes that are characteristic of a species
11. Group of four chromatids

DOWN

2. Body cells
3. Fusion of the nuclei of male and female gametes
5. Pairing of chromatids during prophase I of meiosis
6. Cells that have only one chromosome from each pair
7. Single cell formed by fertilization
8. Special sex cells found in complex organisms

Part II: Content Review

Complete each of the following sentences.

12. Sexual reproduction requires two different parent cells from _____

_____

13. Sexual reproduction produces offspring that are _____

_____

14. In sexually reproducing organisms, a new offspring results when _____

_____

15. Because of meiosis, each gamete has _____

_____

16. The 46 chromosomes in human body cells can be grouped into _____

_____

17. Homologous chromosomes are similar in three ways: _____

_____

18. As the result of two meiotic divisions, each original cell produces _____

_____

19. The process of disjunction occurs during _____

_____

20. By the end of telophase I, there are _____

_____

21. The second meiotic division is exactly _____

22. The events that occur during telophase II include the formation of _____

_____

Part III: Skills Development

Review the skill entitled "Graphic Organizing: Flow Chart" on pages 34–37. Then, complete the flow chart below by filling in the stages of meiosis.

23. | Prophase I | → | | → | | → | | →

| | → | | → | | → | |

MEIOSIS AND SEXUAL REPRODUCTION   CHAPTER **21**
21-2 Sexual Reproduction in Simple Organisms

Part I: Vocabulary Review

In the space next to each vocabulary term, write the definition of the term. In the lettered spaces below each term, write statements that contain the term and help to explain the meaning of the term.

1. conjugation: _____

   a. _____

   _____

   _____

   b. _____

   _____

   c. _____

   _____

2. zygospore: _____

   a. _____

   _____

   b. _____

   _____

   c. _____

   _____

Part II: Content Review

For each statement below, decide whether it relates to conjugation in bacteria, conjugation in spirogyra, or conjugation in paramecia. Write "B" for bacteria, "S" for spirogyra, or "P" for paramecia.

_____ **3.** The filaments are made of haploid cells.

_____ **4.** A mating type, called a donor, gives a copy of all or part of its DNA to another mating type, called a recipient.

_____ **5.** These organisms have plus and minus mating types.

_____ **6.** During conjugation, these organisms stick together at their oral grooves.

_____ **7.** When favorable conditions return, each zygospore undergoes meiosis, forming four haploid cells.

_____ **8.** The amount of DNA that enters the recipient depends on the length of time that conjugation lasts.

_____ **9.** The mating types of this organism are called active and passive.

_____ **10.** The zygotes formed by conjugation are diploid.

_____ 11. Only two of the resulting haploid micronuclei do not disappear.

_____ 12. Usually, conjugation stops before a copy of all the donor's DNA has entered the recipient.

_____ 13. The contents of the active cells flow through the conjugation tube and fuse with the nucleus and cytoplasm of the passive cells, forming zygotes.

_____ 14. During conjugation, the macronucleus disappears.

_____ 15. Only one haploid cell of four survives, and it divides by mitosis, giving rise to a new haploid filament.

_____ 16. These organisms have macronuclei and micronuclei.

_____ 17. During conjugation, the donor passes a copy of some of its DNA to the recipient through a long thin tube.

_____ 18. In reproduction by conjugation, plus and minus mating types join.

_____ 19. During conjugation, two filaments of opposite mating types come to lie side by side.

_____ 20. Micronuclei of plus and minus mating types fuse to form diploid micronuclei.

Part III: Skills Development

Review the skill entitled "Graphic Organizing: Compare/Contrast Matrix" on pages 41–44. Then, complete the compare/contrast matrix below.

21.

CHARACTERISTIC	SEXUAL REPRODUCTION	ASEXUAL REPRODUCTION
Genetic makeup of the offspring		
Effect on amount of variation		
Adaptability to changes in environment		
Effect on survival of species in a changing environment		

MEIOSIS AND SEXUAL REPRODUCTION
21-3 Sexual Reproduction in Animals

Part I: Vocabulary Review

If the statement is true, write TRUE in the space at the left. If the statement is false, make it true by changing the underlined word(s).

_____ 1. The gametes of animals develop in specialized organs called <u>gonads</u>.

_____ 2. The female gonads produce female gametes, which are called <u>sperm cells</u>.

_____ 3. The male gonads are called <u>ovaries</u>.

_____ 4. Ovaries produce <u>ova</u>.

_____ 5. <u>Testes</u> produce sperm cells.

_____ 6. Individual earthworms have both testes and ovaries and therefore are called <u>gonads</u>.

_____ 7. The process by which gametes develop in the gonads is called <u>gametogenesis</u>.

_____ 8. <u>Spermatogenesis</u> takes place in the ovaries.

_____ 9. Formation of sperm is called <u>spermatogenesis</u>.

_____ 10. During the second meiotic division, the secondary oocyte divides unequally into a large cell called a(n) <u>sperm cell</u>.

_____ 11. Sperm develop from immature sex cells called <u>ootids</u>.

_____ 12. When gametes fuse outside the body of the female, it is called <u>external fertilization</u>.

_____ 13. When gametes fuse inside the body of the female, it is called <u>parthenogenesis</u>.

_____ 14. <u>Internal fertilization</u> is common in many insects, including bees, wasps, aphids, and certain ants.

Part II: Content Review

Reorganize the four events in each group in the order in which they would happen. Write 1 next to the event that would happen first, 2 next to the event that would happen second, and so on.

15. _____ Each worm uses the stored sperm from the partner to fertilize its own eggs.

_____ Each earthworm transfers sperm to the sperm receptacle of its partner.

_____ During mating, two earthworms lie next to each other.

_____ The two earthworms separate.

16. _____ Before birth, primary oocytes develop within a baby's ovaries.

_____ At sexual maturity, a primary oocyte completes meiosis and develops into a functional egg about once a month.

_____ By birth, the primary oocytes are in prophase in the first meiotic division.

_____ During an early stage in female embryonic development, oogonia divide many times by mitosis.

17. _____ When the first meiotic division takes place in the primary oocyte, the cytoplasm of the cell
.   divides unequally.

_____ The ootid grows into a mature egg.

_____ During the second meiotic division, the secondary oocyte divides unequally into a large cell called
an ootid and another polar body.

_____ The polar bodies break apart and die.

18. _____ Each primary spermatocyte undergoes meiosis to form two secondary spermatocytes.

_____ Each spermatid develops into a mature sperm.

_____ A spermatogonium increases in size to become a primary spermatocyte.

_____ Each secondary spermatocyte undergoes a second meiotic division, forming four spermatids.

19. _____ The sperm cell nucleus moves through the cytoplasm toward the egg cell nucleus.

_____ The acrosome releases enzymes that dissolve an opening through the protective membranes of
the egg.

_____ The sperm nucleus joins with the egg nucleus to form a zygote.

_____ The sperm nucleus enters the egg, leaving the rest of the sperm outside the egg.

Part III: Skills Development

Review the skill entitled "Graphic Organizing: Concept Map" on pages 49–55. Then, complete the concept map below.

20.

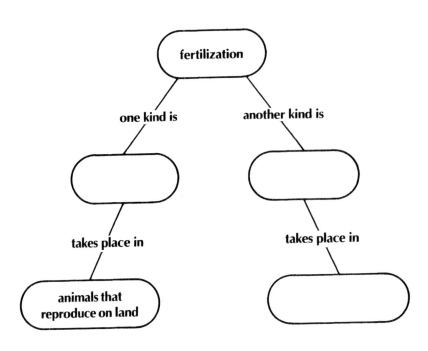

CHAPTER REVIEW

Know the Terms

Match the occurrence with the phase of meiosis. You may use a phase more than once.

a. prophase I   **e.** prophase II
b. metaphase I   **f.** metaphase II
c. anaphase I   **g.** anaphase II
d. telophase I   **h.** telophase II

  1. Disjunction occurs.

  2. Chromosomes (not tetrads) line up at equator.

  3. Crossing-over begins.

  4. Both daughter cells divide, forming haploid cells.

  5. Centromeres divide and sister chromatids separate.

  6. Synapsis occurs.

  7. Centromeres attach to spindle.

  8. Tetrads line up at equator.

  9. Daughter cells form, but chromosomes are in replicated form.

1. _____

2. _____

3. _____

4. _____

5. _____

6. _____

7. _____

8. _____

9. _____

Define or describe the following words.

10. gamete: _____

_____

11. fertilization: _____

_____

12. zygote: _____

_____

13. meiosis: _____

_____

14. follicle: _____

_____

15. synapsis: _____

_____

16. crossing-over: _____

_____

17. conjugation: _____

_____

CHAPTER REVIEW

Understand the Concepts

Answer the following questions in one or two sentences.

1. How is meiosis different from mitosis? _____

_____

_____

2. Why aren't the offspring that result from sexual reproduction exactly like either parent? _____

_____

_____

_____

3. Why is it necessary to reduce the number of chromosomes in gametes by one-half? _____

_____

_____

_____

4. What is the difference between oogenesis and spermatogenesis, and where does each occur? _____

_____

_____

_____

5. What is the main problem associated with external fertilization, and how is this compensated for? _____

_____

_____

_____

6. What is the advantage of internal fertilization over external fertilization? _____

_____

_____

7. Why is sexual reproduction more advantageous than asexual reproduction? _____

_____

_____

8. What is the advantage of unequal cytoplasmic division during oogenesis? _____

_____

_____

_____

ANIMAL DEVELOPMENT
22-1 Embryonic Development

Part I: Vocabulary Review

Compare and contrast the following pairs of terms. First list their similarities, then their differences.

1. development and differentiation: _____

_____

_____

_____

2. embryo and morula: _____

_____

_____

_____

3. cleavage and gastrulation: _____

_____

_____

_____

4. blastula and blastocoel: _____

_____

_____

_____

5. blastopore and primitive gut: _____

_____

_____

6. gastrula and ectoderm: _____

_____

_____

7. endoderm and mesoderm: _____

_____

_____

8. germ layers and embryonic induction: _____

_____

_____

_____

Part II: Content Review

Answer each of the following questions in one or two sentences.

9. What are the two stages that usually result from the cleavage of an embryo? _____

_____

_____

10. How does a lot of yolk affect cleavage? _____

_____

_____

11. How is gastrulation different from cleavage? _____

_____

_____

12. From which germ layer does each of the following develop: the brain, the blood, the liver? _____

_____

_____

_____

13. Where are the first signs of differentiation found in the gastrula? _____

_____

_____

14. What is the role of the nucleus and cytoplasm in determining cellular differentiation? _____

_____

_____

_____

15. How may organizers determine the course of cell differentiation? _____

_____

_____

Part III: Skills Development

Review the skill entitled "Graphic Organizing: Flow Chart" on pages 34–37. Then, fill in the stages of embryonic development in the flow chart below.

16.   [_____] → [_____] → [_____]

ANIMAL DEVELOPMENT
22-2 External and Internal Development

Part I: Vocabulary Review

Complete each sentence by filling in the blank with the correct vocabulary term.

1. As the chicken embryo develops, it forms four membranes that are called the _____.

2. The outermost membrane that lines the inside of the shell of the chicken embryo is the _____.

3. The developing chicken embryo exchanges oxygen and carbon dioxide through the blood vessels of the

_____.

4. The fluid-filled sac that surrounds the developing chicken embryo is the _____.

5. The membrane that surrounds the yolk is called the _____.

6. Among mammals, embryos typically develop within a structure called the womb, or _____.

7. In most mammals, nutrients and oxygen diffuse from the mother's blood into the embryo's blood by a

specialized structure called the _____.

8. The mammalian embryo is attached to the placenta by a structure called the _____.

Part II: Content Review

Complete each of the following statements.

9. In most aquatic animals, fertilization and development take place _____

_____

10. In birds and most reptiles as well as a few mammals, fertilization takes place inside the mother's body

followed by _____

_____

11. The hard shell of the bird egg and the leathery shell of the reptile egg provide _____

_____

12. The four extraembryonic membranes formed by a chicken embryo are _____

_____

13. The chorion aids in the exchange of _____

_____

14. The allantois is a sac-like structure that grows out of _____

_____

15. Two important functions of the amniotic fluid are _____

_____

16. The yolk sac is the source of food for _____

ANIMAL DEVELOPMENT
22-2 External and Internal Development (continued)

17. A high percentage of mammalian young survive to adulthood because they are _____

_____

18. The umbilical cord contains _____

_____

19. The two kinds of nonplacental mammals are _____

_____

20. In marsupials, some internal development takes place in the uterus, but there is no _____

Part III: Skills Development

Review the skill entitled "Reading for Understanding: The SQ3R Approach" on pages 4–7. Then, apply this skill to the paragraph below.

Survey the paragraph below.

EXTERNAL DEVELOPMENT ON LAND

Fertilization inside the mother's body followed by development outside her body takes place in birds and most reptiles, as well as in a few mammals. In these animals, the fertilized egg, which contains a large amount of yolk, is enclosed in a protective shell. The shelled egg is moist inside, which provides the embryo with a self-contained watery environment. The shell is almost waterproof, but is porous enough to allow oxygen from the air to diffuse into the egg and carbon dioxide from the embryo to diffuse out. The number of embryos that survive to hatching is greater for animals whose eggs have a shell than for those whose eggs lack a shell. In fact, animals that lay eggs with a shell produce fewer eggs than animals that lay eggs without a shell. Both the hard shell of the bird egg and the tough, leathery shell of the reptile egg provide protection for the embryo. Reptiles, however, usually leave their eggs whereas bird eggs and young birds are carefully tended by the parents. Thus, the percentage of reptile eggs that survive is less than the percentage of bird eggs that survive. Knowing this, it is not surprising that reptiles lay many more eggs than birds.

Turn the topic heading of the paragraph into a question.

21. Write the question in the space below.

_____

Read the paragraph.

Recite what you have learned.

22. Write the answer to the question you wrote in number 21 on the lines below.

_____

_____

_____

Review what you have learned.

CHAPTER REVIEW

Know the Terms

Match the part of the bird egg with its function.

a. amniotic fluid   d. shell   g. air space
b. chorion   e. albumin   h. amnion
c. allantois   f. yolk sac

1. aids in gas exchange

2. contains amniotic fluid

3. collects metabolic wastes

4. hard protective covering

5. contains food source

6. cushions embryo

7. protein supply

1. _____

2. _____

3. _____

4. _____

5. _____

6. _____

7. _____

Complete the following paragraph, using the list of words below. You may use a word more than once.

blastula   placenta   ectoderm   cleavage
gastrulation   zygote   morula   mesoderm
sperm   blastocoel   fertilization   endoderm
gastrula   ovum   neural tube   differentiation

A male gamete, the __(8)__, combines with a female gamete, the __(9)__, in a process called __(10)__, which results in a __(11)__. This structure begins a series of cell divisions, known as __(12)__. Eventually a solid ball of cells, called __(13)__, forms. As mitosis continues, the ball becomes hollow. It is now called __(14)__. The cavity in the center is the __(15)__. This structure continues to grow and divide and goes through the process of __(16)__ to become a __(17)__. This has three cell layers, the outer layer, or __(18)__, the inner layer, or __(19)__, and the __(20)__. These cell layers then undergo __(21)__, or specialization, to become the various tissues of the body.

8. _____

9. _____

10. _____

11. _____

12. _____

13. _____

14. _____

15. _____

16. _____

17. _____

18. _____

19. _____

20. _____

21. _____

Understand the Concepts

Answer the following questions in one or two sentences.

1. Explain the relationship between the number of embryos produced by a mating and their chances for survival. _____

_____

_____

2. When does differentiation occur? _____

_____

3. Briefly explain the role of DNA in development. _____

_____

_____

_____

4. What is embryonic induction? _____

_____

_____

5. Explain how internal development promotes embryonic success. _____

_____

_____

6. How does cleavage differ in humans and amphibians? _____

_____

_____

7. What do developing embryos require for survival? _____

_____

_____

8. How does the neural tube form? _____

_____

_____

9. How do embryos of pouched mammals develop? _____

_____

_____

HUMAN REPRODUCTION
23-1 Human Reproductive Systems

Part I: Vocabulary Review

Match the terms listed in Column II with the proper definition listed in Column I. Place the answer in the space provided.

COLUMN I

_____ **1.** female gonads

_____ **2.** sac of skin that contains the male gonads

_____ **3.** male gonads

_____ **4.** tube through which an egg travels to the uterus

_____ **5.** storage area for sperm

_____ **6.** process by which an egg is released

_____ **7.** mixture of sperm and fluids

_____ **8.** series of monthly events that includes the thickening of the lining of the uterus in preparation for a fertilized egg

_____ **9.** yellow body formed from a broken follicle that fills with cells

_____ **10.** tube that leads upward from each testis into the lower part of the abdomen

_____ **11.** muscular, pear-shaped organ where a fertilized egg may develop into a baby

_____ **12.** physical traits, such as body hair, that usually appear during adolescence

_____ **13.** narrow neck of the uterus

_____ **14.** involuntary muscular contractions that force semen out of the body

_____ **15.** birth canal

_____ **16.** passageway for excretion of urine

_____ **17.** tiny egg sacs within each ovary

_____ **18.** monthly shedding of extra layers of the uterine lining, the unfertilized egg, and a small amount of blood

COLUMN II

a. oviduct

b. semen

c. menstrual cycle

d. cervix

e. vas deferens

f. ovaries

g. uterus

h. scrotum

i. urethra

j. epididymis

k. vagina

l. corpus luteum

m. menstruation

n. testes

o. follicles

p. ovulation

q. ejaculation

r. secondary sex characteristics

Part II: Content Review

Read each "Cause" and fill in an appropriate "Effect" in the space provided. An example is given below.

CAUSE

19. When the testes secrete the male sex hormone testosterone,

20. If the testes stay within the body,

EFFECT

male secondary sex characteristics

develop.

_____

_____

21. When the outlet of the urinary bladder is closed, _____

22. When an egg matures, _____

23. If sperm are present sometime during the 24 hours after ovulation, _____

24. If an egg is not fertilized, _____

25. When FSH is secreted by the pituitary, _____

26. When the concentration of LH reaches a certain level, _____

27. When the corpus luteum secretes the hormone progesterone, _____

Part III: Skills Development

Review the skill entitled "Graphic Organizing: Line Graph" on pages 30–33. Then, answer the questions, using the information in the graph below.

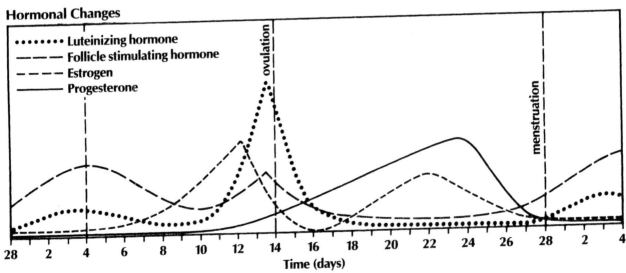

28. Which hormone level is highest at ovulation? _____

29. Which two hormones levels drop at menstruation? _____

30. Which hormone level is highest at the beginning (day 1) of the menstrual cycle? _____

HUMAN REPRODUCTION
23-2 Fertilization, Implantation, and Development

Part I: Vocabulary Review

Replace the italicized definition with the correct vocabulary term.

1. If a woman's oviducts are blocked or she cannot ovulate, *fusion of a sperm and an egg nucleus in a glass laboratory dish* may be tried. _____

2. After *the fastening of the embryo to the wall of the uterus*, the embryo undergoes gastrulation. _____

3. Implantation marks the beginning of *the period during which the baby develops in the uterus*. _____

4. The placenta acts as a barrier that protects the *embryo that is older than about eight weeks* from some harmful substances in the mother's blood. _____

5. In humans, the outer cell layer of the blastula becomes the *outermost of the extraembryonic membranes*.

_____

6. The *temporary organ formed by the chorionic villi and the uterine lining* allows the exchange of nutrients and wastes between the embryo and the mother. _____

7. In humans, the *ropelike structure that connects the developing fetus to the placenta* is tied and cut after the birth of a baby. _____

8. *Fluid within the innermost extraembryonic membrane* protects the fetus, giving it a stable environment and absorbing shocks. _____

9. In humans, *length of pregnancy* is a little over 9 months. _____

10. When the human fetus is ready to be born, *slow, rhythmic contractions of the uterine muscles* begins and the opening of the cervix starts to enlarge. _____

11. *Two people born from the same pregnancy but developed from different eggs* may be of opposite sex.

_____

12. *Two individuals that develop from the same egg* have the same hereditary makeup. _____

Part II: Content Review

Reorganize the events in each group in the order in which they occur. Write 1 next to the event that happens first, 2 next to the event that happens second, and so on.

13. _____ The sperm nucleus fuses with the egg nucleus.

_____ Sperm enter the oviducts.

_____ An egg in the oviduct secretes a chemical that attracts the sperm.

_____ One of the sperm cells breaks through the membranes surrounding the egg.

14. _____ The zygote undergoes cleavage and develops into a blastula.

_____ Implantation occurs and pregnancy begins.

_____ The embryo enters the uterus.

_____ The outer layer of the embryo secretes enzymes that digest part of the uterine lining.

15. _____ Nutrients and oxygen in the blood of the mother diffuse into the fetus's blood; wastes diffuse from the fetal blood into the mother's blood.

_____ The mother's blood is forced into the spaces around the chorionic villi.

_____ Enriched fetal blood travels back to the fetus through veins in the umbilical cord.

16. _____ The baby passes out of the mother's body.

_____ The baby passes from the uterus into the birth canal.

_____ Labor begins and the opening to the cervix gets larger.

_____ The umbilical cord is tied and cut.

17. _____ Two embryos become implanted in the uterus and develop separately.

_____ During the same cycle, two eggs mature and pass into the oviduct.

_____ Fraternal twins are born.

_____ Each egg is fertilized by a different sperm.

Part III: Skills Development

Review the skill entitled "Graphic Organizing: Compare/Contrast Matrix" on pages 41–44. Then, complete the matrix below.

18.

CHARACTERISTIC	CHORION	UMBILICAL CORD	AMNION
Description			
Function			

CHAPTER REVIEW

Know the Terms

Complete the following crossword puzzle.

ACROSS

2. Opening to uterus from vagina
4. Where egg develops
8. Release of an egg
9. Male reproductive organ

DOWN

1. Organ through which embryo receives nutrients
2. Membrane inside shell of a bird egg
3. Developing human embryo
5. Beginning of birth process
6. Egg passageway
7. Site of umbilical cord attachment

Define the word given.

10. epididymis: _____

_____

_____

11. uterus: _____

_____

_____

12. vagina: _____

_____

_____

CHAPTER REVIEW

Understand the Concepts

Answer the following questions in one or two sentences.

1. List in order the four stages of the human menstrual cycle. _____

_____

2. Explain what happens in humans after fertilization. _____

_____

3. Explain what happens in humans if an egg is not fertilized. _____

_____

4. What causes the two types of twins? _____

_____

5. Trace the path of a sperm from where it forms until it leaves the body. _____

_____

_____

_____

6. How is the human menstrual cycle controlled? _____

_____

7. Where does fertilization usually occur? _____

_____

8. What are secondary sex characteristics? _____

_____

9. List the extraembryonic membranes in humans and give their functions. _____

_____

_____

_____

Part I: Vocabulary Review

Complete the following crossword puzzle.

ACROSS

2. Flowering plants
6. Plant life cycle characterized by switching back and forth between haploid and diploid forms
7. Reproductive organ in the male gametophyte of mosses and ferns
9. Nonseed land plants in which the sporophyte is the dominant generation
10. Diploid spore-producing plant generation

DOWN

1. Cone-bearing seed plants
3. Rootlike structures that anchor mosses
4. Female reproductive structure of mosses and ferns
5. Haploid gamete-producing plant generation
8. Nonseed land plants in which the gametophyte is the dominant generation

Part II: Content Review

Complete each of the following sentences.

11. In mosses and ferns, moisture is necessary for _____ .

12. All cells of the gametophyte are _____ .

13. All cells of the sporophyte are _____ .

14. Most botanists believe that plants are related to _____ .

15. Mosses have structures similar in function to _____ .

16. Unlike roots, the rhizoids of mosses _____ .

17. In some mosses, there are separate _____ .

18. In ferns, the dominant generation is the _____ .

Part III: Skills Development

Review the skill entitled "Interpreting Diagrams and Tables" on pages 19–21. Then, use the diagram to answer the questions below.

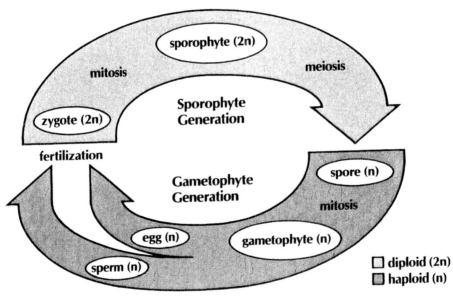

19. What concept is illustrated in the diagram? _____

20. Which plant form is diploid? _____

21. Which plant form is haploid? _____

22. Into what generation does the zygote develop? _____

23. From what is the diploid zygote formed? _____

24. Which generation produces the haploid eggs and sperm? _____

Name _____ Date _____

Part I: Vocabulary Review

Identify the term that fits each of the definitions below. Then, to reveal the biological concept below, transfer the letters that have numbers beneath them to the corresponding numbered blank spaces shown below.

1. young sporophyte of a plant and its food supply ___ ___ ___ ___
   _6_   _34_

2. layer that protects the plant embryo ___ ___ ___ ___   ___ ___ ___ ___
   _27_   _54_   _5_

3. immature, male gametophyte ___ ___ ___ ___ ___ ___   ___ ___ ___ ___ ___
   _57_   _2_ _3_ _59_

4. transfer of pollen grains to the vicinity of female gametophyte

   ___ ___ ___ ___ ___ ___ ___ ___ ___ ___ ___
   _19_   _1_   _33_

5. small opening on an ovule ___ ___ ___ ___ ___ ___ ___ ___ ___
   _10_   _9_   _58_

6. structure formed when the tube cell of a pollen grain grows through the micropyle and into the ovule

   ___ ___ ___ ___ ___ ___   ___ ___ ___ ___
   _47_   _53_   _37_

7. plant part that supports the flower and connects the flower with the stem

   ___ ___ ___ ___ ___ ___ ___
   _50_   _51_

8. leaflike structures that form a ring around the base of the flower ___ ___ ___ ___ ___ ___
   _11_   _32_   _62_

9. complete circle of leaflike structures that encircle the base of a flower ___ ___ ___ ___ ___ ___
   _25_   _46_

10. white or brightly colored flower parts that are above the sepals ___ ___ ___ ___ ___ ___
    _7_   _21_

11. complete circle of petals that surround the reproductive organs of the flower

    ___ ___ ___ ___ ___ ___ ___
    _24_   _13_   _12_

12. male reproductive organs of a flower ___ ___ ___ ___ ___ ___ ___
    _15_ _45_   _38_

13. stalklike part of the male reproductive organ of a flower ___ ___ ___ ___ ___ ___ ___
    _29_   _18_   _60_

14. saclike structure where pollen grains are produced ___ ___ ___ ___ ___ ___ ___
    _35_   _16_

15. female reproductive organ of angiosperms ___ ___ ___ ___ ___ ___
    _4_   _61_   _31_

16. pollen-receiving part of the pistil ___ ___ ___ ___ ___ ___
    _22_   _48_

17. part of the pistil that supports the stigma ___ ___ ___ ___ ___
    ₂₀   ₅₆

18. ovule-containing part of the pistil ___ ___ ___ ___ ___
    ₄₉   ₄₀

19. the ovary of angiosperms develops into this ___ ___ ___ ___ ___
    ₄₄   ₃₀

20. female gametophyte that has seven cells with eight haploid nuclei

    ___ ___ ___ ___ ___   ___ ___ ___
    ₈   ₃₆   ₂₈

21. sugary liquid produced by flowers ___ ___ ___ ___ ___ ___
    ₂₆   ₄₂

22. process in which one sperm fertilizes an egg and the other sperm fertilizes the two polar nuclei

    ___ ___ ___ ___   ___ ___ ___ ___   ___ ___ ___ ___ ___
    ₃₉   ₂₃   ₁₄   ₅₅

23. tissue that stores food for the developing plant embryo ___ ___ ___ ___ ___ ___ ___ ___
    ₁₇ ₄₁   ₄₃   ₅₂

CONCEPT:

___ ___ ___ ___ ___ ___ ___ ___ ___ ___ ___   ___ ___ ___   ___ ___ ___
₁ ₂ ₃ ₄ ₅ ₆ ₇ ₈ ₉ ₁₀ ₁₁   ₁₂ ₁₃ ₁₄   ₁₅ ₁₆ ₁₇

___ ___ ___ ___   ___ ___ ___ ___ ___ ___ ___ ___ ___ ___   ___ ___ ___
₁₈ ₁₉ ₂₀ ₂₁   ₂₂ ₂₃ ₂₄ ₂₅ ₂₆ ₂₇ ₂₈ ₂₉ ₃₀ ₃₁   ₃₂ ₃₃ ₃₄

___ ___ ___ ___ ___ ___ ___ ___   ___ ___   ___ ___ ___
₃₅ ₃₆ ₃₇ ₃₈ ₃₉ ₄₀ ₄₁ ₄₂   ₄₃ ₄₄   ₄₅ ₄₆ ₄₇

___ ___ ___ ___ ___ ___   ___ ___ ___   ___ ___ ___ ___ ___ ___
₄₈ ₄₉ ₅₀ ₅₁ ₅₂ ₅₃   ₅₄ ₅₅ ₅₆   ₅₇ ₅₈ ₅₉ ₆₀ ₆₁ ₆₂

Part II: Content Review

Answer each of the following questions in one or two sentences.

24. What are the two kinds of cones produced by gymnosperms? _____

_____

25. How does pollination occur in gymnosperms? _____

_____

26. Describe the process of fertilization in gymnosperms. _____

_____

27. Name the two cells that make up each pollen grain. _____

_____

28. What kind of fertilization is unique to flowering plants? _____

_____

SEXUAL REPRODUCTION IN PLANTS
24-3   Fruits and Seeds

CHAPTER **24**

Part I: Vocabulary Review

Write the correct vocabulary term that best replaces the italicized definition in each statement.

1. All angiosperm embryos have at least one *seed leaf.* _____

2. In *flowering plants whose seeds have only one cotyledon,* flower petals occur in groups of three. _____

3. In *flowering plants whose seeds have two cotyledons,* flower petals occur in groups of four or five. _____

4. The *part of the embryo above the point of attachment of the cotyledons* usually gives rise to the terminal bud,

leaves, and upper part of the stem. _____

5. In some plants, the *part of the embryo below the point of attachment of the cotyledons* gives rise to the lower

part of the stem. _____

6. In some plants, the *lowermost part of the embryo* gives rise to the roots. _____

7. Many seeds go through a *resting period when seed growth is slowed or stops altogether* before they begin to

grow. _____

Part II: Content Review

Select the best answer and write the letter in the space provided.

_____ **8.** After fertilization, into what does each ovule develop?
  a. a fruit
  b. a seed
  c. a sperm
  d. an egg

_____ **9.** In angiosperms, where are seeds always found?
  a. within petals
  b. within a receptacle
  c. within a style
  d. within a fruit

_____ **10.** What kind of fruit forms when several ovaries are found within one flower?
  a. a simple fruit
  b. a complex fruit
  c. an aggregate fruit
  d. a multiple fruit

_____ **11.** What makes up a seed, or ripened ovule?
  a. the epicotyl, hypocotyl, and radicle
  b. the seed coat, embryo, and endosperm
  c. the hilum and cotyledons
  d. the roots, stems, and leaves

_____ **12.** In addition to one or two cotyledons, what three parts does a plant embryo have?
- **a.** the epicotyl, hypocotyl, and radicle
- **b.** the seed coat, embryo, and endosperm
- **c.** the roots, stems, and leaves
- **d.** the pistil, stamen, and anther

_____ **13.** In a developing corn seedling, to what plant part(s) do the hypocotyl and radicle give rise?
- **a.** the cotyledons
- **b.** the hilum
- **c.** the stem and leaves
- **d.** the roots

_____ **14.** Where are nutrients stored in a mature bean seed?
- **a.** in the seed coat
- **b.** in the cotyledons
- **c.** in the hypocotyl
- **d.** in the epicotyl

_____ **15.** How are the seeds of the snapdragon dispersed?
- **a.** by floating across water
- **b.** by the wind
- **c.** by bursting of the fruit
- **d.** by hooking onto a passing animal

_____ **16.** In species that are native to areas with cold winters, how is dormancy usually broken?
- **a.** by lack of light
- **b.** by physical crushing of the seed coat
- **c.** by lack of oxygen
- **d.** by exposure to low temperatures and moisture

Part III: Skills Development

Review the skill entitled "Graphic Organizing: Concept Map" on pages 49–55. Then, complete the concept map that appears below.

17.

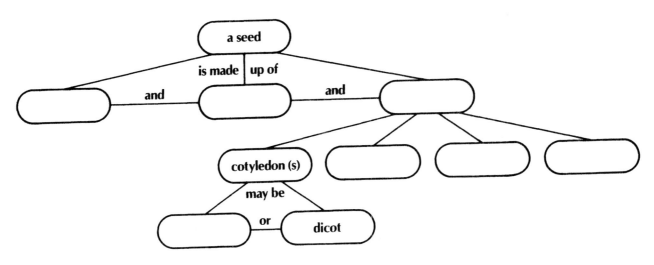

CHAPTER REVIEW

Know the Terms

Match the flower part with its function.

a. pedicel   **d.** sepals   **g.** frond
b. receptacle   **e.** petals   **h.** stamens
c. fruit   **f.** embryo   **i.** pistil

1. forms the corolla   1. _____

2. enclose and protect the flower bud   2. _____

3. female reproductive organ   3. _____

4. male reproductive organ   4. _____

5. support and attachment to the stem   5. _____

6. attachment of all flower parts   6. _____

Complete the following paragraph, using the list of words below. You may use a word more than once.

diploid   sperms   sporophyte
meiosis   haploid   zygote
eggs   gametophyte   fertilization

Plant life cycles with two generations are said to show alternation of
generation. The __(7)__ generation produces __(8)__ and __(9)__. They are
__(10)__ since they contain *n* chromosomes. They combine during the
process of __(11)__ to form a __(12)__. This structure is __(13)__ since it contains
2*n* chromosomes. It grows by mitosis into the __(14)__ generation. Cells
within the reproductive structure then undergo __(15)__ to form spores,
which germinate into the __(16)__ generation.

7. _____
8. _____
9. _____
10. _____
11. _____
12. _____
13. _____
14. _____
15. _____
16. _____

Match the seed or embryo part with its definition or function.

a. epicotyl   **c.** radicle   **e.** seed coat   **g.** fruit
b. hypocotyl   **d.** hilum   **f.** endosperm   **h.** embryo

17. develops into a new plant   17. _____

18. gives rise to lower part of the stem   18. _____

19. food source for the embryo   19. _____

20. gives rise to terminal bud and leaves   20. _____

21. gives rise to roots   21. _____

22. protects the embryo   22. _____

CHAPTER REVIEW

Understand the Concepts

Answer the following questions in one or two sentences.

1. Explain pollination in flowering plants. _____
_____
_____

2. How does fertilization occur in flowering plants? _____
_____
_____
_____

3. What is the advantage of flowers that are brightly colored and have fragrance? _____
_____
_____

4. How do fruits aid in the dispersal of the seeds that they contain? _____
_____
_____
_____
_____

5. What are the major groups of land plants? _____
_____

6. Explain the reproductive difference between the sporophyte generation and the gametophyte generation in plants. _____
_____
_____

7. Which is the dominant generation in seed plants? _____
_____

8. What are the final roles of the zygote, the ovule, and the ovary in angiosperms? _____
_____
_____

MENDELIAN GENETICS
25-1 Mendel's Principles of Heredity

Part I: Vocabulary Review

Complete the paragraphs below by filling in each blank with the correct vocabulary term.

The branch of biology that studies the ways in which hereditary information is passed on from parents to

offspring is called **(1)** _____ . In the first scientific study of heredity, Gregor Mendel crossed

plants that were pure for certain contrasting traits; he called the pure plants the **(2)** _____ .

The offspring of the pure plants that Mendel crossed were the **(3)** _____ . The offspring of

crosses between pure parents showing contrasting traits are called **(4)** _____ . The offspring

produced by the self-pollination of the hybrids made up the **(5)** _____ .

Mendel described the traits that were expressed in the F_1 generation as **(6)** _____ and the

traits that were hidden in the F_1 generation as **(7)** _____ . He concluded that when an

organism is hybrid for a pair of contrasting traits, only the dominant trait can be seen in the hybrid; this conclusion

is called the **(8)** _____ . Another conclusion drawn by Mendel was that the "factors"

controlling each inherited trait occur in pairs and are separated from each other during gamete formation and

recombined at fertilization; this idea is known as Mendel's **(9)** _____ . Today, we know that

each "factor" hypothesized by Mendel is a **(10)** _____ .

Part II: Content Review

The sentences below are incorrect statements. Rewrite the sentences to make them correct.

11. In sexual reproduction, hereditary material comes from only one parent, resulting in offspring that are identical

to the parent. _____

_____

_____

12. During Gregor Mendel's lifetime, much was known about chromosomes and cell division. _____

_____

_____

13. Pea plants were a bad choice for Mendel's investigations of heredity because they were hard to grow. _____

_____

_____

_____

14. Mathematics was of no use in Mendel's analysis of data. _____

_____

_____

15. The importance of Mendel's work was appreciated by many scientists during Mendel's lifetime. _____

_____

_____

16. When Mendel crossed a pure parent plant that was short with a pure parent plant that was tall, all offspring in

the F_1 generation were short. _____

_____

_____

17. When Mendel let the tall hybrid plants self-pollinate, he found that about three-fourths of the offspring were

short and about one-fourth were tall. _____

_____

_____

18. The appearance of tall plants in the F_2 generation showed that the factor that determined shortness was lost.

_____

_____

_____

19. Mendel hypothesized that each trait in an individual was controlled by a mysterious force. _____

_____

_____

20. Mendel believed that both dominant and recessive factors were expressed in hybrids. _____

_____

_____

21. The separation of homologous chromosome pairs during meiosis and their recombination during fertilization

would account for the separation and recombination of the parent plants. _____

_____

_____

_____

MENDELIAN GENETICS
25-2 Fundamentals of Genetics

Part I: Vocabulary Review

If the statement is true, write TRUE in the space at the left. If the statement is false, make it true by changing the underlined word(s)

_____ 1. Different copies or forms of a gene controlling a certain trait are called <u>phenotypes</u>.

_____ 2. If the forms of a gene controlling a certain trait are the same, the organism is said to be <u>heterozygous</u> for that trait.

_____ 3. If the forms of a gene controlling a certain trait are different, the organism is said to be <u>homozygous</u> for that trait.

_____ 4. The word *heterozygous* means hybrid.

_____ 5. An organism that is <u>homozygous</u> for a certain trait has two identical alleles for that trait.

_____ 6. The letters *tt* may be used to represent the <u>phenotype</u> of a short pea plant.

_____ 7. The physical trait that an organism develops as a result of its genetic makeup is called its <u>genotype</u>.

_____ 8. Predicting that you will get about 50 heads and 50 tails if you toss a coin 100 times is an example of the <u>law of dominance</u>.

_____ 9. Each box in a <u>Punnett square</u> stands for a possible union of a male gamete with a female gamete.

_____ 10. Mating an individual of unknown genotype with an individual showing the contrasting recessive trait is an example of the <u>law of probability</u>.

Part II: Content Review

Answer each of the following questions in one or two sentences.

11. To agree with Mendel's findings, what must each body cell of an organism have? _____

_____

_____

12. What were the two different alleles for height in the pea plants that Mendel studied? _____

_____

13. Would a short pea plant be heterozygous or homozygous? _____

_____

14. What is the difference between genotype and phenotype? _____

_____

_____

15. (a) If there are several possible events that might happen and no one of them is more likely to happen than another, what can you predict is likely to happen? _____

_____

   (b) What law governs your prediction? _____

_____

16. What is a test cross used for? _____

_____

17. Using a test cross, what results would indicate that the unknown genotype was heterozygous? _____

_____

_____

Part III: Skills Development

Review the skill entitled "Interpreting Diagrams and Tables" on pages 19–21. Then, use the diagram below to answer the questions that follow.

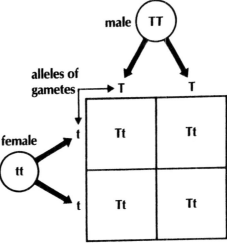

18. What is this kind of diagram called? _____

19. What phenotypes would the male and the female parent plants have? _____

_____

20. What allele would the gametes from each parent plant contain? _____

_____

_____

21. What would be the phenotype(s) and the genotype(s) of the offspring? _____

MENDELIAN GENETICS
25-3 Other Concepts in Genetics

Part I: Vocabulary Review

Compare and contrast the following pairs of terms. First list their similarities, then their differences.

1. monohybrid cross and dihybrid cross: _____

_____

_____

_____

2. law of independent assortment and multiple alleles: _____

_____

_____

_____

_____

3. incomplete dominance and codominance: _____

_____

_____

_____

Part II: Content Review

Select the best answer and write the letter in the space provided.

_____ 4. When Mendel crossed a pure parent plant that had yellow, round seeds with a pure parent plant that had green, wrinkled seeds, all the offspring had
a. yellow, wrinkled seeds
b. yellow, round seeds
c. green, round seeds
d. green, wrinkled seeds

_____ 5. When Mendel let hybrid plants with yellow, round seeds self-pollinate, the least common F_2 generation phenotype was
a. yellow, wrinkled seeds
b. yellow, round seeds
c. green, round seeds
d. green, wrinkled seeds

_____ 6. What did Mendel conclude from his dihybrid-cross experiments?
a. Different traits are inherited together.
b. The same traits are inherited independently of one another.
c. Different traits are inherited independently of one another.
d. Some traits are recessive.

_____ 7. What is the expected phenotype ratio for a Mendelian dihybrid cross?
  a. 9:3:3:1
  b. 1:2:1
  c. 2.97:1
  d. 3:18:1

_____ 8. When red Japanese four-o'clocks are crossed with white Japanese four-o'clocks, what kind of inheritance pattern results?
  a. Mendelian dihybrid cross
  b. codominance
  c. Mendelian monohybrid cross
  d. incomplete dominance

_____ 9. When homozygous red shorthorn cattle are crossed with homozygous white shorthorn cattle, what kind of inheritance pattern results?
  a. Mendelian dihybrid cross
  b. codominance
  c. Mendelian monohybrid cross
  d. incomplete dominance

_____ 10. Among the human species, how many alleles control blood type?
  a. one allele
  b. two alleles
  c. three alleles
  d. four alleles

_____ 11. Among human populations, how many possible genotypes are associated with the ABO blood types?
  a. six genotypes
  b. four genotypes
  c. three genotypes
  d. two genotypes

Part III: Skills Development

Review the skill entitled "Graphic Organizing: Compare/Contrast Matrix" on pages 41–44. Then, complete the matrix below.

12.

CHARACTERISTIC	INCOMPLETE DOMINANCE	CODOMINANCE
How inheritance pattern differs from Mendel's laws		
How genotypes are written		
Which organisms show the pattern for which traits		

CHAPTER REVIEW

Know the Terms

Complete the following crossword puzzle.

ACROSS

2. Physical appearance of an organism
4. Prefix meaning "one"
6. An individual that is heterozygous for a trait
8. One of the two or more forms of the gene
9. The study of heredity

DOWN

1. The genetic make-up of an organism
3. Father of genetics
5. Prefix meaning "two"
7. A distinct unit of hereditary material found in chromosomes

Define or describe the following words.

10. test cross: _____

_____

_____

_____

11. recessive trait: _____

_____

_____

12. law of segregation: _____

_____

_____

_____

CHAPTER REVIEW

Understand the Concepts

Answer the following questions in one or two sentences.

1. Why was Mendel successful in his study of genetics? _____
_____
_____

2. Why was the garden pea plant a good choice for Mendel's studies of genetics? _____
_____
_____

3. Explain the principle of dominance. _____
_____
_____
_____

4. How is incomplete dominance different from complete dominance? _____
_____
_____

5. Explain independent assortment. _____
_____
_____

6. How can one determine whether the genotype of an individual exhibiting a dominant trait is
homozygous dominant or heterozygous? _____
_____
_____

7. Why is it important to carry out a large number of trials in determining probability? _____
_____
_____
_____

8. What is the difference between a homozygous and a heterozygous trait? _____
_____

MODERN GENETICS
26-1 Chromosomal Inheritance

Part I: Vocabulary Review

A. Write the correct vocabulary term that best replaces the italicized definition in each statement.

1. The discovery of two *unmatched chromosomes that determine whether an organism is male or female* confirmed the idea that an inherited trait may be determined by a particular pair of

chromosomes. _____

2. The fruit fly has three pairs of *homologous chromosomes.* _____

3. In the female fruit fly, there are two *rod-shaped sex chromosomes that look the same.* _____

4. The sex chromosomes in the male fruit fly consist of one X chromosome and one *hook-shaped sex*

chromosome. _____

5. In humans, hemophilia is an example of a *trait that is controlled by a gene found on the sex*

chromosome. _____

6. *A condition in which an individual cannot perceive certain colors, usually red and green,* is more common in

males than in females. _____

7. Genes cannot be distributed independently during meiosis if they are part of a *set that includes all the genes*

that are on the same chromosome. _____

8. In a small number of offspring in the F_2 generation, linked genes separate because of *the exchange of pieces*

of homologous chromosomes during synapsis of the first meiotic division. _____

9. The way in which human height is inherited is an example of *the type of inheritance in which two or more*

genes affect the same characteristic. _____

B. Compare and contrast the following pairs of terms. First list their similarities, then their differences.

10. sex chromosomes and autosomes: _____

_____

_____

11. X chromosome and Y chromosome: _____

_____

12. sex-linked trait and color blindness: _____

_____

_____

_____

MODERN GENETICS

26-1 Chromosomal Inheritance (continued)

Part II: Content Review

Read each "Cause" and fill in an appropriate "Effect" in the space provided. An example is given below.

CAUSE

EFFECT

the zygote will develop into a male.

13. In *Drosophila*, when a sperm containing a Y chromosome joins with a female gamete, _____

14. In humans, when a sperm containing an X chromosome joins with a female gamete, _____

15. If a female fruit fly has the recessive allele for eye color on both of her X chromosomes, _____

16. If carriers have a normal dominant allele on one X chromosome, _____

17. If a mother is a carrier for color blindness, _____

18. If a female inherits two alleles for color blindness, _____

19. If a father is color-blind, _____

20. If both parents are color-blind, _____

21. If genes are linked on the same chromosome, _____

22. If plants pure for two linked dominant traits are crossed with plants pure for two linked recessive traits, _____

23. When crossing-over occurs, _____

MODERN GENETICS
26-2 The Genetic Material

Part I: Vocabulary Review

Complete the following crossword puzzle.

ACROSS

4. five-carbon sugar found in DNA
6. basic unit of DNA
7. purine that pairs with cytosine

DOWN

1. pyrimidine that pairs with adenine in DNA
2. purine that pairs with thymine in DNA
3. coiled shape of the DNA molecule
5. pyrimidine that pairs with guanine

Part II: Content Review

Reorganize the four events in each group in the order in which they occurred. Write 1 next to the event that happened first, 2 next to the event that happened second, and so on.

8. _____ Griffith injected a mixture of dead Type S bacteria and live Type R bacteria into mice.

_____ The mice developed pneumonia and died.

_____ Griffith mixed dead Type S bacteria with live Type R bacteria.

_____ Griffith concluded that some factor from dead Type S bacteria could change Type R bacteria into Type S.

9. _____ Cells infected by phages with radioactive DNA showed a lot of radioactivity; cells infected by phages with radioactive protein showed almost no radioactivity.

_____ Hershey and Chase tagged the protein coat with radioactive sulfur; they tagged the phage DNA with radioactive phosphorus.

_____ This experiment proved that phage DNA enters the cells, while the phage protein stays outside the cells.

_____ Large numbers of bacteria were exposed to and infected by the radioactively tagged phages.

10. _____ Bases of free nucleotides fasten onto the complementary bases on each exposed strand of DNA.

_____ Two double-stranded molecules of DNA exactly like the original molecule are made.

_____ When the nucleotides join together, they make a complete complementary strand exactly like the old one.

_____ Hydrogen bonds break, and the two strands of the DNA molecule come apart.

Part III: Skills Development

Review the skill entitled "Graphic Organizing: Concept Map" on pages 49–55. Then, complete the concept map below on the components of DNA.

11.

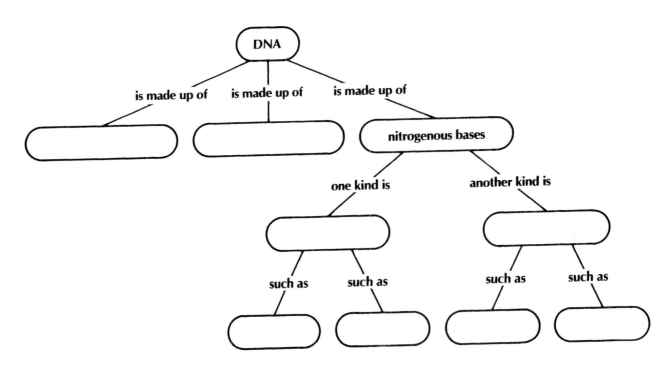

MODERN GENETICS
26-3 Gene Expression

Part I: Vocabulary Review

Write the correct vocabulary term that best replaces the italicized definition in each statement.

1. When scientists found that the synthesis of each polypeptide is controlled by a different gene, they changed the one gene-one enzyme hypothesis to the *hypothesis that states that each gene directs the synthesis of a particular polypeptide chain.* _____

2. Each adenine in DNA is transcribed, or copied, into mRNA as *a nitrogen-containing base found in RNA but not in DNA.* _____

3. To copy the DNA code, the DNA strands separate for a short time and serve as a pattern, or template, for *a strand of RNA that copies the genetic message by matching up complementary bases.* _____

4. *The copying of a genetic message into a molecule of mRNA* insures that each mRNA strand carries the complete message for a single polypeptide in complementary form. _____

5. Most amino acids are specified by more than one *group of three bases on the mRNA.* _____

6. While mRNA may have thousands of nucleotides along its length, *a second kind of RNA* has only about 80 nucleotides. _____

7. In the loop of exposed nucleotides of a tRNA molecule, there is *a sequence of 3 bases that are complements of an mRNA codon.* _____

8. A ribosome consists of protein and *a kind of RNA that is formed in the nucleoli of the cell.* _____

9. By means of *the process by which the information coded in RNA is used for the assembly of a particular amino acid sequence,* the genetic message is used to assemble a polypeptide. _____

Part II: Content Review

Select the best answer and write the letter in the space provided.

_____ 10. In the early 1900s, who suggested the idea that hereditary material controls the synthesis of enzymes?
   a. Garrod
   b. Watson
   c. Beadle and Tatum
   d. Crick

_____ 11. Who suggested the one gene-one enzyme hypothesis based on experiments with red bread mold *Neurospora crassa?*
   a. Garrod
   b. Watson
   c. Beadle and Tatum
   d. Crick

_____ 12. How many polypeptide chains make up hemoglobin?
    a. one
    b. two
    c. three
    d. none of the above

_____ 13. Which is the best statement of the one gene-one polypeptide hypothesis?
    a. One gene controls the decomposition of a particular polypeptide.
    b. One gene controls the synthesis of a particular enzyme.
    c. One gene controls the transport of a particular hormone.
    d. One gene controls the synthesis of a particular polypeptide.

_____ 14. How many bases in a DNA molecule make up one code "word" that specifies an amino acid?
    a. one-base sequence
    b. two-base sequence
    c. three-base sequence
    d. four-base sequence

_____ 15. What nitrogen-containing base takes the place of thymine in a strand of RNA?
    a. adenine
    b. uracil
    c. cytosine
    d. guanine

_____ 16. What kind of RNA is involved with transcription?
    a. mRNA
    b. tRNA
    c. rRNA
    d. a, b, and c

_____ 17. What is a codon?
    a. 2-base sequence of DNA that specifies an amino acid
    b. 3-base sequence of a polypeptide
    c. 3-base sequence of mRNA that specifies an amino acid
    d. 2-base sequence of tRNA that specifies an amino acid

_____ 18. To what part of the tRNA molecule does an amino acid attach?
    a. tail
    b. loop
    c. anticodon
    d. codon

_____ 19. During protein synthesis, where in the cell is a polypeptide assembled?
    a. nucleus
    b. nucleoli
    c. mitochondria
    d. ribosome

_____ 20. What controls the ending of the synthesis of a polypeptide?
    a. The tRNA brings an incorrect amino acid.
    b. The ribosome travels into the nucleus.
    c. The ribosome reaches a "stop" codon.
    d. The messenger RNA disintegrates.

_____ 21. What special kind of protein helps in every step of the protein synthesis?
    a. enzymes
    b. ribosomes
    c. hormones
    d. hemoglobin

_____ 22. What is the name of the process by which information coded in RNA is used to assemble a particular amino acid sequence?
    a. transcription
    b. translation
    c. synthesis
    d. punctuation

Name _____   Date _____

MODERN GENETICS
26-4 Control of Gene Expression

CHAPTER **26**

Part I: Vocabulary Review

Compare and contrast the following pairs of terms. First list their similarities, then their differences.

1. operon and enhancer: _____

_____

_____

_____

2. exon and intron: _____

_____

_____

_____

3. homeotic genes and oncogenes: _____

_____

_____

_____

Part II: Content Review

The sentences below are incorrect statements. Rewrite the sentences to make them correct.

4. Jacob, Monod, and Lwoff discovered how the transcription of certain genes is controlled in bread mold.

_____

_____

_____

5. Jacob, Monod, and Lwoff found that production of lactose-digesting enzymes stops when lactose is present and other sources of energy are not available. _____

_____

_____

6. Jacob, Monod, and Lwoff found that the amino acid sequences of the lactose-digesting enzymes were determined by three enhancers. _____

_____

_____

7. In prokaryotes, the activity of structural genes is controlled by an oncogene. _____

_____

8. In prokaryotes, when a repressor protein binds to a homeobox, transcription of the structural genes starts. _____

_____

_____

9. In *E. coli*, when lactose is present, the operator gene is turned on because the lactose binds to the structural

genes. _____

_____

10. In bacteria, another control gene, called the intron, attracts and binds the enzyme that starts transcription. _____

_____

_____

11. In eukaryotes, related genes are clustered together on the same chromosome. _____

_____

_____

12. When a gene is transcribed, only exons are made into RNA. _____

_____

13. In eukaryotes, different proteins can be synthesized from the same eukaryote DNA segment because enzymes

can cut and splice the DNA in different ways. _____

_____

_____

14. Changes in the amount of coiling or in the shape of RNA can affect the expression of genes in eukaryotes.

_____

_____

15. An ice pack placed on the shaved back of a Himalayan rabbit causes baldness. _____

_____

_____

16. In fruit flies, the development of the embryo is controlled by operator genes. _____

_____

_____

17. If scientists can find a way to switch operons off, they may find a new cure for cancer. _____

_____

CHAPTER REVIEW

Know the Terms

Complete the following paragraphs using the list of scientists below.

Watson and Crick
Punnett and Bateson
Beadle and Tatum
Hershey and Chase

T. H. Morgan
Miescher
Griffith
Sutton

Jacob, Monod, and Lwoff
Avery, MacLeod, and McCarty
Archibald Garrod
Levene

The contributions of Mendel in the middle 1800s began the science of genetics. Many other important contributions followed. __(1)__ discovered and explained sex-linked traits, while __(2)__ studied linked genes. __(3)__ hypothesized that some diseases were caused by the inability to produce certain enzymes. This was confirmed by __(4)__, using neurospora.

DNA was first isolated by __(5)__ in 1869, and its nucleotide components were analyzed by __(6)__ in the 1920s. The question of whether the DNA or protein component of chromosomes controlled heredity was answered by __(7)__ using bacteria, and by __(8)__ using radioactively labeled viruses.

__(9)__ provided the double helix model of DNA, and __(10)__ used bacteria to determine how genes are expressed.

1. _____
2. _____
3. _____
4. _____
5. _____
6. _____
7. _____
8. _____
9. _____
10. _____

Match the following words with their definitions.

a. messenger RNA
b. purines
c. structural gene
d. ribosome

e. nucleotide
f. regulator gene
g. transfer RNA
h. pyrimidines

i. operator gene
j. helix
k. repressor protein
l. gene mutation

11. building block of nucleic acid

12. adenine and guanine

13. thymine and cytosine

14. carries the DNA code to a ribosome

15. copies messenger RNA

16. protein plus two ribosomal RNA molecules

17. DNA segment that codes for a particular polypeptide

18. controls the activity of structural genes

19. controls the activity of an operator gene

20. produces repressors

11. ____

12. ____

13. ____

14. ____

15. ____

16. ____

17. ____

18. ____

19. ____

20. ____

Understand the Concepts

Answer the following questions in one or two sentences.

1. Where are genes found in a cell, and what are they composed of? _____

_____

_____

2. What is meant by multiple gene inheritance? _____

_____

_____

3. Describe the appearance and composition of a DNA molecule. _____

_____

_____

_____

4. What does the sequence of base pairs in a gene determine? _____

_____

_____

5. Explain the process of transcription. _____

_____

_____

_____

6. Briefly explain the sequence of events occurring during protein synthesis. _____

_____

_____

_____

_____

7. Explain the correlation between DNA and protein. _____

_____

_____

8. Explain the relationship between the environment and heredity. _____

_____

_____

APPLIED GENETICS
27-1 Mutations

Part I: Vocabulary Review

Fill in the vocabulary term that best completes each statement.

1. A sudden change in the structure or the amount of genetic material is a _____ .

2. An abnormal change in the structure of all or part of a chromosome or in the number of chromosomes an organism has is a _____ .

3. A change that affects a gene on a chromosome is a _____ .

4. When factors in the environment cause mutations, the factors are called _____ .

5. The transfer of a part of a chromosome to a nonhomologous chromosome is a _____ .

6. When a piece of chromosome is rotated, reversing the order of genes in the segment, it is an _____ .

7. When a piece of a chromosome breaks off and attaches to a homologous chromosome, it is called an _____ .

8. When a piece of a chromosome breaks off, resulting in the loss of some genes, it is a _____ .

9. The addition or loss of an entire chromosome is called _____ .

10. A condition in which cells have some multiple of the normal chromosome number is called _____ .

11. A type of gene mutation in which only a single nucleotide in a gene has been changed is a _____ .

Part II: Content Review

For each statement below, decide whether it relates to chromosomal mutations, gene mutations, or both. Write "C" for chromosomal mutations, "G" for gene mutations, or "B" for both.

_____ 12. Many natural mutations may be the result of random errors in replication of the DNA.

_____ 13. If a single nucleotide is added or removed, all the triplet codons beyond that point are changed.

_____ 14. Beneficial mutations are the source of variations that allow species to meet the needs of their environment.

_____ 15. Nondisjunction takes place when chromosomes that normally separate during meiosis remain together.

_____ 16. Many mutations may be partly the result of mutagens that occur in the environment.

_____ 17. These inherited mutations are usually recessive.

_____ 18. Polyploidy is commonly found in plant cells.

_____ 19. For a mutation to be inherited in a sexually reproducing organism, it must be present in the DNA of a gamete.

_____ **20.** This kind of mutation involves the transfer of a part of a chromosome to a nonhomologous chromosome.

_____ **21.** Sometimes, one base in a DNA molecule is substituted for another.

_____ **22.** Parts of a chromosome may be inverted, added, or deleted.

_____ **23.** De Vries observed this kind of mutation in the evening primrose.

Part III: Skills Development

Review the skill entitled "Reading for Understanding: The SQ3R Approach" on pages 4–7. Then, follow the instructions below.

Survey the paragraph below.

JUMPING GENES

Genes that move or jump from chromosome to chromosome cause another kind of mutation. Although most genes stay in one place, a few are able to move to new locations on the chromosomes during replication. These mobile elements, or "jumping genes," were discovered by Barbara McClintock, an American geneticist. When a gene takes a new position in or near another gene during replication, it often causes an inactivation of that gene. Jumping genes are an important source of variation and are thought to exist in all species. McClintock was awarded the Nobel prize in 1983 for her discovery.

Turn the topic heading of the paragraph into a question.

24. Write the question in the space below.

_____

Read the paragraph.

Recite what you have learned.

25. On the lines below, answer the question that you wrote in number 24.

_____

_____

_____

Review what you have learned.

APPLIED GENETICS
27-2 Human Genetic Disorders

Part I: Vocabulary Review

Complete the paragraphs by filling in each blank with the correct vocabulary term.

To trace the appearance of certain genetic traits in families, scientists may construct a **(1)** _____ , which is a diagram that shows the presence or absence of a certain trait in each member of each generation. An example of a recessive inherited human disorder in which the red blood cells have an abnormal sickle shape is **(2)** _____ . An example of an inherited human disorder that results from an extra copy of chromosome number 21 is **(3)** _____ .

One way that genetic disorders may be detected is by taking a photograph of a person's chromosomes, arranging them into pairs, and comparing them to a normal set of chromosomes; this process is called **(4)** _____ . Another technique used to detect genetic disorders in a fetus is **(5)** _____ , which involves withdrawing a sample of amniotic fluid and examining the cells for abnormalities. A newer method of checking for genetic disorders in a fetus is called **(6)** _____ , _____ , which involves removing a sample of the chorion and examining the cells.

Sound waves may be used to determine the size and position of a fetus by a procedure known as **(7)** _____ . Direct observation of a fetus is possible by means of **(8)** _____ .

Part II: Content Review

Complete each of the following sentences.

9. Carriers of recessive defective autosomal alleles rarely show signs of illness because _____

_____

_____

10. Sickle-cell disease is caused by _____

_____

_____

11. The defective gene that causes sickle-cell disease is more common than expected in African populations because _____

12. Brain damage caused by phenylketonuria (PKU) can be avoided by _____

_____

13. Because Huntington's disease is caused by a dominant autosomal allele, any child born to a parent with Huntington's disease has a 50 percent chance of _____

14. Cystic fibrosis is caused by _____

_____

15. By examining a karyotype, a physician can see that a person with Down syndrome has _____

_____

16. Two kinds of abnormalities that may be detected by amniocentesis are _____

_____

17. During chorionic villus sampling, fetal abnormalities can be detected by examining the cells of the chorion,

because these cells are _____

_____

18. As part of fetoscopy, fetal blood and cell samples may be taken for analysis by _____

_____

Part III: Skills Development

Review the skill entitled "Graphic Organizing: Concept Map" on pages 49–55. Then, complete the concept map below on the major types of genetic disorders.

19.

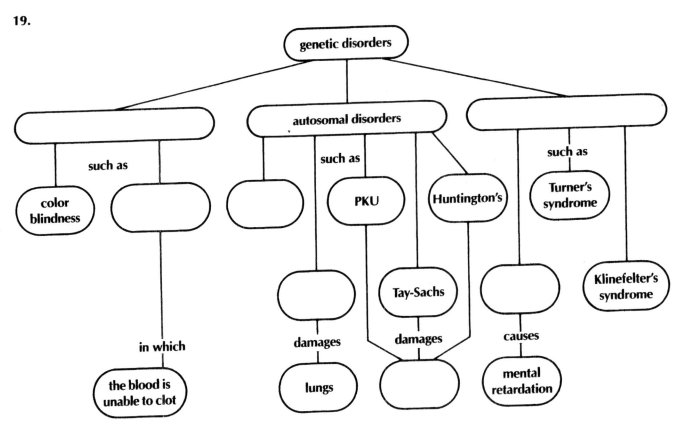

APPLIED GENETICS
27-3 Genetic Engineering

Part I: Vocabulary Review

Replace the italicized definition with the correct vocabulary term.

1. *The process of choosing organisms with the most desirable traits for mating* is often used by breeders in hopes of building up desired traits in a population. _____

2. *The mating of closely related individuals to obtain desired characteristics* is used to produce domestic animals and pets. _____

3. The mule, which is the offspring of a male donkey and a female horse, is an example of *superior traits that are the result of outbreeding.* _____

4. *A group of organisms that has exactly the same genes* is useful for cancer research. _____

5. *The joined DNA from two different species* allows bacteria to become "factories" for making human interferon. _____

6. Large amounts of previously rare substances, such as human insulin, can be produced by using *methods for producing recombinant DNA.* _____

7. One of the long-range goals of genetic engineering is *to correct genetic defects by transferring normal genes to cells that lack them.* _____

8. The first step in any genetic engineering experiment is to isolate pieces of DNA with a desirable gene by using *proteins that cut the DNA molecules into small pieces.* _____

9. One important method of inserting foreign DNA into a host cell involves *small, ring-shaped DNA.*

_____

10. *The intake by living bacteria of DNA from dead bacteria* causes traits of the dead bacteria to show in the living bacterial cells. _____

11. *The viral transfer of pieces of DNA from one bacterium to another* occurs when a virus infects a bacterium and a piece of bacterial DNA becomes part of the virus. _____

Part II: Content Review

Answer each of the following questions in one or two sentences.

12. How do breeders use the process of selection to improve their crops and domestic animals? _____

_____

_____

_____

13. When Mendel let some of the pea plants that he used in his genetic experiments self-pollinate, what kind of breeding method was he employing? _____

14. Why are close relatives prohibited from marrying in many societies? _____

_____

_____

15. How can outbreeding followed by inbreeding be used to produce valuable new lines of plants and animals?

_____

_____

_____

16. How can clones of animals be useful in research? _____

_____

_____

_____

17. Why do polyploid plants usually form separate species? _____

_____

_____

_____

18. What are two ways in which farmers have been helped by genetic engineering? _____

_____

_____

_____

19. What are two ways by which genes can be transferred to bacteria? _____

_____

Part III: Skills Development

Review the skill entitled "Graphic Organizing: Flow Chart" on pages 34–37. Then, complete the flow chart below by filling in the four steps of gene splicing.

20.

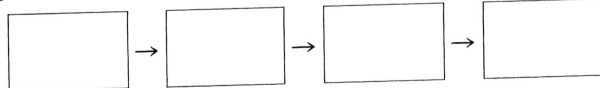

CHAPTER REVIEW

Know the Terms

Match the following genetic disorders with their descriptions.

   a. polyploidy   **e.** Tay-Sachs disease   **i.** cystic fibrosis
   b. Huntington's disease   **f.** hemophilia   **j.** nondisjunction
   c. inversion   **g.** translocation   **k.** Muscular Dystrophy
   d. point mutation   **h.** phenylketonuria   **l.** Down syndrome

1. sex-linked disorder that affects blood clotting   **1.** ___

2. affects breathing by clogging lungs   **2.** ___

3. diagnosed by simple urine test   **3.** ___

4. affects oxygen-carrying capacity in red blood cells   **4.** ___

5. causes plants to have multiple chromosomes   **5.** ___

6. causes muscle tissue to break down   **6.** ___

7. affects Jewish ancestry, infant death   **7.** ___

8. addition or loss of a chromosome   **8.** ___

9. extra twenty-first chromosome   **9.** ___

10. fatal, caused by brain damage, age 30–40   **10.** ___

Define or describe the following words.

11. translocation: _____

_____

12. karyotype: _____

_____

13. point mutation: _____

14. clone: _____

15. deletion: _____

16. pedigree chart: _____

_____

17. mutagens: _____

_____

18. plasmid: _____

19. recombinant DNA: _____

20. mutation: _____

CHAPTER REVIEW

Understand the Concepts

Answer each of the following questions in one or two sentences.

1. How is recombinant DNA made? _____

_____

2. What characteristic of cells may make cloning of animal cells possible? _____

_____

_____

_____

3. What is the difference between translocation and addition? _____

_____

_____

_____

4. Why is inbreeding sometimes harmful? _____

_____

_____

_____

5. Explain the difference between transformation and transduction. _____

_____

_____

_____

6. Distinguish between a sex-linked and autosomal disorder. _____

_____

_____

_____

7. Distinguish between a chromosomal and a gene mutation. _____

_____

_____

8. What is amniocentesis? _____

_____

_____

EVIDENCE OF EVOLUTION
28-1 Evidence from the Past

Part I: Vocabulary Review

Complete the following crossword puzzle.

ACROSS

2. Process by which remains of dead organism are turned to stone
6. Process of change that occurs in species over time
7. Method of determining the order in which events occurred
8. Slow change in the earth
11. Rock formed from layers of particles that settle on floor of a body of water

DOWN

1. Dating method based on rate of decay of radioactive isotopes
3. History of life
4. Hollow form left in rock after the remains of an organism decays
5. Method that determines how long ago an event occurred
9. Traces or remains of an organism preserved by natural processes
10. Fossil formed when an impression made in mud hardens into rock
12. Fossil formed when a mold fills with minerals and hardens, showing external features of original organism

Part II: Content Review

Select the best answer and write the letter in the space provided.

_____ 13. What is a central and unifying theme of biology?
    a. geologic evolution
    b. evolution
    c. petrifaction
    d. unification

_____ 14. What provides the strongest evidence of organic evolution?
    a. study of fossils
    b. study of life
    c. study of biosystems
    d. study of petrifaction

_____ 15. How are the soft tissues of organisms sometimes naturally preserved?
    a. in molds and casts
    b. in sedimentary rock
    c. as imprints
    d. in amber or ice

_____ 16. In which one of the following places would you expect the most fossils to form?
    a. lake and sea floors
    b. forest floors
    c. around volcanoes
    d. mountains

_____ 17. In what kind of rock are most fossils found?
    a. igneous
    b. metamorphic
    c. sedimentary
    d. amber

_____ 18. If layers of rock were undisturbed, where would you expect to find the oldest layers?
    a. top
    b. bottom
    c. middle
    d. above ground

_____ 19. What is the half life of carbon-14?
    a. 5700 years
    b. 10 700 years
    c. 2700 years
    d. 100 years

_____ 20. What isotope can be used to date fossils that are older than 50 000 years?
    a. carbon-14
    b. nitrogen-14
    c. uranium-238
    d. oxygen-18

Part III: Skills Development

Review the skill entitled "Graphic Organizing: Compare/Contrast Matrix" on pages 41–44. Then, complete the matrix shown below.

21.

CHARACTERISTIC	RELATIVE DATING	ABSOLUTE DATING
Purpose		
Method		

EVIDENCE OF EVOLUTION
28-2   Interpreting the Fossil Record

Part I: Vocabulary Review

Fill in the vocabulary term that best completes each statement.

1. By the comparison of rock layers, or by _____ , scientists can determine the relative ages of rocks and fossils in a particular region.

2. Through correlation, geologists have constructed a timetable of the earth's history, known as the _____ _____ , which is divided into eras and subdivided into periods and epochs.

3. Trilobites are good examples of _____ , which allow the relative dating of rocks within a narrow time span.

4. Scientists hypothesize that dinosaurs became _____ , or died out completely, when the earth was struck by an asteroid or comet or when the earth underwent severe volcanic activity.

Part II: Content Review

The sentences below are incorrect statements. Rewrite the sentences to make them correct.

5. If rock layer A is older than rock layer B, it follows that fossils found in layer A are more recent than fossils in layer B. _____

_____

_____

_____

6. Scientists can use correlation of sedimentary rock layers to date fossils even when there are no nearby rocks that are similar. _____

_____

_____

7. Scientists know that sedimentary rocks containing certain trilobite fossils are from a recent epoch. _____

_____

_____

8. Through a correlation of absolute and relative dating of rocks, scientists have been able to construct a history of transitional forms. _____

_____

_____

9. Modern angiosperms first appeared at the beginning of the Paleozoic era. _____

_____

_____

10. The appearance of the earliest humans has been traced back to the Carboniferous period. _____

_____

_____

11. During its evolution from *Eohippus* to the modern horse, the horse has remained about the same size and it

has retained four toes. _____

_____

_____

12. It has been estimated that the number of species alive today is about the same as the number of all the species

that ever lived. _____

_____

_____

_____

13. The disappearance of the dinosaurs 65 million years ago is an example of slow change. _____

_____

_____

Part III: Skills Development

Review the skill entitled "Graphic Organizing: Scale" on pages 38–40 and the chart on page 579 in your textbook.
Then, construct a geologic time scale showing the following eras: Age of Amphibians, Age of Humans, Age of
Mammals, Age of Invertebrates, Age of Reptiles, Age of Fishes.

14.

600

Now

Millions of Years Ago

EVIDENCE OF EVOLUTION
28-3 Evidence from Living Organisms

Part I: Vocabulary Review

Write the correct vocabulary term that best replaces the italicized definition in each statement.

1. *Parts of different organisms that have similar structures and similar embryological development, but have different forms and functions*, are regarded as evidence that some species evolved from a common ancestor.

_____

2. Bird wings and insect wings are examples of *structures that have similar external forms and functions but different internal structures.* _____

3. *The remnants of structures that were functional in an ancestral form* indicate that whales and snakes evolved from four-legged ancestors. _____

Part II: Content Review

For each statement below decide whether it relates to anatomical similarities, embryological similarities, or biochemical similarities. Write "A" for anatomical, "E" for embryological, or "B" for biochemical.

_____ **4.** Embryos of closely related species show similar patterns of development.

_____ **5.** Comparison of a whale flipper with a human hand shows similar structure.

_____ **6.** The early developmental stages of fish and mammals show gill slits, two-chambered hearts, and tails.

_____ **7.** With the Nuttall test, the greater the amount of precipitate, the greater the similarity in protein structure.

_____ **8.** Analogous structures among different animals are regarded as evidence for evolution along different lines.

_____ **9.** Similarities among embryos of different organisms support the idea that these organisms have a common evolutionary origin.

_____ **10.** The human coccyx is an evolutionary remnant of an ancestral, reptilian tail.

_____ **11.** Scientists have discovered that the closer the evolutionary relationship between organisms, the more alike the structure of their DNA and protein molecules.

_____ **12.** Both whales and pythons have vestigial leg bones.

_____ **13.** The sequences of amino acids in the hemoglobin of closely related species are almost identical.

_____ **14.** The more closely related the animals, the longer they continue to resemble each other during the stages of development.

_____ **15.** Evidence for evolutionary relationships is provided by the presence of vestigial organs.

_____ **16.** Homologous structures among different animals are regarded as evidence that some species evolved from a common ancestor.

Part III: Skills Development

Review the skill entitled "Taking Notes" on pages 16–18. Then, read the following passage taken from your text book. The topic sentences, supporting details, and key words and phrases are underlined. On the lines following the passage, organize the important points into a useful set of notes.

BIOCHEMICAL SIMILARITIES

Scientists have discovered that <u>the closer the evolutionary relationship between organisms, the more alike the structure of their DNA and protein molecules.</u> For example, <u>the sequences of amino acids in the hemoglobin of closely related species are almost identical.</u>

<u>The degree of evolutionary relationship between different types of organisms also can be determined with the Nuttall test, which is based on antigen-antibody reactions.</u> (See Chapter 10.) For example, if human blood serum is injected into a rabbit, the rabbit produces antibodies against the proteins in the human blood. If serum from this sensitized rabbit is then mixed with human blood serum, a cloudy precipitate forms, showing an antigen-antibody reaction. The amount of the precipitate can be measured. If serums from a chimpanzee, a baboon, and a pig are then tested individually with serum from the sensitized rabbit, the amount of precipitate formed will be different in each case. The amount of precipitate is an indication of the similarity in protein structure between each of these animals and humans. <u>The greater the amount of precipitate, the greater the similarity in protein structure,</u> and the more closely the animal in question is related to humans.

17. _____

_____

_____

_____

_____

_____

_____

_____

_____

_____

_____

_____

_____

_____

_____

EVIDENCE OF EVOLUTION
28-4 The Origins of Life — Early Hypotheses

Part I: Vocabulary Review

Replace the italicized definition with the correct vocabulary term.

1. *The idea that living organisms arise naturally from nonliving matter* was finally defeated as a hypothesis for how maggots arise from decaying meat when Louis Pasteur showed that microorganisms that developed in a

nutrient broth came from spores and microorganisms in the air. _____

Part II: Content Review

Reorganize the events in each group in the order in which they occurred. Write 1 next to the event that happened first, 2 next to the event that happened second, and so on.

2. _____ Van Helmont concluded that the wheat was changed into mice by the presence of human sweat.

   _____ Van Helmont placed wheat grains in a sweaty shirt.

   _____ After 21 days, the wheat had disappeared and mice were present.

3. _____ Redi saw maggots consume the decaying meat.

   _____ Redi placed meat in open containers.

   _____ Redi observed that the maggots formed pupas.

   _____ Redi saw that the pupas developed into flies.

4. _____ Flies entered the open jars and maggots appeared on the meat; no maggots appeared on the meat in the closed jars.

   _____ Redi hypothesized that maggots developed from eggs laid on meat by flies.

   _____ This experiment proved only that the meat had to be exposed to open air in order to develop maggots.

   _____ Redi placed some meat in open jars and in sealed jars.

5. _____ Redi proved that maggots did not arise spontaneously from decaying meat.

   _____ Flies landed on the gauze and laid eggs on the gauze.

   _____ No maggots appeared inside any of the jars.

   _____ Redi placed meat inside jars covered with gauze, allowing free circulation of air.

6. _____ Needham opened and examined the flasks and found them full of microorganisms.

   _____ Needham boiled flasks of broth for a few minutes to kill any microorganisms in them and then he sealed the flasks.

   _____ Needham concluded that microorganisms develop by spontaneous generation.

   _____ Needham repeated the experiment several times and got the same results.

7. _____ Pasteur's experiment disproved the idea of spontaneous generation.

_____ Pasteur filled flasks with broth and then heated the necks of the flasks and drew them out into a long S shape.

_____ The contents were sterilized by boiling.

_____ As long as the flasks were undisturbed, the contents remained sterile despite their being exposed to air.

Part III: Skills Development

Review the skill entitled "Finding the Main Idea" on pages 8–10. Then, look for the main idea in each of the following paragraphs. If the main idea is stated as part of the topic sentence, underline it. If it is merely implied, express it in your own words in the space provided.

At about the time that Redi was performing his experiments, Anton van Leeuwenhoek (LAY ven huke) made the startling discovery of microorganisms in a drop of water. Soon, it was found that when hay or soil was placed in sterile water, millions of microorganisms appeared within a few hours. Here, surely, was a clear-cut case of spontaneous generation! The controversy that Redi had almost put to rest flared up again and raged for the next 200 years.

8. _____

_____

_____

_____

_____

In order to answer this objection and convince the doubters, Redi performed another set of experiments. In these experiments the containers were covered by fine gauze, as shown in Figure 28-16. The gauze allowed the free circulation of air into the containers but kept the flies out of the containers. Redi observed that the flies attempted to reach the meat by landing on the gauze. The flies also deposited eggs on the gauze, which soon developed into maggots. Still, no maggots appeared inside the jars. Redi had proven conclusively that maggots did not arise spontaneously from decaying meat.

9. _____

_____

_____

_____

_____

EVIDENCE OF EVOLUTION
28-5 The Origins of Life — Modern Hypotheses

Part I: Vocabulary Review

Complete the paragraph below by filling in the blanks with the correct vocabulary word.

One problem with **(1)** _____ , the theory that living organisms originate only from other

organisms, is that it does not explain how the first living things originated on earth. To answer this question,

Oparin set forth the **(2)** _____ , which today is the most widely accepted hypothesis of the

origin of life. In this hypothesis, Oparin suggested that the first life forms developed from aggregates of large

proteinlike molecules, called **(3)** _____ , which formed in prehistoric oceans.

Part II: Content Review

Answer each of the following questions in one or two sentences.

4. What assumption did Oparin make about the conditions on the earth billions of years ago? _____

_____

5. What four gases do scientists believe made up the earth's primitive atmosphere? _____

_____

6. What sources of nonbiological energy are thought to have been present on the primitive earth? _____

_____

_____

_____

7. What evidence did Miller and Urey supply to support the heterotroph hypothesis? _____

_____

_____

8. What contribution did Fox make to the heterotroph hypothesis? _____

_____

_____

9. What ingredients have been used in laboratories to form coacervates? _____

_____

10. What hypothesis concerning the chemical makeup of the first organisms has been proposed by Cairns-

Smith? _____

_____

11. If the atmosphere of primitive earth lacked free oxygen, how did the first organisms carry out respiration?

_____

_____

12. What advantage do aerobic organisms have over anaerobic organisms? _____

_____

13. Why are we less affected by ultraviolet light and X rays from the sun today than during the time when the first

life forms were developing? _____

_____

Part III: Skills Development

Review the skill entitled "Making an Outline" on pages 68–69. Then, outline the following passage taken from your textbook on the lines below.

RESPIRATION AND PHOTOSYNTHESIS

Since the atmosphere of the primitive earth contained no free oxygen, it is thought that the first organisms carried on some form of anaerobic respiration to produce energy. This process would release carbon dioxide into the oceans and atmosphere. As the number of heterotrophs increased, the supply of available nutrients in the environment would decrease. Thus, competitions would arise between existing heterotrophs. Any organism with biochemical machinery that enabled it to use different or more complex nutrients than most other heterotrophs would have a distinct advantage. In this way, organisms containing more and more complex biochemical systems could gradually develop.

14. _____

_____

_____

_____

_____

_____

_____

_____

_____

_____

CHAPTER REVIEW

Know the Terms

Match the best answer with each statement or definition.

a. comparative anatomy	**e.** analogous	**i.** embryology
b. homologous	**f.** radioactive dating	**j.** fossils
c. sedimentary rock	**g.** biochemistry	**k.** vestigial
d. extinction	**h.** index fossils	**l.** petrifaction

1. body parts with similar embryological development

2. remnants of structures that functioned in ancestral forms

3. death of all members of a species

4. evolutionary evidence provided by structural similarities

5. use of carbon-14 to determine the age of fossils

6. traces or remains of organisms

7. body parts with similar function but different development

8. replacement of body parts by minerals in water

9. evolutionary evidence from patterns of development

10. evolutionary evidence from DNA and proteins

1. ____
2. ____
3. ____
4. ____
5. ____
6. ____
7. ____
8. ____
9. ____
10. ____

Define or describe the following words.

11. organic evolution: _____

_____

12. geologic evolution: _____

_____

13. spontaneous generation: _____

_____

14. biogenesis: _____

_____

15. heterotroph hypothesis: _____

_____

16. coacervates: _____

_____

17. heterotrophs: _____

_____

Understand the Concepts

Answer the following questions in one or two sentences.

1. Where do evolutionists derive support for their theories? _____

_____

_____

2. How did Francesco Redi help disprove spontaneous generation? _____

_____

_____

3. Why is sedimentary rock important to scientists studying evolution? _____

_____

_____

4. How is relative dating important to the study of evolution? _____

_____

_____

5. What is the difference between relative dating and absolute dating? _____

_____

_____

6. How did Louis Pasteur help disprove spontaneous generation of microorganisms? _____

_____

_____

_____

7. Name two ways each in which soft and hard tissues may become fossilized. _____

_____

_____

_____

8. Describe the changes in Earth's atmosphere from its beginning through to the present. _____

_____

_____

_____

THE MODERN THEORY OF EVOLUTION
29-1 Early Theories of Evolution

Part I: Vocabulary Review

If the statement is true, write TRUE in the space at the left. If the statement is false, make it true by changing the underlined word(s).

_____ **1.** The result of <u>overproduction</u> would be evolution.

_____ **2.** Darwin suggested that organisms with favorable <u>variations</u> would be better able to survive and to reproduce than organisms with <u>unfavorable</u> variations.

_____ **3.** Any inherited trait that improves an organism's chances of survival and reproduction in a given environment is a(n) <u>speciation</u>.

_____ **4.** <u>Adaptation</u> is the formation of new species.

_____ **5.** According to <u>gradualism</u>, evolution occurs slowly and continuously over thousands and millions of years.

_____ **6.** According to <u>natural selection</u>, a species stays the same for extended periods of time and then changes during a brief period of rapid evolution.

Part II: Content Review

Complete each of the following sentences.

7. According to the first principle of Lamarck's theory of evolution, the more an organism uses a particular part of its body, _____

_____

8. Lamarck assumed that the characteristics an organism developed through use and disuse could be _____

_____

9. By cutting off the tails of mice for 22 generations and observing the offspring in each generation, August Weismann demonstrated that _____

_____

_____

10. Charles Lyell proposed that the earth was very old, that it had been slowly changing for millions of years, and that _____

11. When Darwin compared fossil remains with living animals, he observed similarities that suggested the fossil forms _____

_____

12. Darwin observed that while species on the Galapagos Islands resembled species on the mainland, they were always _____

13. Darwin came to believe that the species on the Galapagos Islands had originally come from the mainland and, because of their isolation on different islands, _____
_____

14. According to the ideas of Malthus, the food supply could not keep up with _____
_____

15. The six main points of Darwin's theory involve the concepts of _____
_____
_____

16. Darwin proposed that in the competition for existence, the individuals that have favorable adaptations to their environment will have a greater chance of _____
_____

17. Natural selection means that, in effect, the environment selects _____
_____
_____

18. According to Darwin's theory, over many generations, favorable adaptations gradually _____
_____
_____

19. Two weaknesses of Darwin's theory of natural selection are that it _____
_____
_____
_____
_____

20. At present, scientists do not agree on _____
_____

21. Gradualists believe that links between species are missing from the fossil record because _____
_____

22. The supporters of punctuated evolution argue that links between species are missing from the fossil record because _____
_____

THE MODERN THEORY OF EVOLUTION
29-2   The Synthetic Theory of Evolution

Part I: Vocabulary Review

Compare and contrast the following pairs of terms. First list their similarities, then their differences.

1. synthetic theory and population genetics: _____

_____

_____

_____

2. population and gene pool: _____

_____

_____

_____

3. genetic recombination and genetic drift: _____

_____

_____

_____

_____

4. genetic equilibrium and the Hardy-Weinberg law: _____

_____

_____

_____

_____

Part II: Content Review

Select the best answer for each question and write the letter in the space provided.

_____ 5. What are the units of natural selection?
  a. populations
  b. individuals
  c. species
  d. genera

_____ 6. According to the synthetic theory of evolution, what units evolve?
  a. populations
  b. individuals
  c. mutations
  d. variations

_____ 7. If 5 individuals in a population of 100 have a certain mutant allele, what is the frequency of that allele in the population?
   a. 50 percent
   b. 10 percent
   c. 5 percent
   d. 1 percent

_____ 8. Who included the idea of mutation as part of the theory of evolution?
   a. Hardy
   b. Darwin
   c. De Vries
   d. Weinberg

_____ 9. What is a major source of genetic variation?
   a. chance
   b. genetic equilibrium
   c. gene frequency
   d. gene mutations

_____ 10. What brings about genetic recombination during meiosis?
   a. crossing-over and independent assortment
   b. homologous chromosomes and centrioles
   c. migration and genetic drift
   d. mutation and segregation

_____ 11. What is the movement of individuals into or out of a population called?
   a. crossing-over
   b. independent assortment
   c. migration
   d. segregation

_____ 12. Why is genetic drift usually harmful to small populations?
   a. It increases variations in the gene pool.
   b. It decreases variations in the gene pool.
   c. It maintains genetic equilibrium.
   d. It stops evolution.

_____ 13. Why does the Hardy-Weinberg law never hold true when applied to populations in nature?
   a. because migration always occurs
   b. because mutations and nonrandom reproduction occur
   c. because genetic equilibrium occurs
   d. because genes recombine and segregate

_____ 14. If the allele frequencies of a population show a large variation from the frequencies predicted by the Hardy-Weinberg law, what would you conclude?
   a. no evolutionary change
   b. sexual reproduction
   c. genetic equilibrium
   d. rapid evolutionary change

_____ 15. Why is the Hardy-Weinberg law important?
   a. It allows us to discover whether or not evolution is occurring in a population.
   b. It is a source of genetic variation within a species.
   c. It allows us to predict whether a harmful mutant allele will become useful to the species.
   d. It explains the theories of Darwin and De Vries.

THE MODERN THEORY OF EVOLUTION
29-3 Adaptations and Natural Selection

Part I: Vocabulary Review

Fill in the vocabulary term that best completes each statement.

1. When an organism has a protective adaptation that allows it to blend into a variety of backgrounds, the adaptation is called _____ .

2. When an organism is protected from its enemies by having a noticeable color pattern that the enemy associates with an unpleasant characteristic, such as a bad taste, the adaptation is known as _____ .

3. One kind of organism being protected from its enemies by its resemblance to another species is an example of _____ .

4. One type of natural selection, in which an extreme phenotype becomes a favorable adaptation, is called _____ .

5. A type of natural selection, where the average phenotype is a favorable adaptation and extreme phenotypes are unfavorable, is called _____ .

6. A type of natural selection, where two opposite phenotypes are favorable adaptations and the average phenotype is unfavorable, is termed _____ .

Part II: Content Review

Read each "Cause" and fill in an appropriate "Effect" in the space provided. An example is given below.

CAUSE	EFFECT
7. If a wet climate changes to a very dry climate,	*plants with a heavy cutin layer are most likely to survive and reproduce.*
8. If an animal hibernates,	_____
9. When a flounder is camouflaged against the sandy ocean floor,	_____
10. Because the viceroy butterfly mimics the appearance of the monarch butterfly,	_____
11. When an organism resembles some part of the environment,	_____
12. Since stabilizing selection limits evolution,	_____
13. If two subpopulations become unable to mate with each other,	_____

Part III: Skills Development

Review the skill entitled "Interpreting Diagrams and Tables" on pages 19–21. Then, use the following diagrams to answer the questions below.

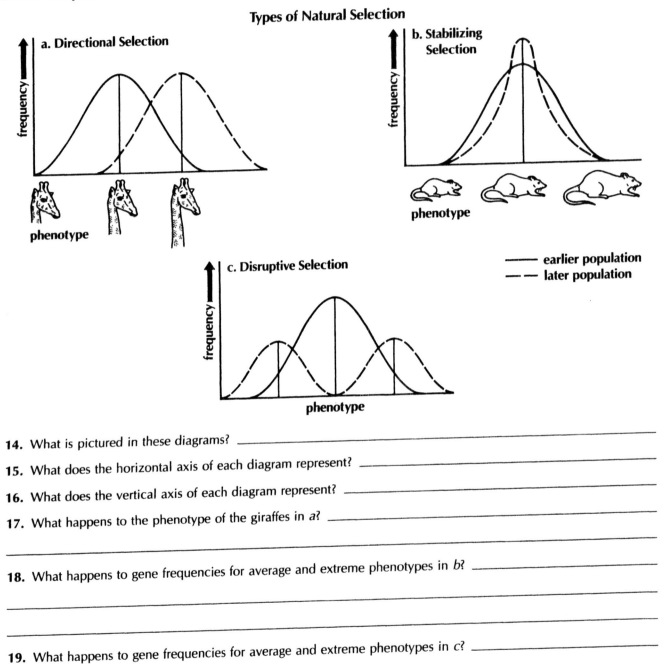

Types of Natural Selection

a. Directional Selection

b. Stabilizing Selection

c. Disruptive Selection

—— earlier population
– — later population

14. What is pictured in these diagrams? _____

15. What does the horizontal axis of each diagram represent? _____

16. What does the vertical axis of each diagram represent? _____

17. What happens to the phenotype of the giraffes in *a*? _____

_____

18. What happens to gene frequencies for average and extreme phenotypes in *b*? _____

_____

_____

19. What happens to gene frequencies for average and extreme phenotypes in *c*? _____

_____

_____

THE MODERN THEORY OF EVOLUTION
29-4 Speciation

Part I: Vocabulary Review

If a statement is true, write TRUE in the space at the left. If a statement is false, make it true by changing the underlined word(s).

_____ 1. The process by which one species evolves into two or more species is called <u>coevolution</u>.

_____ 2. The particular region of the earth where each species is found is called the species' <u>range</u>.

_____ 3. The loss of the ability to interbreed by two isolated groups is called <u>adaptive radiation</u>.

_____ 4. The first step in speciation is <u>reproductive isolation</u>, which occurs when a population is divided by a natural barrier.

_____ 5. The process by which one species evolves into a number of different species with different environments is called <u>convergent evolution</u>.

_____ 6. Natural selection that causes unrelated species to resemble one another is called <u>speciation</u>.

Part II: Content Review

Answer each of the following questions in one or two sentences.

7. Why are the characteristics of a species often different in different parts of its range? _____

_____

_____

_____

8. Why are North American leopard frog populations all considered to be one species even though some subspecies cannot mate successfully? _____

_____

_____

9. How does the isolation of the Kaibab and Abert squirrels illustrate the process of speciation? _____

_____

_____

_____

10. How can scientists tell if species are the result of adaptive radiation? _____

_____

_____

_____

11. What part does the environment of a species play in convergent evolution? _____

_____

_____

12. Why is the relationship between certain flowers and nectar-eating bats considered to be an example of

coevolution? _____

_____

_____

Part III: Skills Development

Review the skill entitled "Making an Outline" on pages 68–69. Then, outline the following passage on the lines below.

COEVOLUTION

Two or more species also can evolve in response to each other through coopera-tive or competitive adaptations. This is called **coevolution.** One example of coevolution is the relationship between flowers and their pollinators. For example, some species of flowers have developed adaptations to attract bees. Bees are active during the day, attracted by bright colors and sweet or minty odors, and usually land on a petal before feeding. Flowers adapted to bees have a sweet or minty odor and are open in the daytime. They have a petal for the bee to land on and are usually bright blue or yellow, because bees cannot see red light. In comparison, bats, which are active at night, feed on the nectar of flowers that are open at night and easily visible in the dark. Coevolution reduces competition between species and benefits both species.

13. _____

_____

_____

_____

_____

_____

_____

_____

_____

_____

_____

_____

THE MODERN THEORY OF EVOLUTION
29-5 Observed Natural Selection

Part I: Vocabulary Review

Replace the italicized definition with the correct vocabulary term.

1. *The development of dark-colored organisms in a population exposed to industrial air pollution* has been

observed among populations of peppered moths in England. _____

Part II: Content Review

Explain why each of the following is important to our understanding of natural selection. The first answer has been written for you.

2. peppered moths: *Industrial melanism has been observed in populations of peppered moths.*

3. industrial air pollution: _____

_____

4. melanin: _____

_____

5. industrial melanism: _____

_____

6. Kettlewell and Tinbergen: _____

_____

_____

7. variability: _____

_____

8. changing environment: _____

_____

9. adaptive trait: _____

_____

10. resistant bacterial strains: _____

_____

_____

11. the Lederbergs: _____

_____

12. *Escherichia coli:* _____

_____

13. streptomycin-resistant bacteria: _____

_____

_____

14. DDT-resistant insects: _____

_____

_____

Part III: Skills Development

Review the skill entitled "Preparing for and Taking a Test" on pages 73–78. Then, practice by preparing to answer the following sample essay question.

What are two examples of observed natural selection?

15. Underline key words and phrases in the essay question.

16. Does the question focus on similarities, differences, examples, reasons, or steps in a process? _____

_____

17. How many parts should the body of your essay contain? _____

18. Fill in the table below to organize your essay.

EXAMPLES	OBSERVED NATURAL SELECTION
1	
2	

Each box in the table corresponds to a paragraph in your essay.

● Pick a box in the table. Enter all the information you want that paragraph to contain.

● Repeat this brainstorming technique until all the boxes are filled in.

● If you run out of time and are unable to finish the essay, you may receive partial credit for the information contained in the table.

19. Compose an introduction, using key words and phrases from the question.

_____

20. Following the organization in Step 18, write your essay. If time permits, correct spelling, punctuation,

and grammar. _____

_____

CHAPTER REVIEW

Know the Terms

Complete the following crossword puzzle.

ACROSS

5. Change that improves chance of survival
6. An adaptation such as migration
7. Resembling another species
8. Differences within a population
9. Formation of new species
10. Developed a theory on evolution

DOWN

1. Group of organisms of the same species
2. Type of selection
3. All the genes in a popultion
4. _____-Weinberg law

Define or describe the following words.

11. adaptive radiation: _____

_____

_____

12. geographic isolation: _____

_____

13. population genetics: _____

_____

CHAPTER REVIEW

Understand the Concepts

Answer each of the following questions in one or two sentences.

1. How are adaptations important in evolution? _____
_____
_____

2. How can geographic isolation result in speciation? _____
_____
_____
_____

3. Explain how two unrelated species in different environments may come to resemble each other. _____
_____
_____
_____

4. Summarize Darwin's theory of natural selection. _____
_____
_____
_____

5. Why might emigration and immigration result in variation within a population? _____
_____
_____
_____

6. Explain the importance of the Hardy-Weinberg law. _____
_____
_____

7. How is industrial melanism a good example of natural selection? _____
_____
_____
_____

MONERANS, PROTISTS, AND VIRUSES
30-1   The Monerans

Part I: Vocabulary Review

Use the clues below to complete the crossword puzzle.

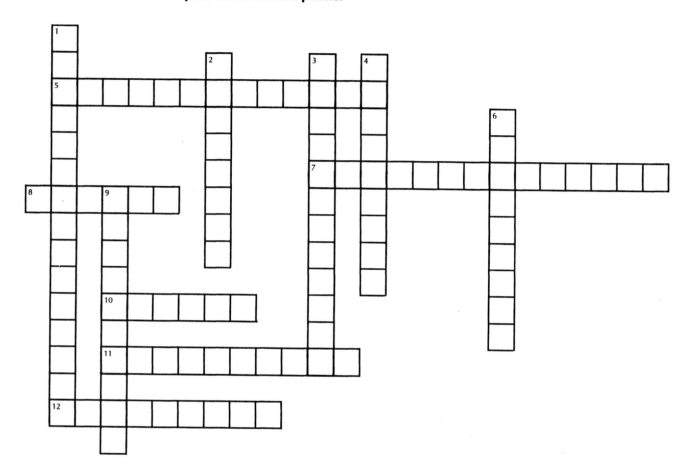

ACROSS

5. Phylum that includes the blue-green bacteria
7. Autotrophic bacteria that live closely with certain marine animals
8. Bacteria are members of this kingdom
10. A spherical bacterial cell
11. Specialized structures enabling some bacteria to withstand unfavorable conditions
12. A spiral-shaped bacterium

DOWN

1. Set of rules that determine whether a specific bacterium causes a specific disease
2. Bacteria that feed on the remains of dead plants and animals
3. Bacteria that retain the stain crystal violet and appear purple under a microscope
4. Harmful, disease-causing bacteria
6. Organisms that live on or in living things
9. Other main branch of the kingdom Monera in addition to the archaebacteria

Part II: Content Review

The sentences below are incorrect statements. Rewrite each sentence to make it correct.

13. Cells that lack a true nucleus, such as bacteria, are called eukaryotic cells. _____

_____

14. Most bacteria are anaerobic, requiring free oxygen to carry out cellular respiration. _____

_____

15. All bacteria reproduce sexually by the process of binary fission. _____

_____

16. A major advance in controlling bacterial disease was the development of tetracycline, the first

antibiotic. _____

_____

17. Bacteria that act as pathogens in the environment are beneficial, as they break down dead plant and animal

tissue into organic substances. _____

_____

Part III: Skills Development

Review the skill entitled "Graphic Organizing: Line Graph" on pages 30–33. Then, after reviewing Section 30-1 in your text, use the graph to answer the following questions.

18. On which axis of the graph is time measured?

_____

19. Are specific units of time represented? _____

20. On which axis is the number of bacteria measured?

_____

21. From the graph, can you determine the exact number of bacteria growing in a culture at a given time? Explain.

_____

22. What does the flat portion of the growth curve represent? Explain. _____

_____

23. What does the entire growth curve reveal about the growth of a bacterial culture? _____

_____

_____

_____

MONERANS, PROTISTS, AND VIRUSES

CHAPTER

30

30-2 The Protists

Part I: Vocabulary Review

Match the terms listed in Column II with the proper definition listed in Column I. Place the answer in the space provided. Each answer may be used only once.

COLUMN I

COLUMN II

_____ 1. photosynthetic, plantlike protists

_____ 2. kingdom consisting of animal-like, plantlike, and funguslike eukaryotes

_____ 3. organisms with glasslike cell walls that are the most numerous of the golden algae

_____ 4. heterotrophic, animal-like protists

_____ 5. rigid outer covering of ciliates that maintains their shape

_____ 6. phylum consisting of the green algae

_____ 7. funguslike protists with a feeding stage characterized by an ameboid plasmodium

_____ 8. animal-like protists that are non-motile and parasitic

_____ 9. single-celled, motile, photosynthetic protists that lack cell walls

_____ 10. protozoa that move and capture prey by means of pseudopods

a. pellicle

b. Euglenophyta

c. Myxomycota

d. algae

e. Chlorophyta

f. Sarcodina

g. protozoa

h. Protista

i. Sporozoa

j. diatoms

Part II: Content Review

Complete each of the statements below.

11. As eukaryotes, members of the kingdom Protista have _____

_____

12. The ciliates are protozoa that use cilia to _____

_____

13. *Trypanosoma gambiense* is a zooflagellate that causes African sleeping sickness in humans by _____

_____

14. Malaria is caused in humans when _____

_____

_____

15. All algae, or plantlike protists, are able to carry on photosynthesis because _____

_____

_____

16. Although the plantlike protist euglena usually carries on photosynthesis, in the absence of light it _____

_____

_____

17. The cell walls of dinoflagellates consist of _____

_____

18. Blooms, known as red tides, are formed when _____

_____

19. The ways in which the funguslike protists resemble fungi are _____

_____

20. The funguslike protists are described as heterotrophs because _____

_____

Part III: Skills Development

Review the skill entitled "Graphic Organizing: Compare/Contrast Matrix" on pages 41–44. Then, complete the matrix below comparing the major characteristics of animal-like, plantlike, and funguslike protists.

21.

CHARACTERISTIC	ANIMAL-LIKE PROTISTS	PLANTLIKE PROTISTS	FUNGUSLIKE PROTISTS
Cell type (eukaryotic vs. prokaryotic)			
Size (unicellular vs. multicellular)			
Nutrition (autotrophic vs. heterotrophic)			
Reproduction (asexual vs. sexual)			
Movement			

MONERANS, PROTISTS, AND VIRUSES

CHAPTER

30

30-3 The Viruses

Part I: Vocabulary Review

Identify the term that fits each of the definitions below. Then, to reveal the biological concept, transfer the letters that have numbers beneath them to the corresponding numbered blank spaces shown below.

1. an RNA virus capable of making DNA from RNA

___ ___ ___ ___ ___ ___ ___ ___ ___ ___
28   9   23   3   1   13

2. cancer-causing genes carried by certain viruses ___ ___ ___ ___ ___ ___ ___ ___ ___
                                                       24   32   17   8   5

3. tiny particles consisting of DNA or RNA surrounded by a protein coat

___ ___ ___ ___ ___ ___ ___
14   4,31   10

4. process in which a bacteriophage attacks, reproduces in, and destroys a bacterial cell

___ ___ ___ ___ ___ ___ ___ ___ ___ ___
12   15   18   26

5. protein coat that surrounds the nucleic acid core of a virus ___ ___ ___ ___ ___ ___ ___
                                                                       27   11,30

6. when a phage and bacterial cell coexist for awhile without destruction of the bacterium

___ ___ ___ ___ ___ ___ ___ ___ ___ ___ ___ ___
20   7   29   33 16   21

7. viruses that attack bacterial cells

___ ___ ___ ___ ___ ___ ___ ___ ___ ___ ___
            19 25   2   6   22

CONCEPT:

___ ___ ___ ___ ___ ___ ___   ___ ___ ___ ___   ___ ___ ___ ___ ___ ___
1   2   3   4   5   6   7   8   9   10 11   12 13 14 15 16 17

___ ___ ___ ___ ___   ___ ___   ___ ___ ___ ___ ___ ___ ___ ___ ___
18 19 20 21 22   23 24   25 26 27 28 29 30 31 32 33

Part II: Content Review

Select the best answer to each question and write the letter in the space provided.

_____ **8.** Viruses are not classified as members of any of the five kingdoms because they
  a. are nonmotile   **c.** lack DNA
  b. are not living cells   **d.** all of the answers given

_____ **9.** Viruses reproduce by
  a. binary fission   **c.** spore formation
  b. mitosis   **d.** attacking living cells

_____ **10.** The genetic makeup of viruses is
  a. DNA only   **c.** either DNA or RNA
  b. RNA only   **d.** both DNA and RNA

_____ **11.** Which of the following is(are) characteristic of viral infections?
  a. are spread in the same ways as bacterial infections
  b. may sometimes be prevented by vaccines
  c. cannot be cured by drugs once they occur
  d. all of the above

_____ **12.** The Sabin vaccine consists of
  a. weakened polio viruses in a flavored drink
  b. polio viruses that have been killed with formaldehyde and then injected
  c. material from cowpox sores used to prevent smallpox
  d. weakened rabies virus used in a series of injections

Part III: Skills Development

Review the skill entitled "Making an Outline" on pages 68–69. Then, outline the following text passage on the lines below.

CHARACTERISTICS OF VIRUSES

Viruses are tiny particles unlike any other living organisms. In fact, scientists do not consider viruses to be living. They are described as somewhere between living cells and nonliving things. Although viruses contain genetic material, they lack all other cell structures necessary for metabolism, reproduction, and growth. A virus consists of genetic material—DNA or RNA—wrapped in a protein coat. Since viruses are not cells, they are not included as members of any of the five kingdoms.

  A virus particle cannot reproduce, or *replicate*, unless it is inside a living host cell. Therefore, viruses survive by attacking a living cell, using the cell's machinery to reproduce. This parasitic invasion of plant and animal cells leads to a wide variety of diseases. In humans, viruses cause many infectious diseases that range from the common cold to rabies and acquired immune deficiency syndrome (AIDS).

13. _____

_____

_____

_____

_____

_____

_____

_____

_____

_____

_____

_____

CHAPTER REVIEW

CHAPTER **30**

Know the Terms

Complete the following paragraphs using the word list below. **You may use a word more than once or not at all.**

fungi	decomposer	Protista	algae
prokaryotic	bacteria	blue-green bacteria	protozoa
viruses	eukaryotic	slime mold	animals
Monera	nucleus	photosynthetic	nonliving

Living organisms on this planet are generally classified as __(1)__ (simplest) or __(2)__ (more complex). Members of the first group belong to kingdom __(3)__ because they lack a true __(4)__. The members that are not photosynthetic are known as __(5)__, and the photosynthesizers are called __(6)__.

The kingdom __(7)__ contains many varieties of organisms. They are __(8)__ because they possess a true __(9)__. The three major groups are the animallike, called __(10)__; the plantlike, which are __(11)__ and are called __(12)__; and the fungilike, most of which are known as __(13)__.

One group of organisms that do not fit in any other group is known as __(14)__. They are considered by some biologists to be __(15)__.

1. _____

2. _____

3. _____

4. _____

5. _____

6. _____

7. _____

8. _____

9. _____

10. _____

11. _____

12. _____

13. _____

14. _____

15. _____

Define or describe the following terms.

16. fission: _____

_____

17. decomposers: _____

_____

18. antibiotic: _____

_____

19. vaccination: _____

_____

20. conjugation: _____

_____

CHAPTER REVIEW

Understand the Concepts

Answer the following questions in one or two sentences.

1. How do scientists classify algae? _____

_____

_____

2. Briefly explain the difference between prokaryotic and eukaryotic cells. _____

_____

_____

3. How are bacteria classified? _____

_____

4. How do viruses reproduce? _____

_____

_____

_____

5. How do bacteria cause disease? _____

_____

_____

6. How can bacterial growth be controlled? _____

_____

_____

7. Upon what basis are protozoans classified into phyla? _____

_____

_____

8. Describe the structure of a virus. _____

_____

_____

9. What is a pathogen? _____

_____

FUNGI AND PLANTS
31-1 Fungi

Part I: Vocabulary Review

If the statement is true, write TRUE in the space at the left. If the statement is false, make it true by replacing the underlined term(s).

_____ 1. In the conjugation fungi, such as *Rhizopus*, digestive enzymes are secreted by rootlike hyphae called rhizoids.

_____ 2. A(n) lichen is made up of an alga and a fungus living together.

_____ 3. The phylum Basidiomycota includes the sac fungi, such as powdery mildews, blue and green molds, and yeasts.

_____ 4. A(n) ascus is formed from a tangled mass of hyphae.

_____ 5. Fungi are nongreen organisms that include yeasts, molds, mushrooms, and rusts and smuts.

_____ 6. The imperfect fungi are members of the phylum Deuteromycota, and are not known to have a sexual phase of reproduction.

_____ 7. Hyphae that grow over the surface of food, giving rise to sporangiophores are called stolons.

_____ 8. Zygomycota are threadlike filaments forming the bodies of most fungi.

Part II: Content Review

Answer each of the following questions in one or two sentences.

9. How do fungi obtain nutrients? _____

_____

10. Why are fungi important in decomposition? _____

_____

_____

11. What are the black dots that are visible in the common bread mold, *Rhizopus?* What function do they serve?

_____

_____

_____

12. What are the two kinds of spores produced by the sac fungi? How do they differ? _____

_____

_____

13. Where are spores located in mushrooms? _____

_____

14. What are some ways in which fungi are beneficial to humans? (Identify at least two.) _____

_____

_____

_____

15. How do both the alga and fungus benefit when living together in a lichen? _____

_____

_____

Part III: Skills Development

Review the skill entitled "Interpreting Diagrams and Tables" on pages 19–21. Then, identify each lettered structure in the diagram below. Complete the chart by filling in the name of each lettered structure and its function.

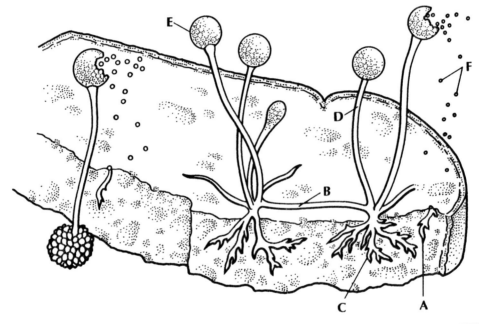

16.

STRUCTURE	FUNCTION
A.	
B.	
C.	
D.	
E.	
F.	

FUNGI AND PLANTS
31-2 Plants

Part I: Vocabulary Review

Compare and contrast the following pairs of terms. First list their similarities, then their differences.

1. Bryophyta and Tracheophyta: _____

_____

_____

_____

2. whisk ferns and club mosses: _____

_____

_____

3. gymnosperms and angiosperms: _____

_____

_____

4. conifers and cycads: _____

_____

_____

_____

Part II: Content Review

Select the best answer to each question and write the letter in the space provided.

_____ 5. Which of the following describe(s) plants?
　　　　a. They are multicellular.
　　　　b. They are photosynthetic.
　　　　c. They all grow and reproduce on land.
　　　　d. a, b, and c

_____ 6. Into which of the following two main groups are plants divided?
　　　　a. bryophytes and tracheophytes
　　　　b. mosses and ferns
　　　　c. gymnosperms and angiosperms
　　　　d. monocots and dicots

_____ 7. Because they lack both vascular and supporting tissues, bryophytes
　　　　a. transport materials by the process of diffusion
　　　　b. must live near water
　　　　c. are usually short
　　　　d. a, b, and c

_____ 8. Which of the following describes whisk ferns, club mosses, horsetails, and ferns?
　　　　a. nonphotosynthetic
　　　　b. spore-dispersing
　　　　c. seed-bearing
　　　　d. nonvascular

_____ 9. In ferns, the roots grow out from horizontal stems called
　　　　a. buds
　　　　b. collars
　　　　c. rhizomes
　　　　d. rushes

_____ **10.** The seeds of angiosperms are enclosed within
  a. flowers
  b. cones
  c. spores
  d. fruits

_____ **11.** The difference between monocots and dicots is that
  a. monocots have exposed seeds
  b. monocots reproduce by means of spores
  c. monocots contain only one seed leaf
  d. monocots are nonvascular plants

_____ **12.** The dominant and most successful plants are the
  a. vascular seed plants
  b. nonvascular plants
  c. nonflowering plants
  d. vascular spore-dispersing plants

_____ **13.** Which of the following is *NOT* associated with gymnosperms?
  a. vascular tissue
  b. seeds
  c. cones
  d. flowers

_____ **14.** Which group of spore-dispersing plants represents the remains of a group of plants that also flourished during the Carboniferous period?
  a. club mosses
  b. whisk ferns
  c. horsetails
  d. ferns

Part III: Skills Development

Review the skill entitled "Graphic Organizing: Word Map" on pages 45–48. Then complete the following word maps for the terms *Bryophyta* and *gymnosperms*.

15.

16.

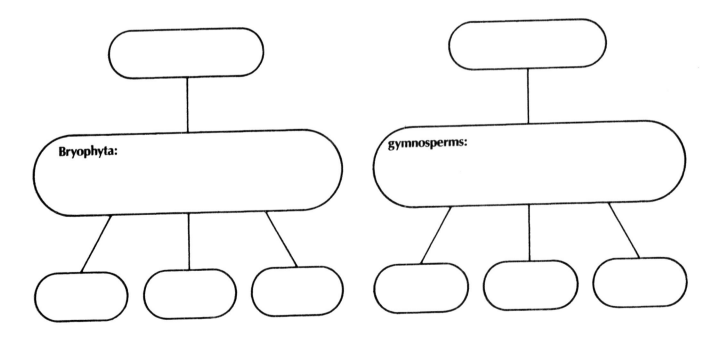

CHAPTER REVIEW

Know the Terms

Complete the following crossword puzzle.

ACROSS

1. Flowering seed plant
4. Bears cones
5. Have leaves coiled in fiddleheads
7. Hyphae that grow over food
8. Top of a mushroom
9. Spore-producing structure
10. Vascular plants

DOWN

2. Nonflowering seed plants
3. Mosses and liverworts
5. Kingdoms, including yeasts, molds, and mushrooms
6. Fungus and alga living together

Define or describe the following words.

11. hypha: _____
_____

12. mycelium: _____
_____

13. rhizoids: _____
_____

CHAPTER REVIEW

Understand the Concepts

Answer each of the following questions in one or two sentences.

1. Explain why bryophytes are generally small and grow where moisture is abundant. _____
_____
_____
_____

2. Why do you suppose that many fungi are saprobes or parasites? _____
_____
_____

3. What features make tracheophytes more advanced than bryophytes? _____
_____
_____
_____

4. Which generation is predominant in the life cycle of bryophytes? _____
_____

5. Which generation is predominant in the life cycle of tracheophytes? _____
_____

6. What adaptations were necessary in plants for life on land? _____
_____
_____

7. What is thought to be the evolutionary relationship between the major plant groups? _____
_____
_____

8. How does reproduction differ in gymnosperms and angiosperms? _____
_____
_____

9. Describe the two major groups of angiosperms. _____
_____
_____

INVERTEBRATES — SPONGES TO MOLLUSKS
32-1 The Animal Kingdom

Part I: Vocabulary Review

Complete the following crossword puzzle.

ACROSS

4. Animal kingdom
5. Type of symmetry shown by the human body
8. Type of symmetry shown by hydra
9. The study of animals
11. Tail end of an animal
12. Animals without backbones

DOWN

1. Belly side of an animal
2. Young animal forms that undergo developmental changes before producing an adult form
3. Type of symmetry shown by the protist rodiolarian
6. Animals with backbones
7. Head end of an animal
10. Upper or back side of an animal

Part II: Content Review

The sentences below are incorrect statements. Rewrite the sentences to make them correct.

13. Kingdom Animalia is the smallest of the five kingdoms of organisms. _____

_____

14. Zoologists divide the animal kingdom into about 30 species. _____

_____

_____

15. When a body is asymmetrical, it can be cut into two halves that have matching shapes. _____

_____

_____

16. A baseball has radial symmetry. _____

17. In spherical symmetry, there is a central axis that runs the length of the animal from top to bottom or from

front to rear. _____

_____

18. Most animals showing radial symmetry either drift in water or are active swimmers. _____

_____

19. Frogs show spherical symmetry. _____

20. Bilaterally symmetrical animals have a dorsal and an anterior side. _____

_____

Part III: Skills Development

Review the skill entitled "Graphic Organizing: Concept Map" on pages 49–55. Then, complete the concept map below.

21.

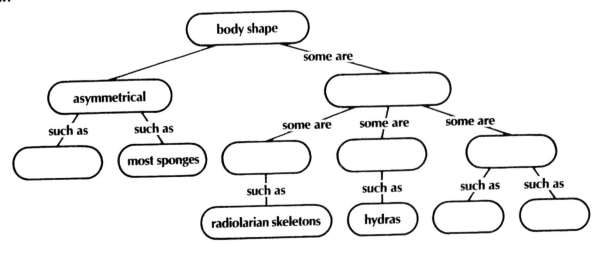

INVERTEBRATES — SPONGES TO MOLLUSKS

CHAPTER **32**

32-2 Sponges and Coelenterates

Part I: Vocabulary Review

Below are groups of terms related to the study of this section. In each group, cross out one word that does not belong and explain the relationship of the remaining four terms.

1. Porifera
pores
polyp
collar cells
spicules

_____
_____
_____
_____

2. collar cells
spicules
spongin
gemmules
cnidoblasts

_____
_____
_____
_____

3. Coelenterata
osculum
polyp
medusa
gastrovascular cavity

_____
_____
_____
_____

4. gemmules
mesoglea
cnidoblasts
nematocysts
planula

_____
_____
_____
_____

Part II: Content Review

Select the best answer for each question and write the letter in the space provided.

_____ **5.** What does Porifera mean?
    a. poorly structured
    b. internal skeleton
    c. pore bearing
    d. dorsal orientation

_____ **6.** In what type of environment do all sponges live?
    a. aquatic
    b. marine
    c. freshwater
    d. land

_____ **7.** How many cell layers are found in a sponge?
    a. one
    b. two
    c. three
    d. four

INVERTEBRATES — SPONGES TO MOLLUSKS

32-2 Sponges and Coelenterates (continued)

_____ 8. Of what substances are the three kinds of spicules made?
   a. calcium compounds, silica, spongin
   b. potassium, mesoglea, amebocytes
   c. carbonate compounds, endoderm, dissolved oxygen
   d. gemmules, jellylike material, cytoplasm

_____ 9. What circulates the water in the central cavity of the sponge?
   a. spicules
   b. spongin
   c. amebocytes
   d. collar cells

_____ 10. What cells finish digesting food and then carry nutrients to other parts of the sponge?
   a. spicules
   b. spongin
   c. amebocytes
   d. collar cells

_____ 11. How do wastes leave the sponge?
   a. through the osculum
   b. through the pores
   c. through the collar cells
   d. through the gemmules

_____ 12. How do sponges reproduce?
   a. only sexually
   b. both sexually and asexually
   c. only asexually
   d. by budding only

_____ 13. Into what structures can some collar cells develop?
   a. spicules
   b. buds
   c. gametes
   d. polyps

_____ 14. What coelenterate body form do jellyfish show?
   a. polyp
   b. medusa
   c. gemmule
   d. asymmetrical

_____ 15. What kind of symmetry do most adult coelenterates show?
   a. bilateral
   b. spherical
   c. radial
   d. asymmetrical

_____ 16. What is the function of coelenterate cnidoblasts?
   a. defense and food capture
   b. filtering water
   c. digestion and food transport
   d. reproduction

_____ 17. What do some nematocysts contain?
   a. gemmules
   b. gametes
   c. poison
   d. digestive enzymes

_____ 18. Where does extracellular digestion take place in coelenterates?
   a. in the mesoglea
   b. in the nematocysts
   c. in the cnidoblasts
   d. in the gastrovascular cavity

_____ 19. What coordinating structures are found in coelenterates, but not in sponges?
   a. brains
   b. nerve cells
   c. tentacles
   d. gemmules

_____ 20. What is the free-swimming larval form of *Aurelia* called?
   a. planula
   b. mesoglea
   c. medusa
   d. polyp

_____ 21. Which form of *Aurelia* reproduces sexually by producing eggs and sperm?
   a. planula
   b. mesoglea
   c. medusa
   d. polyp

INVERTEBRATES — SPONGES TO MOLLUSKS

CHAPTER **32**

32-3   Flatworms and Roundworms

Part I: Vocabulary Review

Replace the italicized definition with the correct vocabulary term.

1. *The simplest invertebrate group showing bilateral symmetry* is also known as the flatworms. _____

_____

2. *The class that contains planarians* includes free-living flatworms with eyespots. _____

3. The *muscular tube that can be extended through the mouth of the planarian* pulls in bits of food into the

digestive cavity of planarians. _____

4. *One class of parasitic flatworms that includes the fluke* has a body covered with thick cuticle and suckers that

allow attachment to the tissues of a host. _____

5. *One class of parasitic flatworms that includes the beef tapeworm* has square body segments, or proglottids,

that produce both eggs and sperm. _____

6. The *segmentlike reproductive structures of the tapeworm* are found below the head and neck of the

tapeworm. _____

7. Members of *the phylum that consists of roundworms* are either free-living or parasitic and have elongated,

cylindrical bodies that are tapered at both ends. _____

Part II: Content Review

For each statement below, decide whether it relates to flatworms or roundworms or both of these phyla. Write "F" for flatworms, "R" for roundworms, or "B" for both.

_____ 8. This phylum contains parasitic worms.

_____ 9. Trichinosis is caused by trichina larvae that are ingested when humans eat undercooked pork.

_____ 10. These animals show bilateral symmetry.

_____ 11. Planaria have no skeletal, circulatory, or respiratory system.

_____ 12. Blood flukes can bore through human skin if the host is wading or swimming in water where the fluke lives.

_____ 13. Pinworms often infect children.

_____ 14. Elephantiasis is caused by filaria.

_____ 15. These worms are the simplest animals with mesodermic layers and organ-system levels of organization.

_____ 16. These worms are the simplest animals having a complete digestive system with two openings and a tube-within-a-tube body plan.

_____ 17. These worms have a nervous system.

_____ 18. Parasitic forms may have life cycles with more than one host.

_____ 19. Indigestible materials are expelled through the mouth in many members of this phylum.

_____ 20. Flame cells are found in some members of this phylum.

_____ 21. Symptoms of hookworm infection include anemia and lack of energy.

_____ 22. Tapeworms are a parasitic member of this phylum.

_____ 23. Schistosomiasis is caused by a member of this phylum.

Part III: Skills Development

Review the skill entitled "Making an Outline" on pages 68–69. Then, outline the following passage on the lines below.

CHARACTERISTICS OF ROUNDWORMS

The phylum **Nematoda** (nem uh TOHD uh) consists of slender, bilaterally symmetrical *nematodes* (NEM uh tohdz), or *roundworms*. Roundworms have elongated, cylindrical bodies that are tapered at both ends and covered with a tough cuticle. Roundworms range in length from less than one millimeter to more than one meter. Many roundworms are free-living, while others are parasitic. The free-living forms are found in fresh water, salt water, and in soil anywhere from the polar regions to the tropics. They feed on algae, plant sap, and decaying organic matter. Parasitic roundworms live on or in most kinds of plants and animals. The actual number of roundworms present in the environment is tremendous. It has been estimated that 1 million or more roundworms are present in one shovel load of garden soil.

24. _____

_____

_____

_____

_____

_____

_____

_____

_____

_____

_____

_____

_____

INVERTEBRATES —
SPONGES TO MOLLUSKS
32-4 Segmented Worms and Mollusks

Part I: Vocabulary Review

Compare and contrast the following pairs of terms. First list their similarities, then their differences.

1. Annelida and Mollusca: _____

_____

_____

_____

2. Oligochaeta and Polychaeta: _____

_____

_____

3. Hirudinea and Cephalopoda: _____

_____

_____

_____

4. parapodia and trochophore larva: _____

_____

_____

_____

5. coelem and mantle: _____

_____

_____

_____

6. Bivalvia and Gastropoda: _____

_____

_____

7. foot and radula: _____

_____

_____

Part II: Content Review

Complete each of the following sentences.

8. Four characteristics of segmented worms are _____

_____

9. In the tube-within-a-tube body plan of segmented worms, the inner tube and the outer tube consist of _____

_____

10. The first and second segments of *Nereis* are called, respectively, _____

_____

11. Two functions of parapodia in *Nereis* are _____

_____

12. Four body systems and functions that are basically the same in *Nereis* and in the earthworm are _____

_____

13. The saliva of the leech has an enzyme that _____

_____

14. The three major classes of mollusks are _____

_____

15. Four characteristics shared by all mollusks are _____

_____

16. Four structures that are found only in mollusks include _____

_____

17. In some bivalves, pearls are produced when _____

_____

18. Water enters and leaves a clam by _____

_____

19. Filter feeders, such as clams, feed on _____

_____

20. The land snail feeds by _____

_____

21. Most cephalopods do not look like other mollusks because _____

_____

CHAPTER REVIEW

Know the Terms

Match each phylum with the appropriate example(s).

a. Porifera   **c.** Platyhelminthes   **e.** Annelida
b. Coelenterata   **d.** Nematoda   **f.** Molluska

1. earthworm   **1.** ____

2. clam   **2.** ____

3. trichina   **3.** ____

4. sponge   **4.** ____

5. hydra   **5.** ____

6. planaria   **6.** ____

7. jellyfish   **7.** ____

8. tapeworm   **8.** ____

9. fluke   **9.** ____

10. leech   **10.** ____

11. snail   **11.** ____

12. pinworm   **12.** ____

Define or describe the following words.

13. invertebrate: _____

_____

14. vertebrate: _____

_____

15. radial symmetry: _____

_____

16. bilateral symmetry: _____

_____

17. dorsal: _____

18. ventral: _____

19. anterior: _____

20. posterior: _____

CHAPTER REVIEW

Understand the Concepts

Answer each of the following questions in one or two sentences.

1. What distinguishes animals from other living organisms? _____
_____
_____
_____

2. Why are sponges considered the least complex animals? _____
_____
_____

3. Distinguish between a polyp and a medusa. _____
_____
_____
_____

4. How are waste removal and gas exchange accomplished in simple animals? _____
_____

5. What characteristics make flatworms more complex than coelenterates? _____
_____
_____

6. Of what medical importance are flukes, tapeworms, and many roundworms? _____
_____
_____

7. What types of structural advancements do roundworms show over the lower animal phyla? _____
_____
_____
_____

8. How are annelids more complex than roundworms? _____
_____

9. How do mollusks protect their soft body tissues? _____
_____

INVERTEBRATES — ARTHROPODS AND ECHINODERMS

33-1 Arthropods: Crustaceans

Part I: Vocabulary Review

Match the terms listed in Column II with the proper definition listed in Column I. Place the answer in the space provided.

COLUMN I

_____ 1. copper-containing respiratory pigment found in crayfish

_____ 2. jaws that crush food by moving from side to side

_____ 3. process in which the exoskeleton is shed and replaced

_____ 4. arthropod class that includes shrimp

_____ 5. delicate, plumelike structures where exchange of respiratory gases occurs

_____ 6. fused head and thorax segments

_____ 7. middle region of an arthropod's body

_____ 8. phylum of invertebrates with segmented bodies; paired, jointed appendages; and exoskeletons

_____ 9. posterior region of an arthropod's body

COLUMN II

a. Arthropoda

b. Crustacea

c. cephalothorax

d. thorax

e. hemocyanin

f. abdomen

g. molting

h. gills

i. mandibles

Part II: Content Review

Answer each of the following questions in one or two sentences.

10. About how many known species of arthropods are there? _____

_____

_____

11. How are arthropod appendages adapted for many different functions? _____

_____

_____

_____

12. What is the exoskeleton of arthropods made of and what is its function? _____

_____

_____

13. Into what three regions are the bodies of most arthropods divided? _____

_____

_____

14. Why are arthropods described as having a well-developed nervous system? _____

15. What kind of circulatory system do arthropods have? _____

16. Why are microscopic crustaceans important to many larger marine animals? _____

17. What substance makes the exoskeleton of the crayfish hard? _____

18. What is the function of the crayfish's carapace? _____

19. What special function do swimmerets serve in female crayfish? _____

20. What body parts can a crayfish regenerate? _____

21. Upon what does the crayfish feed? _____

22. In the crayfish, where does its food get chewed and digested? _____

23. Where does the crayfish excrete the wastes that are removed from the blood by the green glands? _____

24. What blood vessels are lacking in the crayfish? _____

25. In the crayfish, what keeps water flowing through the gill chambers? _____

26. What kinds of sensory organs does the crayfish have? _____

27. In crayfish during what time of year does mating occur and when are the eggs laid? _____

INVERTEBRATES — ARTHROPODS AND ECHINODERMS

33-2 Arthropods: Centipedes to Arachnids

Part I: Vocabulary Review

If the statement is true, write TRUE in the space at the left. If the statement is false, make it true by changing the underlined word.

_____ 1. Centipedes belong to the class <u>Diplopoda</u>.

_____ 2. Millipedes belong to the class <u>Chilopoda</u>.

_____ 3. Spiders, scorpions, ticks, mites, and daddy longlegs belong to the class <u>Arachnida</u>.

_____ 4. The first pair of arachnid appendages are the fang-like <u>pedipalps</u>.

_____ 5. The second pair of arachnid appendages, the <u>cheliceras</u>, is sensitive both to chemicals and to touch.

_____ 6. The respiratory organs of the arachnids are called <u>spinnerets</u>.

_____ 7. There are three pairs of <u>spinnerets</u> at the end of a spider's abdomen.

Part II: Content Review

Select the best answer for each question and write the letter in the space provided.

_____ 8. What is the most common number of pairs of legs in centipedes?
a. about 300
b. about 150
c. about 35
d. about 12

_____ 9. Where would you expect to find centipedes in nature?
a. under a log
b. on the ocean floor
c. in the desert
d. in a stream

_____ 10. How many pairs of legs does each body segment of a centipede usually have?
a. four pairs of legs
b. three pairs of legs
c. two pairs of legs
d. one pair of legs

_____ 11. In what way is the common house centipede helpful to humans?
a. They eat plants.
b. They eat cockroaches and bedbugs.
c. They hide in dark places.
d. They eat dead plant and animal remains.

_____ 12. How many pairs of legs do millipedes usually have on each body segment?
a. four pairs of legs
b. three pairs of legs
c. two pairs of legs
d. one pair of legs

_____ 13. What do millipedes eat?
a. decaying plant matter
b. snails
c. insects
d. scorpions

_____ **14.** How do millipedes protect themselves?
  a. with poison claws
  b. by biting and clawing
  c. by spitting
  d. by rolling up or giving off an unpleasant odor

_____ **15.** What kind of arachnid transmits diseases, such as Lyme disease and Rocky Mountain spotted fever?
  a. spiders
  b. scorpions
  c. ticks
  d. mites

_____ **16.** Why are spiders usually helpful to humans?
  a. They make webs.
  b. They spin silk.
  c. They eat insects.
  d. They lay their eggs outside.

_____ **17.** Which of the following is an example of a poisonous spider that can harm humans?
  a. garden spider
  b. brown recluse
  c. orb-weaving spider
  d. wolf spider

_____ **18.** What main parts make up the body of an arachnid?
  a. cephalothorax and abdomen
  b. head, thorax, and abdomen
  c. legs and abdomen
  d. cephalothorax and legs

_____ **19.** What pair of appendages does a spider use to pierce its prey?
  a. spinnerets
  b. cheliceras
  c. pedipalps
  d. walking legs

_____ **20.** How many walking legs do arachnids have?
  a. 2 legs
  b. 4 legs
  c. 6 legs
  d. 8 legs

_____ **21.** Where does respiratory gas exchange occur in arachnids?
  a. cheliceras
  b. pedipalps
  c. book lungs
  d. cephalothorax

_____ **22.** What are spinnerets used for in spiders?
  a. to transfer sperm
  b. to paralyze prey
  c. to spin silk
  d. to walk

INVERTEBRATES —
ARTHROPODS AND ECHINODERMS
33-3 Arthropods: Insects

Part I: Vocabulary Review

Compare and contrast the following pairs of terms. First list their similarities, then their differences.

1. incomplete metamorphosis and complete metamorphosis: _____

_____

_____

_____

_____

2. nymphs and pupa: _____

_____

_____

_____

_____

3. Coleoptera and Diptera: _____

_____

_____

_____

_____

4. spiracles and ovipositor: _____

_____

_____

_____

_____

Part II: Content Review

Read each "Cause" and fill in an appropriate "Effect" in the space provided. An example is given below.

CAUSE	EFFECT
5 . Because insects have the ability to fly,	*they can travel great distances.*
6. Since there is tremendous variation in insect adaptations for feeding and reproduction,	_____
	_____
	_____

7. Because insects are small, _____

8. When an insect nymph molts, _____

9. When insects undergo complete metamorphosis, _____

10. During the pupal stage, _____

11. When insect larvae secrete the molting hormone, _____

12. When an insect larva secretes the juvenile hormone, _____

13. When scientists use sex attractants called pheromones, _____

Part III: Skills Development

Review the skill entitled "Graphic Organizing: Compare/Contrast Matrix" on pages 41–44. Then complete the matrix below.

14.

CHARACTERISTIC	HONEYBEE	MOSQUITO	TERMITE
Order			
Habitat			
Number of wings			
Mouthparts			
Economic importance			

INVERTEBRATES —
ARTHROPODS AND ECHINODERMS
33-4 Arthropods: Echinoderms

Part I: Vocabulary Review

Replace the italicized definition with the correct vocabulary term.

1. Members of *the phylum that includes starfish, sea urchins, sea cucumbers, and sand dollars* are all marine animals and live mainly on the ocean floor. _____

2. The *network of water-filled canals that is found only in echinoderms* helps starfish move about and get food.

_____

3. *Water-carrying channels* run into each arm of the starfish. _____

4. Extending from the ventral surface of the arms of a starfish are *water-filled tubes, each ending in a suction disk.* _____

Part II: Content Review

The sentences below are incorrect statements. Rewrite the sentences to make them correct.

5. Among the echinoderms, both the larvae and the adults are bilaterally symmetrical. _____

_____

_____

6. Echinoderms lack a coelom. _____

_____

7. The echinoderm skeleton consists of soft plates that are outside of the body. _____

_____

_____

8. In echinoderms, the blastopore becomes the mouth, and the anus forms at a later stage opposite the mouth.

_____

_____

_____

9. The pattern of development of echinoderms is completely unlike that of vertebrates, suggesting no evolutionary relationship. _____

_____

_____

10. The sieve plate of a starfish prevents water from entering the canals of the water-vascular system. _____

_____

11. When the bulb of an echinoderm tube foot contracts, water is forced into the tube foot, causing it to shorten.

_____

_____

12. In feeding, the starfish uses its stomach to pry open its prey. _____

_____

13. The starfish uses the tube feet on its arms to stuff food into its stomach. _____

_____

14. Respiration in the starfish occurs by diffusion of gases across the skin gills and the sieve plate. _____

_____

_____

15. Excretion takes place by diffusion through the anus of the starfish. _____

_____

_____

16. Starfish are hermaphrodites. _____

_____

17. In starfish, fertilization is internal. _____

_____

18. The larvae of starfish are sessile. _____

_____

19. Starfish are unable to regenerate missing parts. _____

_____

Part III: Skills Development

Review the skill entitled "Graphic Organizing: Flow Chart" on pages 34–37. Then complete the flow chart below to show the steps involved when a starfish feeds on a clam.

20.

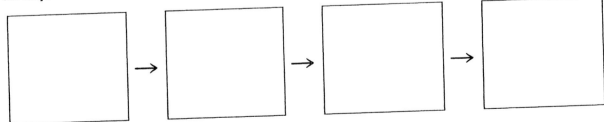

CHAPTER REVIEW

Know the Terms

Match the characteristics or examples with the correct phylum or class. An answer
may be used more than once.

a. Arthropoda   **d.** Chilopoda   **g.** Insecta
b. Echinodermata   **e.** Diplopoda
c. Crustacea   **f.** Arachnida

1. bilateral symmetry (phylum)

2. radial symmetry (phylum)

3. shrimp (class)

4. centipedes (class)

5. jointed legs (phylum)

6. water-vascular system (phylum)

7. segmented body (phylum)

8. spider (class)

9. chitinous exoskeleton (phylum)

10. starfish (phylum)

11. lobster (class)

12. millipedes (class)

13. open circulatory system
    (phylum)

14. six legs (class)

15. one pair of legs per segment
    (class)

16. skin gills (phylum)

17. tick (class)

18. sea urchin (phylum)

19. spinnerets (class)

20. two pair of legs per segment
    (class)

1. _____   11. _____

2. _____   12. _____

3. _____   13. _____

4. _____

5. _____   14. _____

6. _____   15. _____

7. _____   16. _____

8. _____   17. _____

9. _____   18. _____

10. _____   19. _____

                   20. _____

Define or describe the following words.

21. cephalothorax: _____

_____

22. entomology: _____

_____

23. metamorphosis: _____

_____

24. pupa: _____

_____

25. ovipositor: _____

_____

CHAPTER REVIEW

Understand the Concepts

Answer the following questions in one or two sentences.

1. What is the function of antennules on a crayfish? ————————————————————

——

——

2. What is the function of the green gland in a crayfish? ————————————————

——

——

3. What is the ecological value of spiders? ————————————————————————

——

——

4. Why are insects so successful? ————————————————————————————

——

——

——

——

5. Explain the stages of incomplete metamorphosis. ————————————————————

——

——

——

6. Explain the stages of complete metamorphosis. ————————————————————

——

——

——

7. Explain respiration in starfish. ————————————————————————————

——

——

8. Use the development of starfish to explain their place in evolution. ————————

——

——

——

VERTEBRATES—FISHES TO REPTILES

CHAPTER **34**

34-1 The Chordates

Part I: Vocabulary Review

Use the clues below to complete the crossword puzzle.

ACROSS

3. Largest chordate subphylum
6. Warm-blooded
8. Subphylum that includes the lancelets
9. Structure found in pairs in the throat region of all chordates during some part of their lives

DOWN

1. Flexible, rodlike, internal supporting structure characteristic of chordates
2. Dorsal, hollow structure found in chordates
4. Chordate phylum
5. Subphylum that includes the tunicates
7. Cold-blooded

Part II: Content Review

Explain why each of the following is important to gaining an understanding of chordates. The first example has been completed for you.

10. Urochordata and Cephalochordata: *Members of these two subphyla are considered to be more primitive*

than vertebrates. _____

11. nerve cord: _____

_____

12. notochord: _____

13. gill slits: _____

14. tunicates: _____

_____

15. amphioxus: _____

_____

16. vertebrates: _____

17. spinal column: _____

_____

18. brain: _____

_____

19. head, neck, and trunk: _____

_____

20. tail: _____

21. jointed, internal skeleton: _____

22. two pairs of appendages: _____

23. heart with two to four chambers: _____

24. closed circulatory system: _____

25. hemoglobin: _____

26. gills: _____

27. lungs: _____

28. coelom: _____

_____

29. two layers of skin: _____

_____

VERTEBRATES—FISHES TO REPTILES
34-2   The Fishes

Part I: Vocabulary Review

Select the most appropriate words from the following list to complete the paragraph.

operculum   swim bladder
Chondrichthyes   Myxini
Osteichthyes   Cephalaspidomorphi
lateral lines

The most primitive of all living vertebrates are the jawless fishes. One class of jawless fishes, the __(1)_____

_____ , includes the lampreys. The other class, __(2)_____ , includes hagfishes.

The cartilaginous fishes, class __(3)_____ , include sharks, rays, and skates. Sharks are very

sensitive to vibrations because of __(4)_____ , which extend along each side of their bodies.

The bony fishes, class __(5)_____ , are the largest class of vertebrates. The gills of bony fishes

are protected by a bony flap called an __(6)_____ . Most bony fishes have a gas-filled sac

called a __(7)_____   that regulates their buoyancy.

Part II: Content Review

For each statement below, decide whether it relates to jawless fishes, cartilaginous fishes, or bony fishes. Write "J" for jawless fishes, "C" for cartilaginous fishes, and "B" for bony fishes.

_____ **8.** In members of this group, the skeleton is made entirely of cartilage, and traces of the notochord are present in the adult.

_____ **9.** These fishes have long, snakelike bodies and smooth skins with no scales.

_____ **10.** Most members of this group have bony skeletons, paired fins, and protective, overlapping scales.

_____ **11.** Almost all members of this group live in salt water.

_____ **12.** Fertilization is internal in many members of this group.

_____ **13.** These fishes lack paired fins and true jaws.

_____ **14.** The fins of these fishes are made of skin webbing, which is usually supported by bone or cartilage ribs.

_____ **15.** Some members of this group have flattened, winglike bodies with whiplike tails.

_____ **16.** Members of this group have a complex nervous system that includes ten pairs of cranial nerves.

_____ **17.** Almost all members of this group are marine.

_____ **18.** In these fishes, the movement of muscles in the mouth and gill covers maintains the flow of water over the gills.

_____ **19.** These fishes must keep swimming to force water through the mouth, over the gills, and out through five to seven pairs of gill slits.

_____ **20.** In some species, the embryos develop within the body of the mother and are born alive.

_____ 21. Unlike all other vertebrates, the notochord persists throughout the life of these fishes.

_____ 22. Some of these fishes have a larval stage of development.

_____ 23. Most of these fishes have an air bladder in the upper part of their body cavities.

_____ 24. Two classes of this group are the most primitive of all living vertebrates.

_____ 25. Members of this group include sharks, rays, and skates.

_____ 26. Members of this group have a two-chambered heart, consisting of an atrium and a ventricle.

Part III: Skills Development

Review the skill entitled "Making an Outline" on pages 68–69. Then, outline the following passage on the lines below.

THE CARTILAGINOUS FISHES

27. The *cartilaginous* (kart ul AJ uh nus) *fishes, class* **Chondrichthyes** (kahn DRIK thee eez), include sharks, rays, and skates. Almost all members of this group are marine. They range in size from small skates less than 1 meter in length to whale sharks 15 meters long. Manta rays may be 6 meters across and weight as much as 1200 kilograms. In members of this group, the skeleton is made entirely of cartilage, and traces of the notochord are present in the adult. Unlike the jawless fishes, the cartilaginous fishes have movable upper and lower jaws that are equipped with several rows of sharp teeth. These biting jaws enable the cartilaginous fishes to eat a wide variety of food. Like all fishes, members of this class have two-chambered hearts.

_____

_____

_____

_____

_____

_____

_____

_____

_____

_____

_____

VERTEBRATES—FISHES TO REPTILES
34-3   The Amphibians

Part I: Vocabulary Review

Compare and contrast the following pairs of terms. First list their similarities, then their differences.

1. Amphibia and tadpoles: _____

_____

_____

2. nictitating membrane and tympanic membrane: _____

_____

_____

_____

Part II: Content Review

Complete each of the sentences below. The first example has been completed for you.

3. Four kinds of amphibians included in the class Amphibia are *frogs, toads, salamanders, and newts.*

4. For most amphibians, reproduction and development must take place _____

_____

5. It is thought that amphibians evolved from _____

6. Most scientists believe that amphibians were the very first _____

_____

7. The skin of amphibians is generally _____

_____

8. Both the mudpuppy and the axolotl are actually _____

_____

9. Four protective adaptations found in tailless amphibians include _____

_____

_____

10. The three eyelids of the frog are _____

_____

11. When frogs are floating with most of their body underwater, they can breathe air _____

12. In frogs, most digestion and absorption of food takes place _____
_____

13. The cloaca of the frog serves as a passageway for _____
_____

14. The frog has a three-chambered heart made up of _____
_____

15. When a frog hibernates during the winter, its respiratory needs are met by _____
_____

16. The two main parts of the frog's nervous system are _____
_____
_____

17. The five main parts of the brain of a frog are _____
_____
_____

18. The six kinds of sensory organs of a frog are _____
_____
_____

19. The two organs of excretion in the frog are _____

20. After six to nine days, fertilized frog eggs _____

Part III: Skills Development

Review the skill entitled "Graphic Organizing: Flow Chart" on pages 34–37. Then, complete the flow chart below to show the process of frog development from a mass of fertilized eggs to an adult frog.

21.

	→	→	→

VERTEBRATES—FISHES TO REPTILES
34-4   Reptiles

Part I: Vocabulary Review

Select the vocabulary word that best completes the statement and write it on the space provided.

1. A vertebrate that has a dry, scaly skin; does not need water for reproduction; and produces fertilized eggs that are enclosed in thick, leathery, waterproof shells probably belongs to the class known as _____

Part II: Content Review

Answer each of the following questions in one or two sentences.

2. How are reptiles well adapted for life on land? _____

_____

_____

3. Which reptiles have four-chambered hearts? _____

_____

4. What unique characteristic is shown by the primitive tuatara? _____

_____

5. What are the largest reptiles alive today? _____

_____

6. How can you tell an American alligator from an American crocodile? _____

_____

_____

7. What are the upper and the lower shell of a turtle called? _____

_____

_____

8. What reproductive behavior is shared by all turtles, including ocean-dwelling ones? _____

_____

_____

9. What are four ways that lizards differ from snakes? _____

_____

_____

10. What poisonous lizard lives in the deserts of the southwestern United States? _____

_____

_____

11. Why are snakes helpful? _____

_____

12. How are the sense organs of snakes useful in hunting? _____

_____

_____

13. How are snakes able to swallow prey that is much bigger than they are? _____

_____

_____

14. What are four kinds of poisonous snakes that live in the United States? _____

_____

_____

Part III: Skills Development

Review the skill entitled "Finding the Main Idea" on pages 8–10. Then, read each of the following paragraphs and, in the space provided, express the main idea in your own words.

Crocodiles and alligators are the largest living reptiles. They range in length from 2.5 meters to more than 7 meters. They are found in lakes, swamps, and rivers in tropical regions all over the world. Both alligators and crocodiles have long snouts, powerful jaws with large teeth, and long, muscular tails. See Figure 34-24. The tails are used in swimming. These two types of reptiles look very much alike, but their teeth are arranged differently. Furthermore, the American alligator has a much broader snout than the American crocodile. In both alligators and crocodiles, there are nostrils at the tip of the snout. This allows the animals to lie in water, with only the tip of the snout and the eyes above the surface.

15. _____

_____

Lizards and snakes belong to the same order, but there are many differences between them. Most lizards are four-legged, while snakes have no legs. Lizards have movable eyelids and external ear openings, while snakes have immovable eyelids and no external ear openings. In both lizards and snakes, the skin is covered with scales. Both animals shed their skins periodically. Unlike the scales of the lizard, which are almost uniform in size, the scales of the snake vary in size. While scales on the back and sides of a snake are small, on the belly of the snake, there is a single row of large scales. These scales act as cleats to give the snake traction as it moves across the terrain.

16. _____

_____

CHAPTER REVIEW

Know the Terms

Match each of the following classifications or examples with its appropriate description. An answer may be used more than once.

a. chordata	**c.** lancelets	**e.** vertebrata
b. cephalochordata	**d.** urochordata	**f.** endotherms

1. tunicates

2. largest subphylum

3. most advanced phylum

4. amphioxus

5. subphylum of lancelets

6. soft-bodied, sessile, marine

1. ____

2. ____

3. ____

4. ____

5. ____

6. ____

Match each of the following organisms with its classification. An answer may be used more than once.

a. jawless fish	**c.** bony fish	**e.** reptiles
b. cartilaginous fish	**d.** amphibians	

7. sharks

8. perch

9. alligators

10. turtles

11. hagfish

12. bass

13. lampreys

14. frog

15. tortoises

16. lizards

17. eels

18. snakes

19. rays

20. amphioxus

21. salamander

7. ____

8. ____

9. ____

10. ____

11. ____

12. ____

13. ____

14. ____

15. ____

16. ____

17. ____

18. ____

19. ____

20. ____

21. ____

CHAPTER REVIEW

Understand the Concepts

Answer the following questions in one or two sentences.

1. What is the advantage of being endothermic? _____

_____

_____

2. What is a notochord? _____

_____

_____

3. In reptiles, why is a three-chambered heart an advantage over a two-chambered heart? _____

_____

_____

_____

4. Describe metamorphosis in amphibians. _____

_____

_____

_____

5. Why must amphibians live near water or in moist environments? _____

_____

_____

_____

6. Why are reptiles better adapted to a terrestrial environment than amphibians? _____

_____

_____

_____

7. Describe three features of all chordates. _____

_____

_____

_____

Name _____ Date _____

VERTEBRATES — BIRDS AND MAMMALS   CHAPTER

35-1   Birds

Part I: Vocabulary Review

If a statement is true, write TRUE in the space at the left. If a statement is false, make it true by changing the underlined word.

_____ 1. Feathers are one characteristic that distinguish <u>Aves</u> from all other animals.

_____ 2. The thin, hairlike branches spreading out diagonally from the shaft of a feather are called <u>barbules</u>.

_____ 3. Each <u>barb</u> is made up of many tiny hooks.

_____ 4. Pouching out from a bird's small lungs are many <u>syrinxes</u>.

_____ 5. A bird's <u>crop</u> is a thick-walled muscular organ that may contain small stones.

Part II: Content Review

Select the best answer and write its letter in the space provided.

_____ 6. From what group of animals do scientists think birds evolved?
  a. mammals
  b. primates
  c. reptiles
  d. Aves

_____ 7. How are the bones of birds adapted for flight?
  a. The bones are filled with air spaces.
  b. The bones are brittle.
  c. The bones are spindle shaped.
  d. The bones have barbules

_____ 8. How many chambers make up a bird's heart?
  a. two chambers
  b. three chambers
  c. four chambers
  d. five chambers

_____ 9. From what structures in the skin do a bird's feathers grow?
  a. barbs
  b. vanes
  c. quills
  d. follicles

_____ 10. What is the flat part of a typical feather called?
  a. vane
  b. quill
  c. barb
  d. barbule

_____ 11. In late summer, what often happens to a bird's feathers?
  a. They lose their coloring.
  b. They change shape.
  c. They become oily.
  d. They are molted.

_____ **12.** What kind of feathers cover, insulate, and protect a bird's body?
    a. flight feathers   **c.** shaft feathers
    b. contour feathers   **d.** scaled feathers

_____ **13.** How do birds waterproof their feathers?
    a. by zipping them together
    b. by spreading oil over them
    c. by changing their color
    d. by molting

_____ **14.** What increases the efficiency of gas exchange in birds?
    a. two-way air flow through the lungs
    b. the presence of a syrinx
    c. hollow bones
    d. one-way air flow through the lungs

_____ **15.** How would you describe the regulation of body temperature in birds?
    a. ectothermic   **c.** cold-blooded
    b. endothermic   **d.** external

_____ **16.** Into what structure do a bird's rectum, genital ducts, and ureters empty?
    a. cloaca   **c.** gizzard
    b. crop   **d.** proventriculus

_____ **17.** What part of a bird's brain coordinates muscles to allow the precise movements of flight?
    a. hypothalamus   **c.** cerebellum
    b. cerebrum   **d.** medulla oblongata

Part III: Skills Development

Review the skill entitled "Graphic Organizing: Compare/Contrast Matrix" on pages 41–44. Then, complete the matrix on the systems of a bird below.

18.

SYSTEM	MAJOR ORGAN(S)	FUNCTION(S)
Respiratory		
Circulatory		
Digestive		
Excretory		
Nervous		
Reproductive		

VERTEBRATES — BIRDS AND MAMMALS
35-2 Mammals

Part I: Vocabulary Review

Identify the term that fits each of the definitions below. Then, to reveal the biological concept below, transfer the letters that have numbers beneath them to the corresponding numbered blank spaces shown below.

1. class of vertebrates that have hair or fur and nourish their young with milk

   ___ ___ ___ ___ ___ ___ ___
   16   18 75   76

2. teeth specialized for cutting ___ ___ ___ ___ ___ ___ ___ ___
                                    43   69   59

3. teeth specialized for tearing ___ ___ ___ ___ ___ ___ ___
                                    26   33

4. teeth specialized for grinding ___ ___ ___ ___ ___ ___ ___ ___ ___
                                        66   21   78

5. backmost grinding teeth ___ ___ ___ ___ ___ ___
                             60   9

6. egg-laying mammals ___ ___ ___ ___ ___ ___ ___ ___ ___
                        44 71   1   7

7. pouched mammals ___ ___ ___ ___ ___ ___ ___ ___ ___
                     4   51   27

8. mammals in which a placenta forms during the development of the embryo

   ___ ___ ___ ___ ___ ___ ___   ___ ___ ___ ___ ___ ___
           48   50   37   6   55

9. insect-eating mammals ___ ___ ___ ___ ___ ___ ___ ___
                          22 67 58   5

10. largest order of placental mammals ___ ___ ___ ___ ___ ___ ___ ___
                                             36 52   40   57

11. mammalian order that includes rabbits and hares ___ ___ ___ ___ ___ ___ ___ ___
                                                        46   54   38   64

12. mammalian order that includes bats ___ ___ ___ ___ ___ ___ ___ ___
                                         62 73   65   49

13. order of mammals having only molars or no teeth at all ___ ___ ___ ___ ___ ___ ___
                                                              3   63   8   13

14. mammalian order that includes only elephants ___ ___ ___ ___ ___ ___ ___ ___ ___
                                                           56   10   24   70

15. order of hoofed mammals having an even number of toes

    ___ ___ ___ ___ ___ ___ ___ ___ ___ ___
    17   29   12

16. order of hoofed mammals having an odd number of toes

    ___ ___ ___ ___ ___ ___ ___ ___
        47   20   34

17. stomach chamber in which food is stored in ruminants ___ ___ ___ ___ ___
                                                            28   42

18. order of flesh-eating mammals that includes cats and dogs ___ ___ ___ ___ ___ ___ ___ ___
$\overline{35}$ $\overline{25}$ $\overline{23}$

19. order of meat-eating aquatic mammals that includes walruses

___ ___ ___ ___ ___ ___ ___
   $\overline{61}$ $\overline{77}$ $\overline{72}$ $\overline{32}$

20. order of nearly hairless aquatic mammals that includes whales ___ ___ ___ ___ ___
$\overline{11}$ $\overline{41}$ $\overline{30}$

21. order of plant-eating aquatic mammals that includes manatees ___ ___ ___ ___ ___
$\overline{15}$ $\overline{68}$ $\overline{45}$

22. order of mammals having grasping hands and flexible feet ___ ___ ___ ___ ___ ___ ___
$\overline{19}$ $\overline{14}$

23. a thumb opposite other fingers, making it possible to grasp objects

___ ___ ___ ___ ___ ___ ___ ___ ___ ___
  $\overline{39}$ $\overline{53}$ $\overline{2}$ $\overline{74}$ $\overline{31}$

CONCEPT:

$\overline{1}$ $\overline{2}$ $\overline{3}$ $\overline{4}$ $\overline{5}$ $\overline{6}$ $\overline{7}$ $\overline{8}$ $\overline{9}$ $\overline{10}$ $\overline{11}$ $\overline{12}$ $\overline{13}$ $\overline{14}$ $\overline{15}$

$\overline{16}$ $\overline{17}$ $\overline{18}$ $\overline{19}$ $\overline{20}$ $\overline{21}$ $\overline{22}$ $\overline{23}$ $\overline{24}$ $\overline{25}$ $\overline{26}$ $\overline{27}$ $\overline{28}$ $\overline{29}$ $\overline{30}$ $\overline{31}$ $\overline{32}$ $\overline{33}$ $\overline{34}$

$\overline{35}$ $\overline{36}$ $\overline{37}$ $\overline{38}$ $\overline{39}$ $\overline{40}$ $\overline{41}$ $\overline{42}$ $\overline{43}$ $\overline{44}$ $\overline{45}$ $\overline{46}$ $\overline{47}$ $\overline{48}$ $\overline{49}$ $\overline{50}$ $\overline{51}$

$\overline{52}$ $\overline{53}$ $\overline{54}$ $\overline{55}$ $\overline{56}$ $\overline{57}$ $\overline{58}$ $\overline{59}$ $\overline{60}$ $\overline{61}$ $\overline{62}$ $\overline{63}$ $\overline{64}$ $\overline{65}$ $\overline{66}$ $\overline{67}$ $\overline{68}$ $\overline{69}$

$\overline{70}$ $\overline{71}$ $\overline{72}$ $\overline{73}$ $\overline{74}$ $\overline{75}$ $\overline{76}$ $\overline{77}$ $\overline{78}$

Part II: Content Review

Complete each of the sentences below.

24. It is thought that mammals evolved from _____

_____

25. Along with birds, mammals share the following two characteristics: _____

_____

26. A unique feature of the mammals in the order Chiroptera is _____

27. The largest living land animals belong to _____

_____

28. Two unique characteristics of the hands of primates are _____

VERTEBRATES — BIRDS AND MAMMALS
35-3 Human Origins

Part I: Vocabulary Review

In the space provided, write the vocabulary term that best replaces the italicized definition in each statement.

1. *The branch of science that attempts to trace the development of the human species* deals with the physical, social, and cultural aspects of human development as well as the origin of humans. _____

2. *The ability to walk on two legs in an upright position* is characteristic of humans. _____

3. In humans, *the opening in the skull where the spinal cord enters* is under the skull, allowing the head to be balanced on top of the spinal column. _____

4. *A genus of fossil bipedal mammals found in southern Africa* shows more human than ape characteristics and suggests that bipedal locomotion evolved before an increased brain size. _____

5. The earliest members of *the species of modern humans* are believed to have arisen from *Homo erectus* about 250 000 to 350 000 years ago. _____

6. The fossil record indicates that about 35 000 years ago *an early type of Homo sapiens* died out. _____

7. *A type of prehistoric human, considered to be the same as modern humans*, probably gave rise to the three primary human races in the world today. _____

Part II: Content Review

The sentences below are incorrect statements. Rewrite the sentences to make them correct.

8. The human brain is much smaller than that of other primates. _____
_____
_____

9. The human cranium is lower and more squared off than that of other primates. _____
_____
_____

10. Humans have sloping foreheads with bony eyebrow ridges. _____
_____

11. Humans jawbones are heavier than those of other primates and are rectangularly shaped. _____
_____
_____

12. Humans have less distinct chins and generally larger teeth than other primates. _____
_____

13. Humans are the only animals that use two legs instead of four. _____

14. The straight, rod-like structure of the human spinal column is adapted for bipedal locomotion. _____

15. In fossils, the location of the foramen magnum determines whether or not a primate had a large brain. _____

16. The only primates alive today are humans. _____

17. From the fossil record, it is thought that apes began to evolve around 30 thousand years ago. _____

18. Fossil evidence suggests that *Australopithecus* was more apelike than humanlike. _____

19. Compared with *Australopithecus*, *Homo habilis* had more humanlike teeth and smaller brains. _____

20. The first remains that show truly human characteristics appear in the fossil record about 1.5 million years ago and are classified as *A. africanus.* _____

21. From Cro-Magnons on, evolutionary changes were mainly physical rather than behavioral and cultural. _____

22. The number of base differences in the carbohydrate molecules of related species can be used as a measure of time at which the species diverged from a common ancestor. _____

CHAPTER REVIEW

Know the Terms

Match the mammal with the order to which it belongs.

a. Rodentia   **e.** Artiodactyla   **h.** Chiroptera
b. Cetacea   **f.** Proboscidea   **i.** Insectivora
c. Edentata   **g.** Perissodactyla   **j.** Carnivora
d. Lagomorpha

1. bat	**6.** cat
2. armadillo	**7.** porcupine
3. mole	**8.** dolphin
4. elephant	**9.** rabbit
5. horse	**10.** deer

1. _____   6. _____
2. _____   7. _____
3. _____   8. _____
4. _____   9. _____
5. _____   10. _____

Complete the following paragraphs, using the list of words below.

premolars	placental mammals	Mammalia
marsupials	bipedal locomotion	Cro-Magnons
Aves	incisors	canines
anthropology	Neanderthals	monotremes
Homo sapiens	molars	Primates

The two most advanced classes of the subphylum Vertebrata are the birds, or __(11)__, and __(12)__, which is subdivided into three groups. The __(13)__ are reptilelike and lay eggs. They include the duckbill platypus. The __(14)__ are pouched and include the kangaroo. The __(15)__ retain their young within the uterus until embryonic development is complete.

Mammals show many adaptations for survival. They have well-differentiated teeth. The __(16)__ are for cutting, the __(17)__ are for tearing, and the __(18)__ and __(19)__ are for grinding.

Humans, apes, and monkeys belong to the order __(20)__ and have large, well-developed brains. The branch of science that attempts to trace the development of the human species is called __(21)__. Humans are unique in their ability to walk upright on two legs, called __(22)__ Modern humans belong to the species __(23)__. The __(24)__ were an early type of this species but were replaced by the __(25)__, who are believed to be the direct ancestors of modern humans.

11. _____
12. _____
13. _____
14. _____
15. _____
   _____
16. _____
17. _____
18. _____
   _____
19. _____
   _____
20. _____
21. _____
22. _____
   _____
23. _____
24. _____
25. _____

CHAPTER REVIEW

Understand the Concepts

Answer each of the following questions in one or two sentences.

1. What adaptations enable aquatic mammals to survive in water? _____

_____

_____

2. What features would aid a scientist in classifying a fossil as humanlike? _____

_____

_____

3. What are some features that make both birds and mammals the most advanced animals? _____

_____

_____

4. How do molecular geneticists date the divergence of different species from a common ancestor?

_____

_____

_____

5. What two characteristics are unique to mammals? _____

_____

6. Why is it difficult to study the origin of humans? _____

_____

_____

7. How are birds adapted for flight? _____

_____

_____

_____

8. Briefly explain reproduction in birds. _____

_____

_____

BEHAVIOR

CHAPTER **36**

36-1   The Nature of Behavior

Part I: Vocabulary Review

Fill in the vocabulary term that best completes each statement.

1. Any change in the external or internal environment is called a _____ .

2. The series of activities performed by an organism in response to a change in its external or internal

environment is termed _____ .

3. Physiological and behavioral cycles occurring over a period of about 24 hours are known as

_____ .

Part II: Content Review

Read each "Cause" and fill in an appropriate "Effect" in the space provided. The first example has been completed for you.

CAUSE	EFFECT
4. When a hungry dog smells food (stimulus),	*it responds physiologically by salivating.*
5. When a hawk sees a rabbit,	_____ _____
6. When a rabbit sees an attacking hawk,	_____ _____ _____
7. Because of honeybees' form of vision,	_____ _____ _____ _____
8. When a bat uses echolocation to determine whether an object is an obstacle or a moving prey,	_____ _____
9. Because male gypsy moths have a keen sense of smell,	_____ _____ _____ _____
10. Because there are so many stimuli in the environment,	_____ _____

11. The more complex an organism's nervous system and
    structure are,

    _____

    _____

12. When ground squirrels are kept under constant
    environmental conditions,

    _____

    _____

Part III: Skills Development

Review the skill entitled "Graphic Organizing: Line Graph" on pages 30–33. Then use the line graph to answer the following questions.

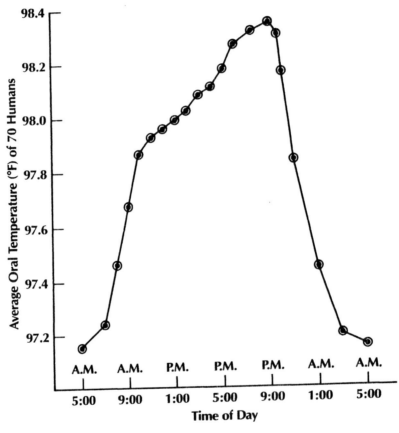

13. What does this line graph show? _____

_____

14. This is an example of what biological phenomenon? _____

15. At about what time of day is a person's oral temperature likely to be the highest? _____

16. Why do you think hospital nurses often take a patient's temperature early in the morning? _____

_____

BEHAVIOR
36-2 Innate Behavior

Part I: Vocabulary Review

Use the clues below to complete the crossword puzzle.

ACROSS

3. Complex, inherited behavior sequence
4. Simple, quick, automatic action that does not require control by the upper brain
5. Annual round trip made by many species between their winter feeding grounds in the south and their spring breeding grounds in the north

DOWN

1. Behavior that is not the result of learning
2. Movement by a simple animal or a protist toward or away from a stimulus

Part II: Content Review

Complete each of the sentences below.

6. Most innate behaviors aid _____

7. Innate behavior results from impulse pathways built into the nervous system; the instructions for the pathways

are carried _____

8. Five environmental factors that may act as stimuli for plant tropisms include _____

_____

9. Plant tropisms are controlled by _____

_____

10. Rapid responses in plants are controlled by _____

_____

11. Examples of a negative taxis and a positive taxis in an ameba are _____

_____

_____

12. A reflex arc consists of _____

_____

_____

13. Reflexes help an organism avoid injury by _____

_____

14. As in the behavior of the praying mantis, sometimes reflex arcs are linked to produce _____

_____

15. Instincts are found primarily in _____

_____

16. Two instinctive behaviors found in spiders are _____

_____

17. An example of an instinctive behavior in which one activity triggers the next occurs in sticklebacks as _____

_____

18. Research has shown that many migratory birds navigate by _____

_____

19. In some animals, reproductive hormones are the physiological stimuli that may lead to three instinctive

behaviors: _____

_____

20. In many birds and mammals that reproduce seasonally, increasing daylight stimulates the hypothalamus,

which in turn stimulates _____

_____

21. As in the case of territoriality in male sticklebacks, once internal conditions have been altered by hormones,

the animal responds to _____

_____

BEHAVIOR
36-3 Learned Behavior

Part I: Vocabulary Review

Compare and contrast the following pairs of terms. First list their similarities, then their differences.

1. learned behavior and conditioning: _____

_____

_____

_____

2. habituation and habit: _____

_____

_____

_____

3. imprinting and insight: _____

_____

_____

_____

Part II: Content Review

Reorganize the four events in each group in the order in which they occurred. Write 1 next to the event that happened first, 2 next to the event that happened second, and so on.

4. _____ Typing becomes easier and faster.

_____ Typing lessons are repeated again and again.

_____ Typing lessons are begun.

_____ Typing becomes a habit requiring little or no conscious effort.

5. _____ Dogs salivate when they hear a bell ring even though no food is present.

_____ Bell is rung every time dog is given food.

_____ Association of bell with salivation is reinforced by presenting food immediately after ringing the bell.

_____ Dogs normally salivate when they smell or see food.

6. _____ Animal associates pushing lever with the reward of food.

_____ Caged animal is hungry and is trying to find food.

_____ Animal pushes lever regardless of whether it is rewarded with food or not (operant conditioning).

_____ By trial and error, animal pushes a lever in its cage and is rewarded with food.

7. _____ Trainer rewards trick by blowing a whistle and giving the whale food.

_____ When whale does trick it hears whistle and gets food; it gets nothing if it does not do the trick.

_____ Whale does a particular trick on its own.

_____ The trick becomes a conditioned response when the whale hears the conditioned stimulus, which is the whistle.

8. _____ Mallard ducklings imprint on decoy.

_____ Mallard ducklings hatch under experimental conditions.

_____ For their first 36 hours, the ducklings see only a wooden decoy duck.

_____ When the ducklings mature, they court and try to mate with wooden decoy ducks.

9. _____ Chimp climbs on top of boxes to reach bananas.

_____ Chimp piles up boxes.

_____ Chimp is hungry.

_____ Chimp is released in a room with boxes scattered on the floor and a bunch of bananas hanging from the ceiling out of reach.

Part III: Skills Development

Review the skill entitled "Finding the Main Idea" on pages 8–10. Then, read the paragraph below and find the main idea. On the lines below, write the main idea of the paragraph and explain why it is the main idea.

10. While innate behavior is controlled by genes, learned behavior is controlled only indirectly by genes. Heredity determines the type and complexity of the nervous system, which controls the ability to learn. Animals with more complex nervous systems exhibit a greater capacity to learn. Animals with long life spans and long periods of parental care exhibit mostly learned behavior as adults. In some animals, parents actually teach their offspring certain behaviors. Lions, for example, teach their offspring how to hunt.

_____

_____

_____

_____

_____

_____

_____

BEHAVIOR
36-4 Social Behavior

Part I: Vocabulary Review

Complete the paragraph by selecting the appropriate words from the following list.

dominance hierarchy   social behavior
pheromones   territory

Animals belonging to the same species exhibit **(1)** _____ , which consists of both helpful

and hostile interactions. Some animals live in societies where a ranking, or **(2)** _____ ,

is established through fighting or displays of aggression. Often the behavior of other members of the same

species is influenced by special chemicals, called **(3)** _____ , which are used as

signals. During breeding season, certain animals, usually males, may claim or defend a particular area, or

(4) _____ , against intrusion by other members of the same species.

Part II: Content Review

Select the best answer for each question and write the letter in the space provided.

_____ **5.** When various species of animals randomly gather around a source of light or water, what are they
collectively known as?
  a. an aggregation   **c.** a dominance hierarchy
  b. a family   **d.** a pecking order

_____ **6.** What behavior is elicited in gulls only when eggs are present and certain hormones are produced in
the parent?
  a. aggression   **c.** courtship
  b. family interactions   **d.** incubation

_____ **7.** What does begging behavior by chicks stimulate a parent bird to do?
  a. incubate eggs   **c.** keep the chicks warm
  b. place food in the chicks' mouths **d.** begin courtship

_____ **8.** What function does mobbing serve?
  a. getting food   **c.** capturing prey
  b. attacking predators   **d.** escaping from an enemy

_____ **9.** Why does aggressive behavior within an animal species seldom cause serious injury or death?
  a. because the behavior is often expressed by "symbolic" displays or postures
  b. because aggressive animals do not claw or bite
  c. because an aggressive animal is often forced to leave the group
  d. because another animal intervenes

_____ **10.** When a wolf presents its neck to a rival, what is it trying to communicate to the rival?
  a. aggression   **c.** subordination
  b. begging   **d.** territoriality

_____ **11.** Why is survival difficult for the lowest ranking bird in a pecking order?
  a. The lowest ranked bird is less likely to obtain enough nourishment.
  b. The lowest ranked bird is the most aggressive.
  c. The lowest ranked bird does not get enough rest.
  d. The lowest ranked bird is usually blind.

_____ 12. How is a troop of baboons protected against attack by predators?
    a. by changing fur color
    b. by submission rituals
    c. by releasing pheromones
    d. by the presence of a clique of dominant male baboons

_____ 13. How do male crickets attract female crickets?
    a. hormones   **c.** pheromones
    b. sound signals   **d.** coloration

_____ 14. Which of the following is an advantage of territoriality?
    a. reducing conflict between members of a species
    b. decreasing the need for communication
    c. eliminating resources
    d. concentrating members of a species in one location

_____ 15. What is the main function of the queen in an insect society?
    a. food production   **c.** reproduction
    b. caring for larvae   **d.** defense

_____ 16. Which members of a honeybee society carry on the essential activities that maintain the hive?
    a. drones   **c.** queens
    b. worker bees   **d.** larvae

_____ 17. How do bees communicate to other bees the direction and distance of food?
    a. by dancing   **c.** by wing position
    b. by pheromones   **d.** by sharing food

Part III: Skills Development

Review the skill entitled "Graphic Organizing: Word Map" on pages 45–48. Then, complete the following word map.

18.

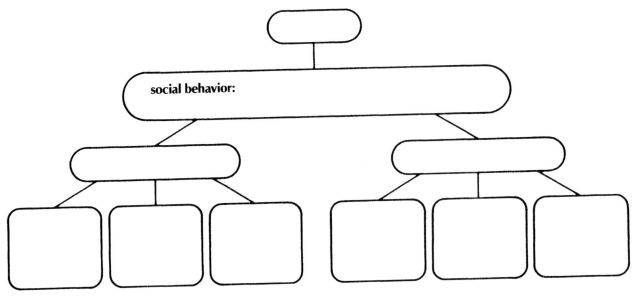

CHAPTER REVIEW

Know the Terms

Match the words with their correct definition.

a. behavior   **e.** insight   **i.** reflex
b. conditioning   **f.** instinct   **j.** stimulus
c. habit   **g.** learned behavior   **k.** taxis
d. imprinting   **h.** migration   **l.** trial and error

1. creating a solution to an unfamiliar problem without a period of trial and error   1. _____

2. a simple form of learning in which behavior is changed through new associations   2. _____

3. an involuntary, automatic response to a given stimulus, not involving the brain   3. _____

4. a complex, inborn behavior pattern   4. _____

5. the series of activities performed by an organism in response to stimuli   5. _____

6. behavior that develops as a result of experience   6. _____

7. any movement by a simple animal or a protist toward or away from a particular stimulus   7. _____

8. in some animals, the forming of an attachment to an organism, object, or other environmental factor soon after hatching or birth   8. _____

9. any factor that causes a receptor to trigger impulses in a nerve pathway, resulting in a change of activity   9. _____

10. learned behavior that becomes automatic   10. _____

Define or describe the following words.

11. circadian rhythm: _____

_____

12. dominance hierarchy: _____

_____

13. habituation: _____

_____

14. innate behavior: _____

_____

15. pheromone: _____

_____

16. social behavior: _____

_____

CHAPTER REVIEW

Understand the Concepts

Answer the following questions in one or two sentences.

1. What is the purpose of a physiological response to a stimulus? _____
_____
_____

2. How are behavioral responses to a stimulus beneficial to an individual and to a species? _____
_____
_____

3. What is the relationship between the complexity of an organism's nervous system and its behavior?
_____
_____

4. What is the role of the sense organs in behavior? _____
_____
_____

5. How does the nervous system function in behavior? _____
_____
_____

6. How is innate behavior important to an organism? _____
_____
_____

7. Why are instincts found primarily in vertebrates and complex invertebrates? _____
_____
_____
_____

8. Why is imprinting on their parents of survival value to the young of a species? _____
_____
_____

Part I: Vocabulary Review

If a statement is true, write **TRUE** in the space at the left. If a statement is false, make it true by replacing the italicized word. The first example has been completed for you.

Ecology _____

1. *Geology* is the branch of biology that deals with the interactions among organisms and between organisms and their environment.

_____

2. *Abiotic* factors include all the living organisms in the environment and their effects, both direct and indirect, on other living things.

_____

3. Water, oxygen, light, temperature, soil and inorganic and organic nutrients are examples of *biotic* factors.

_____

4. *Humus* is the dark, rich organic matter in the topsoil.

Part II: Content Review

A. For each statement below decide whether it describes only abiotic factors, only biotic factors, or the interaction of both factors. Write "A" for abiotic factors, "B" for biotic factors, and "AB" for both in the space provided.

_____ 5. Lichens and other organisms help to break rock into soil.

_____ 6. In deserts, where there is little water available, only plants such as sagebrush and cactus can survive.

_____ 7. The crab spider feeds on small flies.

_____ 8. Humus is formed from the decay of dead plants and animals.

_____ 9. The intensity and duration of sunlight affect the growth and flowering of plants.

_____ 10. At the North and South Poles, the sun never sets during the summers.

_____ 11. The temperature regions north and south of the equator have hot summers and cold winters.

_____ 12. Light is absorbed as it passes through water.

_____ 13. Generally, plants grow best in a mixture of clay and larger particles.

_____ 14. Plant roots, earthworms, insects, and many other animals and protists live in the topsoil.

_____ 15. The energy for almost all living things comes directly or indirectly from sunlight.

B. Describe how each of the following abiotic factors varies in different regions of the earth.

16. light: _____

_____

_____

_____

_____

17. temperature: _____

_____

_____

_____

18. water: _____

_____

_____

_____

_____

_____

Part III: Skills Development

Review the skill entitled "Preparing for and Taking a Test" on pages 73–77. Then, after reviewing Section 37-1 in your text, answer the following multiple-choice questions.

_____ **19.** Where does the earth receive sunlight of the highest average intensity?
   a. at the North Pole
   b. at the South Pole
   c. in areas around the equator
   d. in regions between the equator and the North Pole
   e. in regions between the equator and the South Pole

_____ **20.** How does altitude affect temperature?
   a. As the altitude rises, the temperature rises.
   b. As the altitude rises, the temperature falls.
   c. The temperature stays the same regardless of altitude.
   d. All of the above may be true depending on where you are.
   e. None of the above is true.

_____ **21.** What are the three distinct layers of soil?
   a. topsoil, bottomsoil, bits of rock
   b. humus, topsoil, subsoil
   c. humus, topsoil, bottomsoil
   d. topsoil, subsoil, bits of rock
   e. humus, subsoil, bits of rock

_____ **22.** What is the photic zone?
   a. the layer of water in an aquatic environment through which light passes
   b. the zone in an aquatic environment in which approximately 80% of the earth's photosynthesis takes place
   c. the zone in an aquatic environment where there is no light
   d. both A and B
   e. none of the above

_____ **23.** Which of the following are abiotic factors?
   a. water
   b. oxygen
   c. temperature
   d. light
   e. all of the answers given

ORGANIZATION IN THE BIOSPHERE
37-2   Biotic Relationships in Ecosystems

CHAPTER **37**

Part I: Vocabulary Review

Use the clues below to complete the crossword puzzle.

ACROSS

2. A series of organisms through which food energy is passed

4. All the populations of different organisms within a given area

6. The portion of the earth in which living things exist

9. Animals that feed on dead animals they find

11. A symbiotic relationship in which both organisms benefit

12. The amount of energy available in an ecosystem may be shown in this form.

13. A symbiotic relationship in which one organism benefits and the other is harmed

DOWN

1. Food chains that are connected at different points

3. A symbiotic relationship in which one organism benefits and the other is not affected

5. Organisms that can produce organic compounds from inorganic compounds

7. Animal that feeds on both plants and animals

8. Animals that feed only on plants

10. A community and its physical environment

Part II: Content Review

Select the best answer to each question and write the letter in the space provided.

_____ **14.** Which term below describes all individuals of a particular species within a certain area?
    a. population
    b. community
    c. ecosystem
    d. a, b, and c
    e. none of the answers given

_____ **15.** Of the following heterotrophs, which one eats plants ONLY?
    a. carnivore
    b. herbivore
    c. omnivore
    d. scavenger
    e. none of the answers given

_____ **16.** Which statement below about symbiotic relationships is false?
    a. In a symbiotic relationship, it is possible that neither organism will benefit.
    b. In mutualism, both organisms benefit from the relationship.
    c. In commensalism, one organism benefits from the relationship, and the other is not affected.
    d. In parasitism, one organism benefits from the relationship, and the other is harmed.
    e. All of the statements are true.

_____ **17.** Which of the following are autotrophs?
    a. consumers
    b. decomposers
    c. producers
    d. saprobes
    e. predators

_____ **18.** Which statement below is true regarding food chains within an ecosystem?
    a. Carnivores are first-level consumers.
    b. Herbivores are second-level consumers.
    c. Each consumer always stays on the same level within a food chain.
    d. Decomposers are the final consumers in every food chain.
    e. None of the statements is true.

_____ **19.** What percentage of food energy taken in at one feeding level is passed to the next feeding level?
    a. 100%
    b. 50%
    c. 25%
    d. 10%
    e. 5%

Part III: Skills Development

Review the skill entitled "Graphic Organizing: Compare/Contrast Matrix" on pages 41–44. Then, complete the matrix below, comparing autotrophs and heterotrophs.

20.

CHARACTERISTIC	AUTOTROPHS	HETEROTROPHS
Ability to make own food		
Method(s) by which food is obtained		
Types of organisms		

ORGANIZATION IN THE BIOSPHERE
37-3 Cycles of Materials

Part I: Vocabulary Review

Identify the term that fits each of the definitions below. Then, to reveal the biological concept, transfer the letters that have numbers beneath them to the corresponding blank spaces shown below.

1. microorganisms that can convert ammonia to nitrate and nitrite

___ ___ ___ ___ ___ ___ ___   ___ ___ ___ ___ ___ ___ ___
14   30   22   10   28

2. microorganisms that get energy by converting nitrite and nitrate to nitrogen gas

___ ___ ___ ___ ___ ___ ___ ___   ___ ___ ___ ___ ___ ___
23,39   2   11   18   9   7   21

3. process by which some bacteria, such as blue-green bacteria, convert nitrogen gas directly to ammonia

___ ___ ___ ___ ___ ___ ___   ___ ___ ___ ___ ___ ___
1   26   13   20   16   15

4. microorganisms that can produce ammonia from nitrogen gas

___ ___ ___ ___ ___   ___ ___ ___ ___ ___ ___
8   3   6   33

5. process by which carbon dioxide is removed from the atmosphere by photosynthesis and is returned by cellular respiration

___ ___ ___ ___ ___   ___ ___ ___ ___ ___
25   4   12   35   19

6. process by which oxygen is released into the atmosphere by photosynthesis and removed by cellular respiration

___ ___ ___ ___ ___   ___ ___ ___ ___ ___
5   17   38   34   37 27

7. the cycling of water between the surface of the earth and the atmosphere

___ ___ ___ ___ ___   ___ ___ ___ ___
24 29   32   36   31

CONCEPT:

___ ___ ___ ___ ___ ___ ___ ___   ___ ___ ___ ___ ___ ___   ___ ___ ___ ___ ___ ___
1   2   3   4   5   6   7   8   9   10 11 12 13 14   15 16 17 18 19 20

___ ___ ___   ___ ___ ___ ___ ___   ___ ___ ___   ___ ___ ___ ___ ___ ___ ___ ___
21 22 23   24 25 26 27 28   29 30 31   32 33 34 35 36 37 38 39

Part II: Content Review

For each statement below, decide whether it relates to the nitrogen cycle, the carbon cycle, the oxygen cycle, the water cycle, or all of the cycles. Write "N" for nitrogen, "C" for carbon, "O" for oxygen, "W" for water, and "A" for all.

_____ **8.** This is a biogeochemical cycle.

_____ **9.** Plants make proteins and nucleic acids from ammonia.

_____ 10. Evaporation, transpiration, condensation, and precipitation are involved.

_____ 11. Living organisms incorporate into their bodies substances that are returned to the environment when they die.

_____ 12. The normal balance in this cycle has been changed by the burning of fossil fuels.

_____ 13. Photosynthesis and cellular respiration are involved in the carbon cycle and in this cycle.

Part III: Skills Development

Review the skill entitled "Finding the Main Idea" on pages 8–10. Then, read the paragraphs below and identify the main idea in each one. If the main idea is stated as part of a topic sentence, underline it. If it is implied, express it in your own words in the space provided.

14. In all ecosystems, materials revolve between living things and the environment. Organisms incorporate certain substances from the environment into their bodies. When these organisms die, their bodies are broken down by decomposers, and the substances returned to the environment. If these substances were not returned to the environment, their supply would eventually become exhausted. The cycles of materials between living things and the environment are called *biogeochemical cycles*. Nitrogen, carbon, oxygen, and water are among the substances involved in such cycles.

_____

_____

_____

_____

15. Carbon, in the form of carbon dioxide, makes up about 0.03 percent of the atmosphere. Carbon dioxide is also found dissolved in the waters of the earth. In the course of photosynthesis, carbon dioxide from the atmosphere is incorporated into organic compounds, a process known as *carbon fixation*. Some of these organic compounds are broken down during cellular respiration by photosynthetic organisms. This releases carbon dioxide into the atmosphere. If the plants or other photosynthetic organisms are eaten by animals, the carbon compounds pass through a food web. At each level, some are broken down by cellular respiration, releasing carbon dioxide into the atmosphere. Finally, the remains of dead plants and animals and animal wastes are broken down by decomposers, releasing carbon dioxide.

_____

_____

_____

_____

ORGANIZATION IN THE BIOSPHERE
37-4 Maintenance and Change in Ecosystems

Part I: Vocabulary Review

Fill in the vocabulary term that best completes each statement.

1. Succession of one community by another goes on until a mature, stable community, called a _____ _____ , develops.

2. The process by which an existing community is slowly replaced by another community is called _____ _____ .

3. Succession that occurs in an area in which an existing community has been partially destroyed and its balance upset is called _____ .

4. When succession occurs in an area that has no existing life, it is called _____ .

Part II: Content Review

Reorganize the following events in each group in the order in which they would occur during ecological succession. Write the numeral *1* next to the event that would happen first, *2* next to the event that would happen second, and so on.

5. SUCCESSION ON LAND

_____ Mature trees may shade out the sun so that seedlings of the same type cannot survive.

_____ Pioneer organisms appear, further breaking down the rock, and adding organic matter to developing soil.

_____ Seedlings of other trees grow well in the shade.

_____ Grasses and annual plants grow in areas where organic material has accumulated.

_____ The shrubs may shade the grasses, killing them.

_____ A climax community develops.

_____ Tree seedlings may take root, eventually shading out the shrubs.

_____ Weathering breaks large rocks into smaller and smaller pieces.

_____ When grasses and annual plants die, the soil becomes richer; small shrubs begin to grow, and their roots break rocks apart.

6. SUCCESSION IN LAKES AND PONDS

_____ As succession continues, the lake becomes a marsh.

_____ The increased number of plants and animals contribute organic material to the sediment, which hastens the filling-in process.

_____ Sediment, fallen leaves, and other debris gradually accumulate on the lake or pond bottom, decreasing its depth.

_____ As the lake fills in, it becomes rich in nutrients that can support a large population of organisms.

_____ The marsh fills in, forming dry land.

_____ The size of the lake decreases as the moss and plants gradually extend the banks inward.

_____ The filled area becomes part of the surrounding community.

_____ Land communities replace aquatic forms.

_____ At the edges of the lake, sphagnum moss and many of the rooted plants grow out into the shallower water.

Part III: Skills Development

Review the skill entitled "Making an Outline" on pages 68–69. Then, outline the following text passage on the lines below.

CONDITIONS IN AN ECOSYSTEM

7. For an ecosystem to be stable and self-sustaining, certain conditions must exist. First, there must be a constant source of energy. For almost all ecosystems on earth, the source of energy is light from the sun. Only a few ecosystems are based on chemosynthesis. In these ecosystems, the producers derive energy for the synthesis of organic compounds from chemical reactions involving various inorganic compounds. Second, there must be organisms within the ecosystem that can use incoming energy (light) for the synthesis of organic compounds. This role is filled by green plants and algae, which are the producers of the ecosystem. Third, there must be a cycle of materials between living organisms in the ecosystem and the environment. The producers incorporate inorganic compounds from the environment into organic compounds, which may then pass through a food chain or food web. Eventually, however, the decomposers break down the remains of dead organisms, releasing the inorganic substances back into the environment for reuse.

_____

_____

_____

_____

_____

_____

_____

_____

_____

_____

_____

_____

CHAPTER REVIEW

CHAPTER **37**

Know the Terms

Match the words with their correct definition.

a. carbon cycle   **e.** herbivore   **i.** producer
b. commensalism   **f.** niche   **j.** decomposer
c. consumer   **g.** parasitism   **k.** scavenger
d. ecology   **h.** habitat   **l.** mutualism

1. the branch of biology that deals with all the interactions between organisms and their environment

1. _____

2. the particular way in which a species functions in an ecosystem

2. _____

3. a type of symbiotic relationship in which one organism benefits from the association and the other is not affected

3. _____

4. a carnivore that feeds on dead animals that it finds

4. _____

5. an organism that produces organic compounds from inorganic compounds; an autotroph

5. _____

6. the pathways by which carbon is circulated through the biosphere

6. _____

7. an organism that obtains nutrients by breaking down the remains of dead plants and animals

7. _____

8. a heterotroph; an organism that obtains nutrients from other organisms

8. _____

9. a heterotroph that feeds only on plants

9. _____

10. a symbiotic relationship in which one organism benefits from the association and the other is harmed

10. _____

Define or describe the following terms.

11. biotic factor: _____

_____

12. biosphere: _____

_____

13. climax community: _____

_____

14. food web: _____

_____

15. nitrifying bacteria: _____

_____

16. population: _____

_____

Understand the Concepts

Answer the following questions in one or two sentences.

1. Why are the abiotic factors of a region important? _____

_____

2. How are heterotrophs dependent on autotrophs? _____

_____

_____

3. How do animals obtain the nitrogen they need for their life functions? _____

_____

_____

4. How might the light conditions of a region affect its biotic factors? _____

_____

_____

5. A protozoan population lives in the gut of termites and digests the wood the termite eats. Some of the byproducts of this process provide food for the termite. What type of symbiotic relationship is this?

_____

_____

6. What factors determine an organism's niche? _____

_____

7. How are decomposers important to an ecosystem? _____

_____

8. Why are there only a small number of feeding levels in an ecosystem? _____

_____

_____

9. What types of events might destroy a climax community? _____

_____

BIOMES OF THE EARTH
38-1   Terrestrial Biomes

Part I: Vocabulary Review

Match the terms listed in Column II with the proper definition listed in Column I. Place the answer in the space provided.

COLUMN I

_____ **1.** region characterized by a low average temperature and a short growing season, lying south of the Arctic ice caps and extending across North America, Europe, and Siberia

_____ **2.** regions too dry to support grasses, with poor, sandy soil, and rainfall of less than 25 centimeters per year

_____ **3.** large geographical region that has a particular type of climax community

_____ **4.** regions in Europe and eastern North America that have hot and humid summers, cold winters, and an average rainfall of 75–150 centimeters per year

_____ **5.** region with cold winters and a growing season of about 120 days; characterized by a belt of evergreen forest extending across North America, Europe, and Asia

_____ **6.** regions found in the interiors of North and South America, Asia, and Africa, with deep, rich, soil and an average rainfall of 25–75 centimeters a year

_____ **7.** regions around the equator that have a uniform climate and a constant supply of rainfall throughout the year

COLUMN II

a. biome

b. taiga

c. tundra

d. grasslands

e. temperate deciduous forests

f. deserts

g. tropical rain forests

Part II: Content Review

Complete each of the sentences below.

8. The major terrestrial biomes are _____

_____

9. The layers beneath the topmost layer of soil in the tundra are called _____

10. The average precipitation in the tundra is only about 10 to 12 centimeters a year, yet during the warm season

the region is wet with bogs because of _____

11. There are no trees in the tundra because of _____

_____

12. In the taiga, the dominant vegetation is _____

13. Three animals found in the taiga are _____

_____

14. The species present in deciduous forests vary with _____

15. Grasslands have become the most productive farmlands of the earth because _____

_____

16. In the past, the grasslands were populated by _____

_____

17. Two special adaptations desert plants have for conserving water are _____

_____

18. Tropical rain forests are found in _____

19. In a tropical rain forest, treetops form a _____

_____

20. Many animals of a tropical rain forest have adaptations that allow them to _____

_____

21. Plants, such as cacti and ferns, that grow on other plants but are not parasites are known as _____

_____

Part III: Skills Development

Read the skill entitled "Graphic Organizing: Compare/Contrast Matrix" on pages 41–44. Then, after reviewing Section 38-1 in your text, complete the following table.

TERRESTRIAL BIOMES

22.

CHARACTERISTIC	TUNDRA	TAIGA	TEMPERATE DECIDUOUS FORESTS	GRASS-LANDS	DESERTS	TROPICAL RAIN FORESTS
Climate	low average temperature; short growing season of about 60 days	cold winters; growing season of about 120 days		temperate or tropical		
Vegetation			varied; common trees are oak, maple, hickory, beech, chestnut, and birch		varies from none to a variety of plants adapted for water con-servation and reproduc-tive cycles (eg. cacti)	

BIOMES OF THE EARTH
38-2 Aquatic Biomes

Part I: Vocabulary Review

Use the following clues that describe terms related to your study of aquatic biomes to identify each term and write it in the space provided. Then find the term in the word search below and circle it. Answers may appear across, up, down, or backwards.

_____ 1. nonphotosynthetic planktonic protists and planktonic animals

_____ 2. organisms that live on the ocean floor

_____ 3. area along the shoreline that is covered by water at high tide and uncovered at low tide

_____ 4. photosynthetic planktonic organisms

_____ 5. free-swimming organisms living in the oceans

_____ 6. shallow waters above the continental shelf

_____ 7. small organisms that float near the surface and are carried by ocean currents

```
K  N  O  T  K  N  A  L  P  O  T  Y  H  P
Y  S  A  B  D  O  N  Q  B  M  P  T  G  B
I  N  T  E  R  T  I  D  A  L  Z  O  N  E
W  U  I  N  N  K  C  S  L  P  C  A  L  V
N  E  K  T  O  N  F  D  N  E  A  U  X  I
R  S  D  H  F  A  O  I  M  P  Y  B  Z  W
X  E  N  O  Z  L  A  R  O  T  T  I  L  J
Q  B  E  S  A  P  I  L  F  G  O  N  Y  V
R  U  Z  O  O  P  L  A  N  K  T  O  N  Q
```

Part II: Content Review

Select the best answer for each question and write the letter in the space provided.

_____ 8. Which of the following is NOT an example of a body of standing water?
   a. lakes
   b. ponds
   c. swamps
   d. bogs
   e. streams

_____ 9. Where can wetlands be found?
   a. lakes
   b. ponds
   c. swamps
   d. bogs
   e. streams

_____ **10.** The zones of the ocean, from shallowest to deepest, are the
   a. littoral zone, intertidal zone, open ocean.
   b. intertidal zone, littoral zone, open ocean.
   c. intertidal zone, open ocean, littoral zone.
   d. littoral zone, open ocean, intertidal zone.
   e. open ocean, intertidal zone, littoral zone.

_____ **11.** Freshwater biomes differ from the marine biome in that
   a. organisms in freshwater biomes excrete less water than those in the marine biome.
   b. the marine biome shows less temperature change than do freshwater biomes.
   c. the volume of water in freshwater biomes is more than that of the marine biome.
   d. organisms in freshwater biomes are more numerous than those in the marine biome.
   e. all of the above answers

_____ **12.** Which of the following statements is NOT true?
   a. Lakes are usually larger than ponds.
   b. An acidic environment exists in a bog.
   c. Ponds are usually too deep for light to reach the bottom.
   d. The bottom of fast-moving streams is made of rocks and gravel.
   e. The main producers in areas of deep water are phytoplankton.

Part III: Skills Development

Read the skill entitled "Graphic Organizing: Word Map" on pages 45–48. Then, after reviewing Section 38-2 in your text, construct word maps for the following terms: (a) benthos, (b) nekton.

13.   **14.**

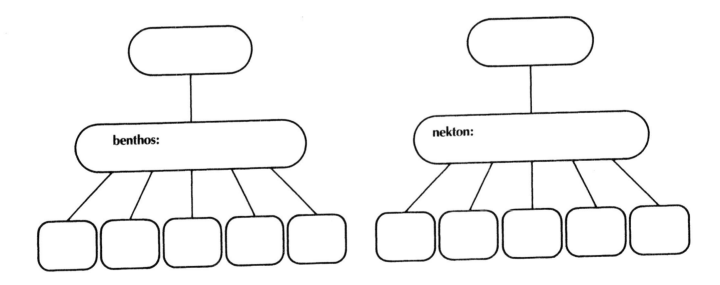

CHAPTER REVIEW

Know the Terms

Complete the following paragraphs using the list of words below.

zooplankton	plant life	desert	tropical rain forest
freshwater	taiga	tundra	temperate deciduous forest
terrestrial	permafrost	marine	phytoplankton
plankton	grasslands	benthos	biomes
epiphytes	nekton	latitude	

The earth is divided into large geographical regions that show particular types of climax communities, called __(1)__. In land, or __(2)__, biomes, the climax community is defined by its dominant type of __(3)__. The biome known as the __(4)__ is characterized by low average temperatures and plants such as lichens, mosses, and grasses with few, if any, trees. Only the upper layers of soil thaw in the summer, while the layers beneath, called the __(5)__, remain continually frozen.

Moving southward, the vegetation gradually changes, and evergreen forests become the dorminant plant life. This biome, called the __(6)__, has cold winters but warmer summer temperatures. Pines, spruce, and firs are the dominant vegetation. South of this biome, in eastern North America and in Europe, one finds the __(7)__ with hot, humid summers and cold winters. Common trees are oak, maple, and hickory, and common animals are wolves, foxes, and deer.

The __(8)__ biomes usually cover large areas in the interior of a continent and have from 25 to 75 centimeters of rainfall per year. The animals of the North American part of this biome are the badger, rattlesnake, and jackrabbit. The __(9)__ receives less than 25 centimeters of rainfall per year and has wide-ranging temperatures. Plants in this biome have special adaptations for water conservation.

The __(10)__ biomes are found around the equator and receive between 200 and 400 centimeters of rainfall a year. Temperatures remain around 25 degrees Celsius, and there is an enormous amount of plant and animal life.

Aquatic environments are also considered to be biomes. The two aquatic biomes on earth are the saltwater, or __(11)__, biome and the __(12)__ biome. The first of these biomes is one of the richest in the world. Organisms that live on the ocean floor are called __(13)__, and organisms that float near the surface are known as __(14)__. This latter group can be divided into two groups. Those that are photosynthetic are called __(15)__, while those that are not photosynthetic are called __(16)__.

1. _____
2. _____
3. _____
4. _____
5. _____
6. _____
7. _____
   _____
   _____
8. _____
9. _____
10. _____
    _____
    _____
11. _____
12. _____
13. _____
14. _____
15. _____
16. _____

CHAPTER REVIEW

Understand the Concepts

Answer the following questions in one or two sentences.

1. What factors distinguish one type of biome from another? _____
_____
_____
_____

2. Why aren't there clear-cut boundaries between biomes? _____
_____
_____
_____

3. Why are there few, if any, trees in the tundra biome? _____
_____
_____
_____

4. Explain the progression of biome as one travels north from the equator. _____
_____
_____
_____

5. Why aren't mountainous regions included in biome classifications? _____
_____
_____
_____

6. With all the lush vegetation found in the tropical rain forest biome, one would think that the soil would be rich in organic matter. Why is this not the case? _____
_____
_____
_____

7. Why is the marine biome the most stable of all biomes? _____
_____
_____
_____

HUMAN ECOLOGY
39-1   Causes of Environmental Damage

Part I: Vocabulary Review

If the statement is true, write TRUE in the space at the left. If the statement is false, make it true by replacing the italicized term.

_____ 1. *Human ecology* deals with the relationship between humans and their environment.

_____ 2. A *carrying capacity* is some factor, such as a lack of food, that halts any further growth in a population.

_____ 3. The movement of the population from rural areas to cities is called *urbanization*.

_____ 4. The removal of soil by wind and water is called *eutrophication*.

_____ 5. Adding anything to the environment or affecting the environment in a way that makes it less fit for living things is called *pollution*.

_____ 6. *Thermal pollution* involves loud sounds that can cause hearing loss.

_____ 7. *Biodegradable* materials can be broken down by bacteria and other decay organisms into simpler substances.

_____ 8. *Erosion* is an accelerated aging process in a lake or pond in which the body of water becomes reduced in size.

_____ 9. *Biological magnification* is the accumulation of substances in higher and higher concentrations in the bodies of organisms at each higher level of a food chain.

_____ 10. *Aerosols* have tiny solid particles or liquid droplets that remain suspended in air.

Part II: Content Review

Read each "Cause" and fill in an appropriate "Effect" in the space provided. The first example has been completed for you.

CAUSE

11. If the human population continues to grow indefinitely,

12. If the number of births equals the number of deaths in a population over a period of time,

13. If land is overfarmed or overgrazed,

14. If sewage and other organic materials are discharged into the water in large quantities,

EFFECT

it will eventually reach a point at

which the environment cannot

support it any longer.

_____

_____

_____

_____

_____

15. When hydrocarbons react with nitrogen oxides in the   _____
presence of sunlight,

16. When a layer of cooler, denser air is trapped below a layer   _____
of warmer air,

Part III: Skills Development

Read the skill entitled "Graphic Organizing: Circle Graph" on pages 22–24. Then, after reviewing Section 39-1 in your text, answer the following questions.

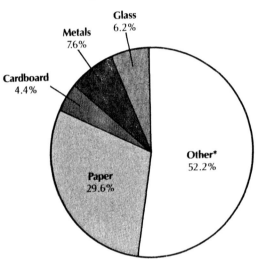

**Composition (by weight) of
Average Sanitary Landfill**

Glass
6.2%

Metals
7.6%

Cardboard
4.4%

Other*
52.2%

Paper
29.6%

*Includes yard waste, wood, demolition debris, plastics,
and miscellaneous wastes

17. What information does the graph contain?

_____

18. What does the number in each wedge-shaped section signify?

_____

19. What percentage of the material found in the landfill is glass?

_____

20. Disregarding the "Other" category, which category makes up the largest percentage of material found in the
sanitary landfill?

_____

21. Which category makes up the smallest percentage of material found in the sanitary landfill?

_____

HUMAN ECOLOGY
39-2 Restoring the Environment

Part I: Vocabulary Review

Compare and contrast the following pairs of terms. First list their similarities, then their differences.

1. renewable natural resources and nonrenewable natural resources: _____

_____

_____

_____

2. terracing and contour farming: _____

_____

_____

_____

3. windbreaks and dams: _____

_____

_____

4. crop rotation and fertilizers: _____

_____

_____

_____

5. sustained-yield tree farming and reforestation: _____

_____

_____

_____

Part II: Content Review

Select the best answer to each question and write the letter in the space provided.

_____ **6.** Which of the following is NOT used to control pollution?
  a. emission controls for automobiles
  b. cover crops in farming
  c. sewage treatment plants
  d. special sites for toxic waste disposal
  e. banning the use of aerosol sprays

_____ **7.** Which of the following is a renewable natural resource?
  a. water
  b. coal
  c. oil
  d. natural gas
  e. metals

_____ 8. Which of the following is a nonrenewable natural resource?
    a. air
    b. trees
    c. soil
    d. minerals
    e. bacteria

_____ 9. Which of the following is NOT a technique used in soil conservation?
    a. cover crops
    b. strip cropping
    c. pheromones
    d. terracing
    e. contour farming

_____ 10. Methods of sustained-yield tree farming include
    a. block cutting
    b. strip cutting
    c. selective harvesting
    d. replacement planting
    e. all of the preceding answers

_____ 11. Species extinctions are
    a. increasing
    b. decreasing
    c. staying about the same
    d. partly caused by city and suburb growth
    e. both a and d

_____ 12. Which of the following are examples of wildlife conservation practices?
    a. restricted hunting and fishing laws
    b. game and bird preserves
    c. restricted use of pesticides
    d. protection of wetlands
    e. all of the preceding answers

_____ 13. How can the damage caused by insects be controlled?
    a. crop rotation
    b. luring insects with pheromones
    c. releasing sterile males into the population
    d. importing natural enemies
    e. all of the preceding answers

Part III: Skills Development

Read the skill entitled "Graphic Organizing: Word Map" on pages 45–48. Then, after reviewing Section 39-2 in your text, construct concept maps for the following terms: renewable natural resources and nonrenewable natural resources.

14.

15.

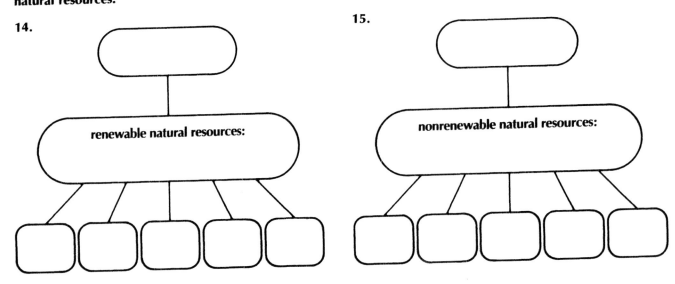

renewable natural resources:

nonrenewable natural resources:

Know the Terms

Complete the following crossword puzzle.

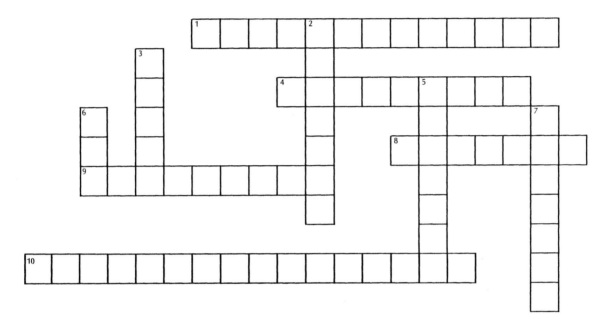

ACROSS

1. Can be broken down by microorganisms
4. Makes the environment less fit for living things
8. Tiny particles suspended in air
9. Farming practice used on hillsides
10. A large area where refuse is dumped into a trench

DOWN

2. Deals with the relationship between living things and their environment
3. Crops planted to prevent erosion
5. Pollution by changing water temperature
6. Example of pesticide
7. Farming practice used on uneven landscapes

Define or describe the following words.

11. human ecology: _____

_____

_____

12. carrying capacity: _____

_____

_____

13. renewable natural resource: _____

_____

_____

CHAPTER REVIEW

Understand the Concepts

Answer the following questions in one or two sentences.

1. Why has the mean (average) age of human beings increased over the past century? _____

_____

_____

_____

_____

2. What role do limiting factors play in nature? _____

_____

_____

3. What effects are we now experiencing as a result of a lack of concern for natural resources? _____

_____

_____

_____

4. How does acid rain form? _____

_____

_____

5. What can we do now to help alleviate our present ecological problems? _____

_____

_____

_____

6. How have chemical pesticides been beneficial? _____

_____

7. How have chemical pesticides been harmful? _____

_____

8. What are some sources of water pollution? _____

_____

_____